OUR LIVES FOR OURSELVES

OUR LIVES FOR OURSELVES

WOMEN WHO HAVE NEVER MARRIED

NANCY L. PETERSON

G. P. Putnam's Sons
New York

Copyright © 1981 by Nancy L. Peterson
All rights reserved. This book, or parts thereof,
must not be reproduced in any form without permission.
Published simultaneously in Canada by Academic Press
Canada Limited, Toronto.

Library of Congress Cataloging in Publication Data

Peterson, Nancy L.
    Our lives for ourselves.

    1. Single women—United States. I. Title.
HQ0800.4.U6P47 1981   305.4'8   80-23101
ISBN 0-399-12476-4

PRINTED IN THE UNITED STATES OF AMERICA

This book is lovingly dedicated to
my grandaunt, Myrtle Dimm Lilley

CONTENTS

ACKNOWLEDGMENTS

Literally hundreds of people were involved directly in the writing of this book. They range from the many never-married women who, at the request of a stranger, shared with me a precious gift, the stories of their lives, to the dozens of people who offered material or moral support and cheered me on my way.

Special mention must be made of special friends. Rose B. Packard encouraged the original impetus for this book and helped me over certain hard spots, especially the composition of the final format. Many other friends contributed ideas, helped me along. They include Carol Wilder, Lynne Dubrofsky, Irma Honda, Ruth Solomon Freeman, Ruth Miller, Regina Sneed, the Gus Schultz family, Florence Perman, Ann Frechette, Nadia Derkach, Norma Hauanio, Gert Broadman, Joan and Rob Hongen, Susan Page. In Stockholm, Berit Rolen and Inga-Maja Ericksson gave a helping hand.

Commissions on the Status of Women in several states helped me locate women to interview, as did several branches of the Young Women's Christian Association. My thanks to the worthy women of these organizations.

My employer in the person of Michael W. Murray, Principal Regional Official, Department of Health and Human Services, Region IX, made the writing of this book possible by granting me an extensive leave of unpaid absence from my job. However, HHS has no official involvement in or support of this project.

Special kudos are owed my agent, Susan Urstadt, and my editor,

Elisabeth Jakab, who believed in this idea strongly enough to take a chance on an unknown and untested writer. They have been among its most faithful supporters, along with my typist and transcriber, Gwen Bantowsky, who also offered useful comment.

A study grant from the Swedish Institute, Stockholm, Sweden, originating from Lars Malmstrom, Swedish Information Service, Los Angeles, enabled me to get an international perspective on this subject. Although not reflected in the text, field work was also done in Nairobi, Kenya, through the good offices of Sweden's Ambassador Cecelia Nettlebrandt and her staff. An indication of Sweden's continuing commitment to the interests of the women of the world, this support symbolizes to me a living tie between the Old World and New, a precious link, a valued heritage which I trust informs and enlightens my own work.

Albany, California   NANCY LEE PETERSON
August 1, 1980

OUR LIVES FOR OURSELVES

INTRODUCTION

It was an August afternoon in the early sixties when the world was very beautiful and you sensed the promise of your life opening before you. I was on the Santa Fe Chief, crossing New Mexico. The open expanses of the high desert had given way to the reaches of the Sangre de Cristo mountains and the early waters of the Rio Grande in their foothills; Spanish and Indian pueblos edged the tracks, reaching back again into the mountain crevices. Someone had tipped the porter, and the strains of Dvořak filled the dome car. To be twenty-two and alive to the afternoon was to sense the richness of life and feel that all things are possible.

I had completed graduate summer school at the University of California at Los Angeles, and then returned to Michigan to visit my parents. Now I was headed for Gallup to resume my second year of teaching on the Navaho reservation in the checkerboard area of San Juan County. My old Buick was parked at the depot, and a four-hour drive would return me to Lake Valley, to the quonset huts and trailer where one other teacher and I maintained a small boarding school.

The country outside the window somehow seemed hospitable and gracious, reassuring me that my gamble in coming to this wild and western place had been a risk well taken.

Those were good and happy times—perhaps the best, in certain respects, to be a young woman setting forth in the world. Many of the comfortable "givens" of the fifties were still with us; the changes that would characterize the sixties were only beginning to emerge. There was not then a women's movement, nor could we even imagine one; our concepts about ourselves and our lives as women were based on assumptions we rarely challenged.

We were taught to realize ourselves through the traditional roles of women. We attended college that we might "enrich ourselves and serve others"; perhaps we would "pick up a skill" like teaching or nursing in case we would want to work. We were encouraged to cultivate our bodies and our looks, acquire domestic skills, overcome our sexual hang-ups. For ahead of us was a certainty we never questioned: We would marry and have children. Our future happiness would be found through men: men to date, men to love, *a man we could marry*. Surely, we would live out our lives much as our mothers had—within the bounds of domesticity, secure and warm.

Yet in retrospect, I can now see there were some small rents in the marital veil enveloping young womanhood, even in 1961, the year I graduated from DePauw University. The "girls" in our graduating class at Alpha Omicron Pi quietly congratulated themselves that at our house, at least, not one senior was engaged—quite the opposite at the Tri Delts or Alpha Chis or Alpha Phis, where they most likely congratulated themselves if the whole graduating class was engaged, or at least within reasonable prospect of soon being married. No, we told ourselves, we were more individualistic than that; everyone knew we were the least conformist house at DePauw, and we would bow off the campus proving it. So Ginnie went to Chicago to become an interior-design trainee for Marshall Field; Jane would teach in Long Beach; Barb enrolled in a Methodist seminary preparing for the ministry; Beth entered graduate school at the University of Chicago to study psychology. I left for New Mexico to begin what was to become a career in the Indian service, my choice being alternately regarded by my peers as either odd or idealistic. But in the back of all of our minds—we more doughty individualists and our more compliant campus classmates— remained an assumption that none of us seriously challenged. A period for a fling as a career girl was allowed, but basic goals didn't change; ultimately, women married. And indeed, within a very few years I had received the requisite number of wedding invitations from my sorority classmates, followed in a year or two by baby announcements; each of them had joined the ranks of the married.

Options in life-styles existed in those times, but we rarely thought to seek them out, or even examine the ones at hand. The inevitability of it all—a good education at the best school you could get into, perhaps a summer in Europe for the affluent and/or determined few, a brief but exciting career, then marriage.

We thought we knew what the alternative to marriage was. We

thought we saw it in the familiar yet threatening facade of spinster-hood, exemplified in the glimpses we had of the lives of our unmarried college instructors, whom we often admired personally and certainly respected professionally, but whose dinner invitations to gracious but modest apartments, whose trips to professional conferences here and there, whose summer vacations spent in the Rockies with each other or with aged relatives only projected an image which chilled us.

I remembered my grade school teachers. There was Miss Jackson, who complained bitterly to the class about the impoverished surround-ings of the boardinghouse where she felt her low salary compelled her to live, and her occasional irrational outbursts against children she especially disliked. And there was Miss Webb, who was buxom and blonde, and who suddenly left our school in Peoria one January to go live in Arizona midst our mothers' whispers implying that she might be pregnant. In high school, there were the Hedstrom sisters—so patient and friendly, understanding with even the most reluctant French conversationalist, and Miss Sperling, who bestowed on those of us willing to work for it a wonderful facility in "Sperlinian" English. Some of us had single aunts and cousins, outside the "normal" circle of the family, and we had neighbors, or knew other single women, like Miss Hoffman, the local branch librarian, who once traveled to South America to study wildlife. . . . No, we knew what staying single meant, and we didn't want any part of it.

By the time I was in my mid-twenties I was in Los Angeles, engrossed in my career, setting up an apartment, going to night school, traveling, and involved with activities and friends. I had loyally helped launch many a wedding and knew quite well the tightened throat, the defensive feeling of going down yet another reception line, alone. But on another level, I sometimes had a curious sense of dislocation and mild confusion—I couldn't quite understand my place in the scheme of things. At cocktail parties after the requisite what-do-you-do part of the conversation was over, I had a disquieting sense of not knowing just who it was that I should present to my conversational partner; in fact, I wasn't certain *who* I was. I knew my uncertainty turned around the fact that I was single, and that the images which directed women's lives prescribed that women of my age should be married. But I seemed to know nothing about being single; beyond the pragmatic aspects of day-to-day living, I didn't quite understand how I should be.

Educated people are taught to "consult the literature" and so I did, what little there was of it. In the more academic and scholarly libraries I consulted, I could find literally nothing under the caption "single women" that applied to the complexities and puzzlements I was facing.

When I reviewed the more popular literature, I found that for the most part there was no such thing as singleness as an end in itself, that all of us in this category were really premarital. The life of the single woman was represented in terms of how to end her singleness, and most texts dealt with a vast and clever stream of information about how to attract and hold a man.

One book that was willing to discuss the situation of women who remained single was Dr. Marian Hilliard's *A Woman Doctor Looks at Life and Love.* Published in 1957, it reflected a prefeminist and highly moralistic view of women's lives and sexuality and dealt at length on the special situation of the unmarried women. Herself ever-single, Dr. Hilliard presented a chilling rendition of a brave but pathetic existence. Single life was hard. "Nothing will again be as painful as the moment [the single woman] realizes that she will live all her life alone, no moment will ever hurt so much," she wrote. Sexuality must be repressed, she advised, and when a single woman felt the "real distress of desire" she should "read a mystery story—visit a friend with five children under ten years of age. Take a very hot bath and plan your next vacation." Dr. Hilliard condemned love affairs with married men. If a single woman were to enter into one, she "would have to give up all her friends and clubs and go into social and moral retreat—she loses caste and has a sense of sickness in her soul." A lurid passage describing an encounter between Dr. Hilliard and an unmarried woman who found herself pregnant described Hilliard's reaction to abortion. ("'I can't have a baby! I can't!' one career woman shrieked at me. 'You've got to do something. This will ruin me!' 'You'll emerge from this a better woman,' I said gently.")

She strongly implied that a good dose of masochism might be in order when she began her book with a heartrending tale of her rejection years before by a man she hoped to marry and her subsequent acceptance of his request that his wife become her obstetrical patient. "Nothing else in my life has ever or will ever hurt so much," she wrote. "On Mother's Day, in the early morning, that I might miss no overtone of human longing or resignation, the child was born. If I could accept that and survive, and I could, then I could withstand anything."

Alone. Aloneness, singleness, loneliness. In those days, you lived in a conventional—oh-so-conventional—marriage and nuclear family, or you were alone, outside, not living as a normal person should. Marriage is normal and normal is right, isn't it?

In a different vein, *Sex and the Single Girl* was published in 1962, causing comment because of its exposition of an assertive life for single women and its more open view of sexuality. No one has ever called Helen Gurley Brown a feminist; some of her views on women would make any sensitive person wince. "Some girls 'hate' men because they secretly envy their 'superior advantages,' their jobs, their ability to exploit. Manhaters may secretly envy men's penises. If you sustain any of these hates, you need help, probably professional, to find out how much nicer it is to be a woman."

Brown had a strongly materialistic orientation and her views of human relationships were often manipulative; she seemed particularly exploitative of men. But *Sex and the Single Girl* began with a chapter entitled "Woman Alone? Oh Come Now" and in a warm and intimate tone described a dynamic life for single women. Brown championed careers, encouraged less conventional views of sexuality, allowed for abortion, and concluded "You may marry or you may not. In today's world that is no longer the big question for women. Those who glom on to men so that they can collapse with relief, spend the rest of their days shining up their status symbols and figure they never had to reach, stretch, learn, grow, face dragons or make a living again are the ones to be pitied. They, in my opinion, are the unfulfilled ones."

The Feminine Mystique was published in 1963, and despite the exhilarating effect it had on those of us who were now beyond the Hilliard or Brown message, Betty Friedan did not deal with the issue of marital status. Her thesis framed fulfillment and self-realization for women through careers and other fully demanding adult pursuits *together with* the more conventional roles of wife and mother. Herself divorced and the mother of adult children, Friedan has never directly focused on the impact of marital status in women's lives, although she allows for alternative life-styles and implies the acceptability of singleness, as do many writers who address women's affairs.

In 1967 the National Organization for Women (NOW) was founded, amid much derisory speculation and the many misconceptions that marked the early days of the women's movement. I resolved to resist joining it. I could not see feminism as a significant or valid issue. I believed it was unnecessary and might undermine the human rights movement for minorities. But then I recalled the troubled remark of another woman Congress of Racial Equality activist who had one day commented that if we really wanted to take on a task to improve the human condition, if we truly wanted to tackle a demon in the field of social inequality, then we ought to begin with the equality of women.

Within three months of NOW's founding I was a convert, albeit a covert one. For about two years I went around confessing to feminism as this "new thing" I was into. Friends smiled indulgently, noncommittally; my proclivity for social causes was well known; perhaps this was a passing fad that they could experience and test out vicariously, through me. I discovered the reorientation required of many liberal women of that day as we turned from advocacy on behalf of "them" to advocating for ourselves. I went through a long process of recognizing—working through—acknowledging and finally owning the special situation faced by women. It was difficult for me, at first, to learn to say "We women need. . . ."; the effect of a statement like that in an office staff meeting at first startled other women as much as it did me. Last of all came the recognition and acknowledgment of self-need; I, who had seen myself as privileged and advantaged, now had much to learn.

I struggled and still struggle toward the individual and social consciousness implicit in the women's movement. I know that the ramifications of feminist proposals are radical and revolutionary, and I become awed and frightened by the dimensions of what will surely become a lifetime struggle. As all women in the movement must, I become wearied by the insidious nature of sexism, and by the gross and often wasteful expenditure of human energies that must be used to ensnare and reverse its course. Yet there is real change, real progress, and sometimes, in the moment of accomplishment, real joy. Revitalized, I draw on the strength the movement itself has given me, and move on.

Open and honest communication among women may be an emphasis of the women's movement, but when my sorority friends and former classmates from DePauw and I met at class reunions and alumni meetings, we weren't very open, and our conversations were polite and brief. My assumption was that all was well in the suburbs where married people live; that the children were developing on schedule; that the mortgage would be paid off in thirty years. They, in turn, politely reflected that indeed my career was interesting, my trips adventurous, my social life rich and full; there was also an unspoken assumption that it was just a matter of time. . . .

But I knew something of the private lives of married men away from their families and had few illusions about marital fidelity, and I could guess at the restlessness and upheavals behind the facade of the women I had known so well only a short time ago. In time the dreaded announcement of separation and divorce came, slipped into conversations or on the backs of Christmas cards.

The women's movement might be the place to deal with what Friedan called "the problem that has no name," but for some illusive reason, the movement shared with my friends and me a curious reticence to address the life-style and circumstances of never-married women. Conferences were called, books were published, learned articles were produced, and consciousness-raising sessions without number probed marriage and coupling of every description; coping with divorce, managing as a single parent, surviving widowhood, and finding acceptance for lesbian women, not to mention a multitude of spin-off problems associated with all these statuses. The failure to even acknowledge the concerns of ever-single women were particularly striking because of the extraordinary degree of participation of single women in the Movement. Six o'clock Thursday evening might find Claudia, Nancy, Gail, and Jean refining a contract with a day-care center while drinking a beer at the Rathskeller, but Claudia, Nancy, and Jean were ever-single and childless, and Gail was single too, divorced and without children.

It is very evident to me that the time is past due to deal with the subject of the never-married woman. Even the nomenclature surrounding the subject is problematic; we hardly know what to call ourselves. The historical terms are inaccurate and pejorative: spinsters don't spin anymore and old maid is a term of derision. My grandmother referred to such women as maiden ladies, but the term is quaint and condescending. Bachelorette is more modern, but is nevertheless cute and offensive and may be an attempt to hitchhike on the higher value placed on the status of bachelor. Never-married has the disadvantage of negatively defining people, by telling what they are not and inferring a standard or norm. Ever-single is positive and brief, though perhaps has a slightly romantic ring to it. Single is a nonspecific term, embracing all categories not presently married.

"The Singular Woman" was once used as a conference title to embrace all women not attached, but sociologist Jessie Bernard objected to it, pointing out that it made such women seem odd and apart from others, and besides, the number of women not affiliated in a marital union was too high to consider them very singular. She endorsed "women on their own," a title which suggests independence and self-reliance but includes single women without regard to previous marital status.

In this book I use some of the above terms interchangeably, hopefully with the meaning intended. Despite its acknowledged clarity and strength, the English language has the problem of being notoriously weak in human relational words. Just try to find a word to describe the second wife of a man with grown children (Mother won't do) or words which untangle the skein of in-laws or cousin statuses strewn across family lines.

As mentioned earlier, scholarly research and literature also reflect the neglected status of the single woman. The topic of womankind has been so generously covered in the research tomes of academia and government that special study departments, libraries, and subject indexes have had to be devised to contain it all. But one can thoroughly research every catalogued piece of material on the ever-single woman in a day or two: *Women and Society—A Critical Review of the Literature with a Selected Annotated Bibliography* contains some 3,600 inclusions on women, of which only 10 are addressed to "spinsters" or "single women." No volumes of research are known to focus wholly on this subject area, despite the global implications of the topic for researchers in psychology, social psychology, sociology, demography, economics, law, and other fields. The substantial number of ever-single women working in these fields of inquiry who have somehow never identified the topic for academic research further illuminates the extreme difficulty women have had in confronting this subject.

Our Lives for Ourselves—Women Who Have Never Married is intended to be the book I looked for all these years and never found. I have been ambivalent about undertaking this project, and weighed the pros and cons of it for a long time. The ambivalence I felt was partly a reflection of the ambiguity I was experiencing about my own marital status, and I knew I would have to resolve my own conflicts in order to be able to handle the topic adequately, present my own story, and address the material other single women might share with me. To deal in a very public way with aspects of one's life that are very personal and private would take great resolve; it was a commitment that I at first sought to avoid.

Besides, I told myself, I am not a professional writer and such an assignment would be a formidable one indeed: There were other areas of the women's movement which demanded my attention, areas where my skills as an organizer might be more aptly applied. I knew this project would snowball and become all-consuming—and it has. But the proposed title of the book rang in my mind; it posed a challenge that would not go away, a need no one else could or would address as I intended.

I have written *Our Lives for Ourselves* because I want readers to know about women who lead lives of positive autonomy. I want people to know about the life experiences of ever-single women: the quality of our lives, the choices we must make, the contentment or the difficulties we find in a life that is "different." Perhaps, in its way, it will offer a charting for a course which once puzzled me and which may now also puzzle other women; perhaps we need not always have to discover anew and alone if others have been there before. In this time of upheaval and urgent reevaluation in women's lives, we will tell each other what we have learned, how we might live.

Sharing is marked by no small sense of pride—pride in self, pride in our small group, who comprise no more than five to seven percent of all women, who understand the societal norms pressed upon us, and who live our lives another way.

I also believe that what I have learned from never-married women may have a predictive value; what is happening in our lives now may foreshadow changes which may come in relationships in the future, and may perhaps forecast changes in the nature of society itself.

In a larger sense, *Our Lives for Ourselves* is another accounting about a segment of society that ultimately reflects the human whole; it is about conflict, ambivalence and resolution, decisions to be made, disappointments faced, triumphs to be savored. This is a book about looking at other ways, about taking the road less traveled.

I

WHEN ALL THINGS SEEM POSSIBLE

I started this book in the most basic and fundamental way I knew: by asking and listening. Over a course of three years I broached the subject of never-marriedness to hundreds of people: to never-married women like myself, to never-married women very unlike myself. Would you like to know more about this subject? Yes, definitely. Would you be willing to share some of your experiences with me? Yes, usually. Do our experiences have something in common, are there common themes among us? There are.

To married women: Would the subject of never-married women interest you? Yes, frankly, I've always wondered what might have happened if I hadn't married and had these children. And I see single women around me; I wonder what their lives are like.

And to separated, divorced, and widowed women: Our lives must be similar in many respects, but without the factor of marriage at all?—different too. Yes, I'd like to know.

I asked men, too, of many backgrounds. A few saw it as a challenging, worthy project and asked what I was learning about never-married women. But for most it was an uncomfortable subject, one to shy away from; they quickly turned the conversation to the technicalities of writing and publishing a book. I wondered why they wanted to avoid discussing the topic; I sensed they felt there was something menacing, maybe even subversive in opening this subject, as though I were dealing with a vested but not quite acknowledged interest. I learned to mention it in a careful offhand way to men I knew, and especially men I cared for. But women were always interested, wanted to know more.

I interviewed, in depth, a group of eighty women. I wanted a group that would represent the great variety among us: They should be of all ages, of various backgrounds and (tiresome word) life-styles, different ethnic and racial groups, come from different parts of the United States. The last issue was of special importance: a Midwesterner myself, I know that women who live west of the Hudson and east of the San Francisco Bay often resent the way the two coasts dominate media attention. New York and San Francisco have their points, but I know that women in Denver and Des Moines and Knoxville and Farmington and Springfield would have fully as much to share.

About age: The United States Census defines never-marriedness as beginning at age thirty and at first it made sense to me to start there; after all, adult life is well established by then and there would be much to report. But my friend Karen Keisling had a better idea: She pointed out that critical marital decisions are often made at a young age; eighteen-year-olds might find the experiences of a woman of thirty remote and inapplicable. I remembered receiving a letter as a college sophomore from my friend Linda, age twenty: "All our high school friends are married. I feel like an old maid."

So this survey begins with women in their twenties, chosen because they were living their lives in an autonomous way: developing plans for the future, not expecting a knight on a white horse to come along and answer all their questions, "make their lives complete." The youngest woman in this survey is twenty, the oldest is seventy-eight.

About ethnic and racial groups. We know cultural values, religious differences, and community norms heavily influence attitudes and behavior about marital status. But the role of culture and ethnicity in singleness is a topic of encyclopedic range, far beyond the scope of this book. Here I can only touch on it to give a flavor of the variations among groups.

I define my sample group as women who never have been legally married. It didn't matter whether they chose to be unmarried or not, or if they intended or hoped to be married in the future. My purpose was to look at their life experiences up to the present time. I looked for women who were interesting, articulate, and insightful; in return for their confidences, I guaranteed anonymity.

A few categories of never-married women have been excluded. Nuns are not included (although several former nuns are): their vocational commitment places them in a unique and exclusive role, not unlike a marital commitment; indeed, they are referred to as "brides of Christ." Women who have maintained continuing relationships of many years duration with one man or one woman who are recognized by the community as common-law wives are not included (although it would be interesting to know why the latter have maintained their single status).

The things I have learned are best understood when considered by life stages. The age categories themselves are approximate because life events flow and intertwine differently for each person, and birthdays are milestones only generally indicating the passing of life events. One woman's crisis at thirty-five is another's at thirty-two or forty or perhaps not at all.

So, on a smoky fall afternoon in Pennsylvania, I sat on the porch of a farmhouse, and, to the sound of apples being crated, talked with a retired teacher. "What is the best thing about being single? the worst? Your relationship with the banker—tell me more about it. If you were twenty again, is there anything you'd do differently?" To a thirty-seven-year-old legislative assistant in Indianapolis: "What do children mean to you? Have you thought of remaining single and raising a child? How would you feel about bearing a child without being married?" And, yes, with a woman advertising executive in New York: "Does your marital status affect your relationship with your clients? With other women? Has anyone thought you were gay? Why do you *really* think you've remained single?"

The women spoke of many things. The kinds of families they came from, how their families felt about their ever-single status. Careers, vocations, and the importance of work in life. Social relationships of all kinds—love affairs, friendships, and being alone. The Man I Should Have Married—and the man, thank God, I didn't. My niece, who means everything to me—the child I bore and gave up. Opening the first progressive day-care center in Omaha. Closing the finest restaurant in Baton Rouge. Several times I was told stories of such self-revealing poignancy that their bearer could only utter them, and then ask me not to use them. I haven't.

In looking for the things single women share in common, I learned something about the role parents and close relatives play as permission-givers—people who say, in effect, "It's okay to remain single." I looked for commonalities in childhood and family background—the quality of parental married and family life, other related factors which might or might not influence singleness. I wondered about role models, and childhood expectations of the future.

I was interested in matters of self-concept and self-esteem. How did never-married women see themselves, how did they compare themselves to other women? And I tried to check out some of the stereotypes and rumors about us. Are we tied to parental apron strings? Unattractive in appearance, blemished in personality? Unduly fond of cats? Secretly gay? Is our old age spent in a corner, regretful, lonely and alone? We shall see.

I found that never-married women in their twenties were a different and more interesting group than I had at first imagined. They were the group I had to study most closely, the women I had the most to learn from. I had somewhat naively assumed they must be like my friends and I were ten or fifteen years ago. I couldn't have been more wrong.

They are a new generation, stronger and braver than their sisters only a few years distant. Not all their concerns are different; educations must still be completed, careers begun, a niche found in the adult world. But emphases and attitudes have shifted. Values affecting what's to be done and how it's to be accomplished are different. Young women today have a sense of wanting to find their own identities, expressing them and fulfilling them in ways which were never done before.

Social relationships are looked at in a fresh way; commitments are made stressing changed priorities. And the question of men and marriage appears in a new context.

Marta Cardenas

One gets a sense of Marta Cardenas—"Marty" to her friends—in her direct gaze, her quick smile. She is the oldest of three daughters, raised primarily by her mother, a successful Chicana administrator of the Texas Employment Commission. Marty lives in a modest studio apartment near downtown Houston where she "pursues a happy life." She is exceedingly pretty.

She completed high school two years ago and entered a training program in electronics construction. "The main thing with me right now is to finish this training. I'm learning a certain type of electronic construction. Our company makes teletype printers and transmitters, and once you get out of training, you can work your way up in the plant fairly fast. I want to become a supervisor, although I have this dream, too, of opening an electronics supply store. It's a good field, because lots of people are into electronics as a hobby, and many businesses need electronic parts.

"My other plan is to save up and go to college and get a degree in electrical engineering. I could do it if I could get the money together, at least enough to get started. Then I could run that plant!" She laughs.

We sat in her living room, a cheerful amalgamation of finds from import houses and things Marty has borrowed from her mother's home. A woven Mexican rug garnished with huge crepe-paper flowers covers one wall; a profusion of houseplants is banked against the other. Prized possessions—a stereo set, a sewing machine, a guitar, a ten-speed bike—are displayed around the room. Marty smiles and hugs her knees.

"I've always been good with my hands and I like to make things. I like to fix up things in general: my car, my stereo, this apartment."

En route to her plans and dreams, Marty enjoys herself. "I come and go as I please, and concentrate on having a good time. I'm not accountable to anybody, *any way.* I like the sociability of my work, but I like to spend time alone in my little place. I feel free here. I can run around without any clothes on, get out my guitar and sing, sit and sew half the night.

"My girl friend was over last weekend, and we were fixing our cars— soldering the radiator on hers, and rewiring the cassette player in mine. We changed the spark plugs and the oil. The two guys we're going with came over about five and we went to the Spaghetti Factory, and out dancing at this cowboy bar outside of town. A more or less typical weekend."

Marty's world is peopled by an assortment of friends from work, from high school, a neighbor with a baby, and a strong, affectionate relationship with her mother. She sees her mother—"My only true role model and the person I admire most"—once or twice a week. Her relationship with her boyfriend, Joe, a Cuban fellow trainee, is "casual and fun, sort of on-again, off-again. My tennis and swimming buddy." Her decision to embark on a three-day drive to Los Angeles with him sparked "about the only major confrontation I've had with my mother lately. She said she didn't like the looks of the thing, which means she doesn't know how involved I am with him. She shouldn't sweat it. Not really."

Other relationships with men have been more meaningful. Sent for initial training to a factory in Kansas, Marty met Caleb, another trainee. He was good-looking and "different" with an offhand manner. They began spending time together, and because they lived near each other in trailers at the training site, Marty engineered a meal-sharing arrangement. Soon they were living together. Caleb was Marty's first lover, an experience she describes as "not great but good, since I had all this curiosity about sex and that initiated me. Caleb and I were pretty close. I wondered if I loved him, and at times I thought maybe I did. Or maybe it was more that he needed me, and since I was out to find out a few things, well, everything was fine with him. I don't know. It doesn't matter. I was taken with him partly because he was older, twenty-five. I still like him and I see him once in a while, but I don't give our relationship a lot of thought. Even when I felt close to Caleb I realized I was pretty interested in some of the other guys around, and I saw I was restricting myself from them."

Marty is more sagacious than many younger women about love, about men, about marriage. "Maybe it's because of my parents splitting up, or because I see what my mother has been able to do for herself and us kids since she's been single. I know she'd have a heart attack if I told her I was in a real heavy place with a guy and was thinking about getting married. Hey! I guess that's what might have been in the back of her mind when she got mad at me for taking off to L.A. with Joe!" Her expression indicated a familiar theme had been repeated.

"But I get that from some of the men out at the plant, too. They tell me they envy me, they wish they hadn't gotten married and could run around. At the rate I hear about people out there getting divorced, I guess they really mean it. I'd bet one in ten marriages are really happy, those being the long-term marriages, where people have been together like forever. I myself have never really seen a fairy-tale love story."

She paused, and fingered an advertisement for a trip to New Orleans folded inside a utility bill, and an unopened flyer offering a variety of courses in adult night school. She looked around her apartment and smiled expansively.

"Still, you never know," she said. "I might like to try it sometime—get married, that is. It's something I haven't done, and I'm curious about it. Yes, it might be real interesting.

"The thing I have to do now is finish this training, and tend to what I think of as my real business in life."

When one is twenty, one has plenty of time.

Kris Adair

Summer heat imparts a languorous quality to the streets of Omaha. Big cars still favored by Nebraskans move more slowly; sound seems to hang in the air. In an aging neighborhood near the center of town, racially mixed groups of children mill in the street, eyed by neighbors in metal lawn chairs, taking the cool from the grass. On the side porch of a once-grand Victorian house, Kris Adair talks with her tenant.

At twenty-six, Kris conveys an impression of disciplined energy. She is high-spirited and gregarious, yet her social awareness, her purposefulness, immediately come through. As she talked the phone rang continuously; friends called with news or information, others sought advice. She dispatched each with humor and efficiency, her bangle bracelets clinking as she waved her arm to emphasize each point. Finally she took the phone off the hook and discussed improving the house, perhaps modernizing the tenant's kitchen.

"It's more a question of financing than anything else; I want to do it. I'm not sure I've held this place long enough to qualify for a second mortgage. Still, it makes a good argument to say that increasing the value of the property or bringing in more income further secures the loans." Kris looked into space and smiled thoughtfully.

She works as a receptionist and sales trainee for a small local realtor. Her income, modest by any standard, has been channeled into the down payment on this house, and into making monthly payments and occasional improvements. Her own apartment is only partly furnished; a refrigerator braces a corner of the dining room; a spinet piano, chair, and sofa occupy the living room.

Kris emphasizes that the house is not only a personal plunge into real estate investment and speculation. "I mean, it *is* that, because I'm convinced real estate is a good long-term investment." Her interests are social as well as monetary. She sees the eventual restoration of her once-elegant home as a way of strengthening the inner city, easing the reputation of racially mixed neighborhoods as a haven for trouble-makers, and showing that private concern and investment can maintain neighborhoods of cultural and historic value.

Accordingly, Kris works with several groups which pursue these goals. She serves on the board of two, ACORN, a local action group concerned with neighborhood renovation, and the Fund for an Open Society, which works for integrated neighborhoods. She also works with Home, Incorporated (Home Opportunities Made Easy), which offers guidance in home ownership to needy families. Kris is helping a divorced black mother learn how to finance a home of her own. "I can see the difference owning a home has meant to me; I know it can mean a lot to her, too. What I stress in real estate is helpfulness and counseling; I'm not in this to be money-hungry. I want to prove to myself I can accomplish a whole range of goals through real estate."

Kris was raised in a small agricultural town in southeast Nebraska, the daughter of a farm implements mechanic and his wife, who raised their six children in the sturdy values of the rural midwest, flavored by their Methodist faith. "I was and still am very close to my mother, a traditional homemaker in every sense of the word. I had a happy childhood. Kids in small towns have fewer distractions and I think we grow up more home and family centered. Mother taught me the skills of homemaking and emphasized a very high sense of personal responsibility and morality. My father and I are less close. He stresses his role as family breadwinner and head of the family with us children.

But he and mother are very loving. I've never questioned their happiness. I know Mother expects that I too will be married and have a family. But she supports my present situation and is solicitous of my feelings. When my sister was married last summer, I was home a good deal, helping with the showers and wedding plans. It was making me edgy, all right; an unmarried woman of my age at a small town wedding has plenty of reason to feel out of place. My girl friends from high school have shoulder-high children by now. My 'differentness' feels very conspicuous. It was a relief to get back to Omaha."

Kris attended college for a year, but dropped out, uncertain of her purpose, and burdened by the loans she would have to repay after graduation. She went to Omaha and found work as a cashier, then became a sales representative for a trade school. She joined a church group for young adults, and there met Keith.

"I was twenty years old at the time and I thought I knew my way around. Keith was a talker—he sold insurance for a living—and something of a manipulator. In my worst moments I still think he spotted me as a naive little virgin he could break in. Well, he moved in on me all right. I was sleeping with him a month after I met him. I felt a little uncomfortable about sex outside of marriage, but he was good in bed, and I'll give him credit—he taught me well, broke me in right. I had some vague ideas about birth control, which mostly consisted of wanting to be reassured that everything would be all right if he pulled out. Well, he reassured me real well, and I was pregnant by January.

"It was like the floor fell out of my world. I quit my job and went home, telling my folks I was pregnant, but I had fallen in love with Keith and we intended to be married anyway. I tried to convince myself that this was so, but when Keith came down to Milford, the truth was up: He didn't fit, he wasn't right for me, he wasn't what I wanted. My father sat in hurt silence: I think he saw through me all the time. He compounded my hurt by reminding me of his values about sex outside of marriage— 'Don't you think we were right all along?' He disallowed my more tender feelings for Keith and the child I was carrying. My mother and I went down to see the minister, and he referred me to the state family service agency."

Kris was placed with two different families in Lincoln, where she served as a household helper and sitter, and did part-time work at a printer's office. The summer months passed quietly, with occasional visits from her mother and Keith. Upset by her pregnancy, Keith blurted out that he was illegitimate himself. In some way he mixed his defensive, possessive feelings for his mother with Kris' pregnancy. Sometimes he would get drunk and harangue her with barely intelligible outbursts, compounding her own sense of anxiety and guilt. She realized these meetings must stop and ended her relationship with Keith, who subsequently left the state.

The baby, a boy, was born in September; Kris released him for adoption when he was three days old, stipulating only that he be placed in a home like her own. She returned to Milford to rest and be comforted by her mother and close friends.

But the surrender of her son left Kris with a feeling of emptiness. "I felt so painfully deprived; I literally sat alone in my bedroom and wept until my eyes were dry. The social worker assured me that the placement had been made according to my wishes, but that didn't help much. I had almost never let myself think about keeping him during the time I was pregnant; I simply didn't see how I could raise a child alone. No one ever mentioned the possibility of some kind of public aid or program which might allow me to consider it; I began to feel I had been trapped into giving him up. My parents were all in favor of relinquishment; they wanted me to have a fresh chance and were concerned about social appearances. I already felt like a maverick and didn't know if I could bear being seen as some sort of deviant."

Her sense of distress deepened; she could not resume a normal life. Keith's menacing voice of doubt and anger seemed to call to her, giving voice to her guilt and unresolved conflict.

She reconsidered. "I began to feel I had misjudged the situation. There were stories in the paper of young mothers raising their babies alone with assistance from special programs; I looked at the pictures of those mothers and their babies and I felt so bad. Who could be a better parent to my boy than I, who could care for him better than I could?" Four months after his birth, Kris filed a court petition to reclaim him. A psychiatrist testified that she was "under extreme mental duress, suffering from acute and prolonged postpartum anxiety."

Seven months later, the court reviewed the case. Calling her into his private chambers, the judge quietly explained that his first consideration must be for the welfare of the child, then for the adopting parents, then for her. He could not rule to return the boy, but spoke of the possibility of a reunion when he was grown. He encouraged her to rebuild her life, look to a time when she might consider having other children. At first deeply disappointed in the court's rejection, Kris later realized the ruling had cleared the air, closed the matter for her. "My religious background came to the fore, and I accepted the decision as painful, but as part of God's will for my life, and that of my son.

"Besides the question about the baby, the pregnancy aroused feelings I didn't expect. I wanted to come out of this a sexual woman, yet I was a little paranoid—was I too sexy, a whore? I wanted romance, yet feared I would not find a trusting, affectionate relationship. And I wanted my figure back—I wanted to wear a bikini—but I saw a look of disapproval cross my mother's face. I wondered if I were tainted by my pregnancy."

She returned to Omaha and found work. She got an apartment, and later bought her house, became active in church, involved herself in community organizations. She resumed her friendships and established new ones. Her dating life, prolific for a while, has mellowed into a steady relationship with one man.

"It's one of those relationships that's on again, off again. Actually, I'm not all that sure what I want from Rod. It's a mix of friendship, love, sex, whatever. I once felt close enough to propose to him, but I realized I wasn't ready and was afraid of being tied down. And I really fear divorce.

"He sees another woman sometimes and yet feels guilty about being involved with both of us. I want attention, sex, and affection, yet I don't want him around a lot. He can fulfill me sexually, yet abuses me by wanting to have sex and leave without satisfying me. He encourages me with my real estate and career and advises me about money, my car, my relations with my sister. He helps me out with this house.

"My girl friend and I were sort of hashing over my relationship with Rod the other day. We decided a lot of relations with men are like this one—mixtures of love, companionship, sex, things you don't particularly like, things that are really great. It's hard to know where the relationship is going. I think the thing to do is to lean back, live it out, day by day, and emphasize the good points. Time will tell.

"I value my private space, my personal freedom, the sense of direction in my life. I know my need for elbowroom and space. I educate people to the fact that I keep busy and can't easily give up time. I lead my life for myself—so I can be free for my responsibilities, so I can work towards my goals. That's what I want; to do my best by all these good things I have going for me."

Julia Hawkins

"I always thought I'd like to be in my twenties for about twenty years—figured I'd have time enough to do all the things I needed to do, strength enough to accomplish them, and have something left over for some other things that needed doin' too!"

The twenties have been described as a time "when all things seem possible." Julia Hawkins, at twenty-seven, lives as though these words were written for her.

The New South has spawned some New Women, Julia among them. She describes herself candidly as part of a generation of blacks whose talents and abilities have been supported by the benefits of affirmative action. She sits in her law office late one night, high above the city. Simply dressed and unpretentious, Julia exudes an air of spirited optimism.

"What I'm here to do is to establish myself as a trial lawyer. This firm has made its reputation on civil rights cases—we've handled some of the landmark decisions in Georgia—but people just don't come through the door with many of those anymore. Because I'm the only woman on the staff, I tend to get the domestic cases, the 'weepin' women.' This staff is unusual for the South—about half black, half white."

She sees herself moving into community affairs, becoming the woman behind the scenes. To this end, she serves on a number of boards—YWCA, World Affairs Council, Urban League, and as vice-president of the Black Lawyers' Guild. "I don't see myself becoming an elected official—just the person people think to call when they want, say, to get through to a congressman, or bring in an ambassador from the U.N. A string puller—well known, respected in the community."

Julia is from Savannah, Georgia. Her parents were teachers, separated when Julia was six. Wishing to avoid having her daughter attend the school where she taught, Mrs. Hawkins enrolled Julia in a private church-run girls' school. Her excellent grades and test scores attracted the attention of college recruiters.

"In the late sixties, Ivy League schools decided there were intelligent black students, and it was time that they got some, or lose federal money. I was interested in a Seven Sisters type school, and decided I liked Smith—the brainy reputation, and all. I got a call from a recruiter—a black woman—and decided I'd go when I learned I *wasn't* being considered under the special admissions program. I didn't see my application as needing special consideration: I wasn't ghettoized, deprived, or poor; just wanted an education, that's all.

"The thing that's great to me about Smith is that it teaches you to believe *you can do anything.* The mix of students was unbelievable: wealthy society types, shy little WASPS, Jewish girls interested in clothes and grades. Many of the other black women were from the ghetto, or said they were, and came in with the idea that the school owes us something because our forefathers were trampled on and we're going to make up for that. But four of us in our dorm didn't go along with them—we had similar backgrounds from professional families—and we stayed away from the idea that we had to be rabble-rousers.

"But the dichotomy disturbed me. My group lived in Commerlyn Hall, and they called us 'Com Toms.' I went home at Thanksgiving with a new little Afro—nearly caught my death of pneumonia getting it—and my mother and grandmother about had a fit. I also had bought a bikini, and talked a line about Black Power. Everyone in Savannah thought I was crazy. My mother decreed I could *not* wear a swimming suit like that in the state of Georgia! Her idea of education was strictly realistic—take plenty of teaching courses. She told me I wasn't at Smith to 'find myself' like the white girls—I must get out there and DO!"

Julia's idea of "doing" was to get a law degree, and she decided to return to the South to earn it. Duke had a national reputation for academic excellence; Julia liked the idea of living in North Carolina; the climate is pleasant, and she felt the region would grow and progress. "Blacks today realize the South is a land of opportunity. Besides, it's my home and I'll stay and fight for what I want it to be." She finished Duke and passed the bar exam on her first try.

But the issue Julia faces now is marriage.

"Marry Richard? You better know there's a *moratorium* on that action right now! I asked him Saturday night if we were deciding if we were marrying each other, or if we were deciding if we were marrying anyone ever, and he said he assumed we both want to marry somebody sometime. I didn't say anything."

Richard's star rises in his world as surely as Julia's does in hers. An engineer with an advanced degree in business, Richard is a young executive with an international communications corporation. As an active member of the Baptist Church, he invited Julia to speak at his church about the Bakke decision. Then they began to date regularly. "He was interested in the fact that he had found somebody he could really talk to, that I had something to say; I was interested in his corporate world, a carry-over from law school, I suppose, and the fact that he was all wrapped up in his church, which I just couldn't imagine. But I liked him, I really did. Then all of a sudden he wants to get married and I couldn't *believe* that. Ridiculous, because we had just met each other. His company puts great emphasis on executives having wives—entertaining customers is a big part of his job—and he's going to go *far* in that corporation. He's smart, he's charming, he has a great sense of humor—and I love him, but I kept saying we just met each other, and kept putting it off and putting it off. I was dating another guy and Richard and I had a big blowup on my birthday because the other guy was here. It got real messy. Well, I finally said yes, I will marry him, and then I always back out and start to get cold feet about the idea. This month it's 'We're thinking about it.' We're going to make the final decision at the end of the month.

"I really don't know if I'll marry this guy. I really don't. He wants me to subjugate my life to him and his interests and do all the things a businessman's wife is supposed to do. And I keep saying, what about my career, I can't do that, and he talks about having children and I say, 'Children? What are they?'

"Richard's next promotion will probably take him overseas. As his wife, I'd be expected to do a very substantial amount of entertaining, and sort of aid and support the other families with the corporation there. So what happens to my career? I don't think I can practice overseas. And all that entertaining jive does nothing for me—small talk and the perfect canapé are not my element, and Tuesday afternoon at the tennis court or bridge table is definitely not where I'd rather be.

"A couple of months ago I was supposed to attend a reception the company was having but I got tied up in court. Richard's boss asked him where I was and he just hemmed and hawed around about it and later jumped all over me. I laid down the law. 'Look,' I said, 'there's no way on God's earth I can or ever shall walk out on my client to attend any party. If it matters so much to your boss, you're just going to have to spell it out to him. Or tell them nothing at all. They don't own me, not yet.' He feels uncomfortable about it, but when the issue came up again last week, he said, 'She's just not able to be here.'

"But I do love him—he's such a *good guy*. I just feel he may be trying to submerge my personality, hold me back. If we get married, I'm sure it will be a turbulent relationship, but I think if I decide to do it, I'll just fight and keep myself. He's going to have to verbalize to me that he's at least willing to make some concessions. If he can *say* it, then I can hold him to it.

"My mother is not really encouraging this relationship. She's uneasy about Richard because she thinks he won't make me happy—she feels I'll try to please him and in the process lose my own happiness. Like when I was a child, bending over backwards to please the other person to make him happy and in the process, pushing myself all out of shape. She liked the guy I went with—George—who loved me more than I loved him, who put himself all out for me. She doesn't want to see me hurt, so she looks at the relationships I have where I do the making up after a fight, and thinks instead of George, who would just never fight with me, and would go out of his way to do nice things for me, as she perceived it.

"Mother never pushes about my marital status or wanting grand-children. Basically she treats me like an adult, although sometimes she makes me feel guilty because she's had a hard life as a single parent. We've had some low-blow fights about who Julia dates and who Mother dates, but our relationship is okay! She thinks I may be just interested in Richard for sex, which I could get anywhere. George, on the other hand, is a *good man*."

She continued, in a more reflective way. "I see I'm now less concerned with the expectations of others, including Mother and Richard's company. If I decide I want to commit myself to him and his interests that's my decision, but I don't owe it and nobody can lay that on me. *That realization is a freedom I have come to enjoy.*"

Living together is a less common arrangement in the South, yet it seemed a middle ground for Julia's position. "Richard was spending time here and once he said, 'I'm living here.' I had to pull back and say, 'The hell you are. You don't pay the rent or the utilities *or* buy the food *or* clean up the place *or nuthin.* You come here and sleep and that's all.' I had to tell him that and that's not a thing I like to do, it's throwing finances in a man's face and black men are supersensitive about that."

She reflected a moment and looked aside. "Here I come from an all-female family, went to an all-female high school and college, then I'm thrown into a mostly white male law school. Now I'm the only woman in this firm! I'm not always sure I learned how to assuage the delicate black male ego.

"But I think anyone I care enough to live with, I may as well be married to. There's no half step. When I make that commitment, I'll be doing it totally, and will expect the same from him.

"So why haven't I married? Because I haven't found someone I thought was going to let me be free enough to let me do what I'm going to do or someone I wanted to be tied down to do the things I think I *have* to do to make the marriage work. Marriage means accepting the responsibility of sharing your life with another person. And I haven't found the person that I want to do that with yet, or whom I wanted to accept that responsibility for. And in accepting that mutual responsibility, still allow myself the freedom I need to do free, maybe even crazy things. I still haven't found anybody I thought I'd have all that give-and-take with yet, so I haven't done it.

"And to be single is to be selfish, and I haven't decided I'm not going to be selfish anymore. 'Cause you give up so much. Maybe I have the wrong view of it, but I perceive marriage as giving up a lot. And a lot of people I know, especially men, say 'Don't do it. Wait till you're thirty-five, or you'll be sorry, so just don't do it.' So there's really no rush."

She got up, glanced down the hallway, and closed the door. "And I've seen a lot of married guys run around—they run to me sometimes—and I don't accept it. I don't think I could stand for it. I'm not sure I could trust anybody to be faithful. I've finally decided that men are just going to play around, that's their nature. So I've sort of mellowed out about the idea that if they take care of business at home, it really doesn't matter. Just as long as I don't find out about it. But you see, I'm not sure I totally accept that view since my first premise was when you marry somebody, it's till death do you part, and that's it. I haven't worked out how I'm going to accept that yet. I don't think I could have a husband who's just running around and flaunting it in my face.

"And then there are times when I'd desperately like to have somebody and that's when I do think about living with somebody. Then I'd have control over that person and when I'd get tired of him I'd say, go home! But you can't have that in marriage. So I still think, do I want to get married or not? What does it have to offer? Not financial security—I can do that myself—and not to have children, 'cause I could just get pregnant or adopt. And for companionship? I can have companionship for the rest of my life. A constant fear is getting tired of it—you get tired of anybody after a while, and you'd have to keep rejuvenating your relationship.

"I've considered all those things and I just don't *know*. I don't know if it's worth it. I've seen so many bad marriages and divorces in here and I listen to the things people say about why their marriage broke up and I know I'm not infallible, I'm just another person, so what would make my marriage so different from all the ones I hear about? And it's just *scary*, I don't know. And then people say, 'Well, it's a risk, everything in life is a risk,' but I think it's a *big* risk because you're playing with your life and somebody else's life and you can do irreparable damage to yourself and to another person, or to your children."

A pause, and sigh. "If I'm unhappy and I'm by myself, well, it's my fault. I can't blame it on another person. And I can't *count on* another person for my happiness, either.

"And then you think about immortality, and having children and having grandchildren. There's still some propriety which requires having a spouse when you have a child.

"So, I stick my toe in and pull it out. And maybe my whole foot, and maybe one day I'll just fall in, I don't know. And sink or swim!

"These are not answers, they are all questions."

Ambiguity and conflict. Conflict and ambiguity. These themes will rise and fall, appear, disappear, and reappear throughout this book. Ambiguity about the nature of marriage itself. Conflict about a given relationship with a particular man. The desirability of having a family; doubts about the unknowns, the "what ifs" of the future. Especially for younger women, these questions are often underlaid with a sense of seismic shifting, of being an explorer in what increasingly becomes a Brave New World for women in their relations with men. For the women's movement and the rise of feminine consciousness fosters new concepts of self, of woman's identity, of the nature of women's relations with men. However much these questions rage in the ideologic sense, or as a function of social theory, their actual resolution will occur around the question of marriage.

It will appear, that is, as one issue within the elaborate context of life strategies for single women in their early and mid-twenties. For the issue that presents itself most strongly among them is not the resolution of marital status or questions concerning relationships with men, but the larger and grander designs of launching adult life, with the question of men and marriage as part of the whole. Completing an education and finding a vocation; establishing oneself in a job or career pattern, beginning to build a reputation "in the field." Establishing a home, or at least a way of living: the basic material possessions one must have. A place in the community, or at least a place in the scheme of things. Life-styles and life-strategies. Social relationships, with peers and parents, women and men and all those people social scientists label "significant others."

Most women in their twenties enjoy a rich variety of relationships. Sue, a writer, spoke of a complex, intimate circle of women friends involved in creative work similar to hers, who supported and stimulated each other with a network of communication and practical assistance. Most women emphasized the special importance of other women as companions and friends. But relationships with couples and families, acquaintances from school and work, from neighborhood and community groups, with older people and with children, were also highly valued.

Relations with men seem to include every conceivable option. Terry lived with two gay men for a year to "enjoy male company in a friendly, pressure-free environment." Maria met Jorge at a political rally, drove him home through a heavy fog, and stayed the night. Later they drew up a friendly "rental contract" to spend time together, and she added "with an option to buy." Monica steadily dates a lifelong friend, now divorced, willingly accepting the conservative norms affecting a teacher in a black Alabama farm community.

Their relationships seemed characterized by a freely arrived-at choice, and a sense of being in control. Terry explained it best. "Look, I know it's not usually thought of as the thing to do, but it happens that if you want to meet men in a small town like this, you go to a bar after a ball game. I know I'm there on my own terms. I'm in control. If I initiate something, I decide what I'm going to do—or not do. And you know, *it's okay*, it works out just fine."

When younger women discuss relationships, the word "commitment" is often heard. When Sue spoke of the problem of "turning an uncommitted relationship into a committed one" she was referring to both the quality and kind of relationship she hoped to achieve. Intimacy is seen as the key to that commitment.

Partnership and equality are greatly valued, indeed, almost demanded. Someone with whom I can share my feelings: Let's be there for each other. Someone to share domestic arrangements and economic burdens. Someone who fully supports my career, who sees my plans as being equally important as his own. Sue spoke of her need to work out dependency/independency feelings: the "take-care-of-me thing" versus the pride she feels in having built a life of her own.

For most of these women, the relationship they seek is described as marriage, quickly followed by a caveat: but not the kind of marriage her parents had! Marriage is felt to be a public statement of a previously private relationship, a socially recognized commitment to the future. Its limitations are felt and expressed, but women are optimistic that adjustments can be made, individual requirements met. Often there is a desire to establish a home and family, although we shall see later that the desire for house and children does not always correlate with a wish for marriage.

Still, it should be emphasized that when women in their early and mid-twenties speak of marriage, they usually speak of it in conditional terms. It all depends, they stress, on finding the right person, the right circumstances, the right relationship. For the largest group of women this age, marriage is one goal, ranked among others. It assumes a greater importance when a certain man in a certain situation presents himself; at other times it is of little or no importance; other matters are dominant and all-absorbing.

There is a second, smaller group of single women in their early and mid-twenties who are deferrers. Usually they are deferring in favor of highly valued educational and career plans. Clear the tracks! I've got to finish this residency and establish a practice! Then I'll think about a relationship. Wait until I become district manager! I'll work twelve hours a day till I make it! There's always time for men. The deferrers tend to see things as either/or. Either Fred or this promotion, either law school or marriage. One senses they protect their career aspirations (read: identities) against an imagined onslaught by marriage: If only the first can be built strong enough, it can withstand the second. In comparison, the first group of women are integrators, perhaps more able to balance out and weigh different values, more able to take things as they come.

Despite the paradoxes of these times and those that are inherent in entering adult life, younger never-married women display a remarkable sense of "getting on with it." They are often willing to make difficult commitments for long-term gains: to quit a promising job to enter a long course of training in a different field, and to go deeply in debt, if necessary, to pay for it; to struggle, at considerable sacrifice, to become established in a new field. Even in small ways, they proceed. These are not women who hole up in a dreary furnished apartment marking time "until my real life begins"; if they buy Arabia or Waterford or whatever, it's to be used and enjoyed now, not saved for an anticipated "more important time."

The sense is often a confident one—the future will take care of itself, despite an uncertain job market and troubling economic indicators. A sense of groundedness and clarity, straightforwardness and pragmatism. And not valuing certain defined relationships—for example marriage—as an end in themselves, but for their particular value for the individuals involved.

However, special circumstances sometimes present themselves. Characteristically, younger women respond in individualistic and unexpected ways. Randy Howard's story, while unusual, shows the resourcefulness, the coping ability, the kinds of values which influence younger women today.

Randy Howard

"I remember having a very clear vision of my father's death—which greatly frightened me—and the boding sense that my mother wouldn't be around either. My father died just as I had dreamed it, when I was fourteen, and my mother passed away five years ago when I was twenty-one. I took on full responsibility for my two younger sisters as a matter of course.

"I had been sort of brainwashed to believe that a Howard can do anything, and besides, I had rehearsed the role during the years of my mother's widowhood. Our family roots had been strong, traditional. I had been encouraged to be studious and good, in the traditional Catholic sense of moral goodness. My father was like that, in his straightforward way. Nearly every Sunday, we'd go to Mass at six A.M. then drive to the country for walking and picnicking. Dad saw the equivalent of God in nature, but never spoke of the beauty of nature, he just presented it.

"When he died Mother was still very dependent and frightened by the responsibilities she had to assume. She had never worked; Dad even did the grocery shopping. I assumed a coresponsibility—I was growing up and so was she—or maybe she was getting younger. She lost weight, became happier, took hold, and even thought about dating before her death. Together we hassled with housework, haggled over used cars, went to Sharon and Susan's school plays. Upon her death I took over as a matter of course. I felt I had been given so much that it was time to give something to my sisters." Randy was named coguardian with her brother Donald, a college student a year older than she.

Donald couldn't cope with the responsibility and promptly left for school in Florida, not even waiting to close his mother's estate. Although Randy wanted and needed his help, he made it clear he had his own life to lead. Hurt by his withdrawal, she realized Don had not fully come to terms with his father's death, and was now further disoriented by the loss of his mother and the new responsibilities assigned to him.

Susan was twelve, Sharon, fourteen. Suddenly, Randy, at twenty-one, was no longer an adolescent, but found herself on the other side of the generation gap. Where she had asked questions, now she must give answers—about sex, boys, school, drugs. The first questions she must answer were economic.

"The remaining estate was very small, and we were slow in getting government benefits started. Friends helped with cash and groceries, but we were soon hundreds of dollars in debt. Eventually, the VA and Social Security came through; even then the three of us had less than five hundred dollars a month to live on. I had to seek work immediately. I was close to a B.A. at the University of Tennessee. I thought about working in juvenile justice. But I was getting enough 'juvenile' at home. The unemployment rate in Knoxville was sky-high the spring of 1975; it was just the pits for new college graduates. I tried substitute teaching, but ended up mostly waiting tables, earning between five and thirty dollars a night.

"The girls were good about the big things—curfew, money and all, but there were many small crises. I know now I overcompensated and did too much for them. They dumped on me in many respects and got away with it. The television would be on till bedtime. I had no private time; I would come home from work or a date and my sisters would always be around, wanting help, needing attention. I felt I had no choice but to respond to their constant requests. I developed a real siege mentality. It was me against the world, on behalf of my sisters. I just never saw that there was any way to give myself some space.

"We went through a period when the girls had a lot of pets; that added to the confusion. The pets were everywhere, including my bedroom—on top of my bed, chirping in the corner, crawling in between the covers. That's what I mean about being too close and having no space—everything was just too much."

Sometimes she would contact Don, asking for help; he would lean on her instead, asking for loans. She resented it; she needed help, he was family. Later she realized Don had not been prepared to manage the girls as she had been when their mother was alive. Perhaps he should have been included then, so she could have more easily relinquished some control, some responsibility.

Despite her circumscribed social life, Randy became significantly involved with two men who asked to marry her. "Many times I wished someone would say, 'Randy, you don't have to worry about it anymore.' But I felt acutely uneasy when men made decisions about the girls and decided I'd rather do it myself, although it exhausted me. It was my 'control' problem; I just couldn't let go.

"And they didn't really fit my needs. I had a deeper sense of apprehension that the relationship might become another burden upon me, something more for me to carry as I was carrying the girls. Underneath it all I knew I was struggling—for a sense of myself, freed up, with space to take care of my own needs, which had been completely set aside.

"My closest friend through all this was Jason. We've known each other five years and lived together, on and off, though we've almost never had a monogamous relationship. He was married for nine years and has two children. He offered tons of support with the girls and was a sympathetic critic of my mothering efforts. I didn't always like to hear what he had to say, but he did give me objective insight.

"The girls used to want me to have a baby—which I think was their way of wanting to reestablish a family. Then they took to calling me Grandma Howard. I empathized with them in the loss of their parents. I was sad for myself as well, and grieved for my mother. I knew if she could somehow see me or come back, she'd be pleased with my efforts, identify with my struggles." Randy looked aside, paused, and shifted. "Christmas was especially hard. We spent it with some other parentless friends. We felt like—orphans—in the traditional sense of the word. After we owned our loss, we coped with it better."

Eventually, Sharon entered college, and Susan moved in with family friends. Randy saw her chance to "get space" and left for San Francisco. She knew she had become burned-out, overstressed.

"I heard San Francisco General Hospital had a funded program for tubal ligation. I had spent twenty-five years in and out of my family and I had absolutely no desire to raise another. I felt good because the two thousand miles to California had given me the beginning of a self-definition. I had broken out of the nest and shed my mother image. Having a tubal ligation seemed a way of assuring my gains."

But the tubal ligation became abscessed. A hard-to-treat viral infection set in and Randy was in bed for four months. Three gay men took her in and took care of her. She was the only straight and the only woman in the household. "They brought me meals and nurtured me—it was like my body said 'wait!' so I let someone else take care of me—I slept a lot, and allowed myself the luxury of rest and care. Every day they brought me flowers and changed my bed; when I was really ill they never left me in the house alone. I had a sense that my body and my whole psychic being had just about had it.

"Staying with these men was one of the most important things that ever happened to me. I noted my real equality with my nurses—it wasn't the kind of equality I'd had with the hetero men I knew in Knoxville. I already had some idea of the restrictions of sexual roles—that having boobs on your chest cuts down on the idea of your intelligence, your integrity—everything comes down to sex. But with the gay men it was never like that. They never tied a tag on anyone; when one guy wasn't working, he did the domestic stuff; they cared about the way they lived and easily exchanged tasks, sometimes humorously playing at traditional male and female roles and 'picking' at them.

"I thought, Well, that's what it really means to be masculine. They were very independent, very healthy. Two were construction workers with beautiful bodies. I never saw effeminate behavior I had sometimes noted among the few gays I knew in Knoxville, who I think were sort of forced into it by the repressive antigay environment. These guys were free to live as they saw fit in San Francisco, and I thought they were really beautiful people."

Randy got well and reluctantly left, pulled back to Knoxville by guardianship responsibilities and household possessions. Her brother took Susan for a summer and began to reestablish a tie with them, realizing his need for a family link. Randy resumed her relationship with Jason, but senses her relationship with him is ending, that she's grown past him. The issue of sex roles rankles. "He expects a meal on the table when he's not working and I am. He's limited by being from this area, I'm ready to break free." Randy wants to return to San Francisco permanently and resume her own life. Susan wishes to come with her, but Randy is reluctant to be pulled back again towards her mothering role.

"I see myself arriving at 'my time' in terms of my identity and potentiality that will come from a lack of restriction. This is just the start of a lot of things—I want to travel, pursue art and drawing, and especially get into women's studies and counseling. I shall be responsible for *only me*. I was exposed to feminism in college, but it's only recently that it's really sparked with me. I find I quickly get resentful of men—odd, because I have mostly male friends—and I'm tired of not being listened to. I feel restricted. When I lived with the gays on Castro Street I was treated as a person and not in the traditional woman's role. God! When I became executor of my parents' estate and custodian of my sisters, the lawyers doubted I could handle it 'because she'll spend all the money on clothes.' My lawyer—MY lawyer—later apologized that he had asked such simple questions during the hearing. After all I was 'such a pretty lady.'

"As a single woman, I see marriage as largely for creating a family, so having my tubes tied is my statement about that. Yet I can't say I'd *never* marry though it's hard now to imagine there'd be men exceptional enough to meet my needs, or adequate reason—I see myself getting more and more adamant about my need for space.

"In ten years, I hope I'm recognized for myself—a public recognition—beyond my role with the girls. I hope I've found a trade to work at and master. I hope I've traveled some. I want to continue to be a role model for the girls, and I hope they'll be proud of me.

"Happiness, as I see it, is to be pleased with myself."

Susan Martin

"I came to New York City with the guy I'd been crazy about since high school, and I guess I owe him credit for helping my career, giving me the support and stamina to get going. I fell right into a good job at a fashion magazine—I was a section editor there at the age of twenty-one. But, within three months it was all over between Marshall and me."

Susan Martin, twenty-nine, looked at me across her small West Side apartment. She seemed tired, in the manner of a disciplined athlete who accepts fatigue as a matter of course. The aging neighborhood she lived in was made up of warehouses and storage docks; the building was painted battleship gray, inside and out.

"I had never envisioned a future without Marsh. I had done all my firsts with him—dropped acid, sex, Woodstock, the March on Washington. The strict issue that broke us up was marriage: I wanted it, he wanted us to live together. It seems funny now, but I just couldn't face my family with it. *I* didn't mind, in terms of my commitment to him, but it wasn't something I could face at home. I was made to feel guilty, weak, and disloyal, and that perverted the relationship. I overcompensated, and that doomed it.

"I came from a rural area in western Pennsylvania. My mother was a bright, frustrated housewife whose life became much happier after she returned to college and became a teacher. She did not steer me toward marriage, but expected all of us children to have careers, and pushed me in particular to high achievement. I know attempting to please her and winning her praise are a part of my achievement orientation.

"My career took off like a house on fire, and I immediately found myself swept up in the vortex of the New York fashion industry publishing scene. You have to appreciate the difference between the city and my tiny-town origins and college environment.

"Young people in New York tend to have a tremendous identity problem. You become somebody very fast through your job and position. I might be having lunch at the Four Seasons with the president of a belt manufacturing concern hoping to influence copy of, say, Springtime Waists or some damn thing. Then it's back to the blue jeans and drawing board, living the scruffy life of the staff for $175.00 per week. I found the constant emphasis on style tiresome—handbags and belts and shoes had nothing to do with my own values, although I remained committed to working competently and well. I had to weigh the value of cashing in on the glamorous name of the magazine against the expoitative nature of my employment situation.

"So I eased out, taking a three-day-a-week job in public relations, and did freelance writing two days a week. That was even less gratifying. Then I picked up a contract to collaborate on writing a book. Then I signed a second book contract and quit my other jobs altogether. Since then, I've done a string of collaborations. But I find collaboration inherently unsatisfactory—after all, it's somebody else's story. I plan to move away from it and do things that leave room for my own voice.

"What I want to emphasize is that I've worked very, very hard over the past three and one-half years to get a writing career going, and made heavy sacrifices to do it. Everything on my life agenda that was not related to work got set aside, deferred, dropped, so at times I could literally work eighteen hours a day, seven days a week.

"For example, there's the matter of friends and a social life. If you work in an office, that kind of setting tends to keep you in contact, generates social action. New York has a peculiar social pattern—many people don't live well, we pay incredible rent for not much, so the nature of things is to go out to dinner and movies and move around the city. But I meet few people; my financial resources are very limited and constant work has caused me to lose my old friends. I don't invest energy or time to reciprocate, so gradually they stop calling. I do rent a house in Woodstock with four other people I feel close to; several summers ago, I went by myself to Vermont and upper New York state and camped out and canoed in places I had been with Marshall. I found that not everything done alone is necessarily fun.

"And I see too that perhaps less consciously I've chosen to be involved with a man who made only limited demands on me. Whitney told me from the beginning he didn't want a committed relationship, and I realized he was emotionally accessible to only a limited degree.

"Thank God I'm coming to the end of this period. My last two collaborations will be published soon. I expect to do well on them financially and will almost certainly be able to pull out of this neighborhood, substantially improve my whole standard of living. Recently, I've felt lonely for almost the first time in my life. I've always lived alone; I used to think I couldn't feel lonely because I was such interesting company for myself. So now I discipline myself to socialize, not work. And, as my time has opened up more, my relationship with Whitney has come into crisis. Now I have time and more interest to do things. I want to be more active, but he doesn't want to do this, or that, or anything much. Part of this evolution involves thinking about my happiness and having time for other parts of my life; I sense that my time with him is just about through. I don't identify with the term never-married because I believe I'll marry in my thirties; that marriage has been deferred for me in favor of writing, just as other goals have. But I recognize now that everyone I have is at arm's length from me, and I see myself moving into a balance with the kind of recognition a career brings and the knowledge that meaning in life will come from someone close to me. That someone will surely be a family, or so I think.

"But I wouldn't mind remaining single—as long as I can have the rewards of freedom, such as the adventurousness I associate with all this; the moving-around spirit, a sense of collecting on what I've rightfully earned.

"As a writer, I've always wanted to live creatively, even experimentally. I value new insights and want to test out new kinds of relationships, including those with other women.

"A couple of years ago I was in a woman's consciousness-raising group and my sensitivities were very high. I had a lot of intellectual ideas about sleeping with women. And I was especially down on sex with men then. So many of them are ignorant about sex with women, they don't know anything about satisfying you. It was always strained, teaching them something they should already know. So I had an intellectual idea that sleeping with women would be more satisfying, and a feminist attitude about women loving one another.

"A very sensual thing got going. I had never much thought about sex with women before, but now it began to be on my mind a lot. I dreamed erotically about women I knew and worked with. I talked it over with my boyfriend—we were having trouble in our own relationship, so we gave some thought to sleeping with a third person—a woman— together. There was one woman at my office who attracted me, and Dave as well, who we both felt was loose enough to approach.

"One day I approached her, in sort of a ha-ha fashion, suggesting she could take this seriously or not. I sort of played the devil's advocate. When she expressed some shock, I argued all the reasons why women should sleep with women—not that I had ever come close to doing it. I kept prompting her. I would send her poems which were sensual or loving in nature, all the while making myself nervous with the possibility of maybe having to come to terms with the whole thing. It made me real upset.

"Well, one night she showed up at my door saying she had slept with a woman. Apparently she had made the first move, after being loosened up with a certain amount of Quaaludes. And it had been the most wonderful thing they'd ever done and they both felt like they'd lost their virginity for the second time and on and on.

"I felt a little jealous, but from then on, the other woman lived a bisexual life, expressing a more or less equal interest in partners of both sexes. But our relationship had become sexually charged. It was impossible to be at ease with one another.

"Finally, my boyfriend and I rented a house. He wasn't coming up for the weekend and knowing full well what I was doing, I invited her up. And we did, in fact, after hesitating for one night, sleep together. It had been a real obsession with me—dreaming, thinking, fantasizing— and in terms of a first-night relationship, it was the best first night I've ever known. It was wonderful in terms of a woman's ability to understand another woman's sexuality and sexual response, after this awful awkwardness of working up to it. We slept together one more night and then quite a bit after that.

"Afterwards, I had no interest in doing it again. Not that it was unpleasant, or that I was embarrassed or uptight about doing it. Apparently breaking the taboo had a tremendous amount to do with it. And once I had crossed over that a lot of obsessive desire went out of it. And besides, she was not a woman I would want a long-time relation- ship with. She's a little flaky in ways which would not make her a satisfactory long-term lover for me.

"But I wouldn't rule out the possibility of sleeping with a woman again. I just don't think I'd ever have a long-term relationship with one. There is something about men, about the male being I want to fulfill my needs. A male gay friend of mine suggested that it was more than just sex, that a whole range of masculine aspects are important to me."

Susan continued. "You know, in considering the lives of single women, I flashed on something last week I want to comment on. I got a letter from an old friend of mine, a cheerful little note written on personalized stationery, commenting that she'd broken the seven-minute mile—we both run. Well, that's nice, but you know, I resented it. She's married to a very affluent guy, not working, doesn't have kids, and I thought, 'If I had somebody to pay the rent and didn't have to work all day, I could run a seven-minute mile too.' If she had children I wouldn't resent it; what I hate is the idea of living off the fat of the land. I can't understand a man who would fully support a woman anymore; I think there's something basically wrong with it; there should be a trade-off somewhere. But then I cooled off a little and thought, 'That could be a lovely setup for me. I could write when I wanted to, live well, there'd be so much less pressure'—then I thought about her living arrangements and mine here, and got upset all over again. But I do recognize the conflict of thinking—so quickly—how nice it could be for me."

In mentioning her married friend, Susan touches on a subject not unfamiliar to never-married women in their twenties, the changes between friends as some marry, others remain single. A film by Claudia Weill, *Girlfriends*, sensitively touches on the pivoting of relationships as marital status changes. A higher and newer loyalty to a spouse and perhaps a child threatens the old intimacy between girl friends; the sense that one member of the comfortable duo has graduated to a new and more valued status sometimes causes the other to feel a sense of loss and displacement.

Not all marriages of friends bring readjustments, however. Some report easier transitions, sometimes involving the incorporation of the new spouse into the old partnership arrangement. Other younger women reported that because of a low incidence of marriage among friends or because old college friends were far away, the issue only rarely presented itself.

Contrasted to the "new" generation, now in its twenties, are the women of my own generation, so conformist in nature, so concerned with the subtleties of every "given," every "should." The locksteps we so thoughtlessly adopted, the assumptions we so casually embraced. If we launched the women's movement to end our own kind of behavior and usher in the New Generation, for that alone the struggle was worth it.

And the odd part is, we didn't even much notice. Perhaps it is a habit of women to go through life observing those who are older and ahead of us, a way of clueing ourselves about what may lie ahead in our own lives. Perhaps we ignore those behind us; that part of our lives is finished, we think; maybe we feel vaguely uneasy about watching someone else live through where we have been. Probably we assume they are living as we did, merely resaying our lines, playing our parts. With this generation, that is not so. Only in a few ways were the women in their twenties like me or my peers, only ten or so years ago.

Yet consider the differences. To be twenty-five today means to have been an adolescent in the turmoil and upheavals of the late sixties; to have endured your mother's consciousness-raising while you were in junior high; to have been raised by Spockian methods. A changed role and a changed consciousness for younger women is largely a "given," the self-assurance and ease these women display about new roles and vocations are rooted in a generation that did not face reassessment and change, but were instead raised within a new context.

But the "upness" of all this, the assertive confidence, does not continue indefinitely. Although there have been periods of confrontation and "downs" before, and although a variety of life crises can erupt through the twenties, near the end of the decade a certain vague uneasiness, a hazy sense of all not being well, begins to set in.

The issue it concerns is marriage, and it appears, often symbolically at first, with an underlying menacing power it hadn't held before. "I tried on a sari a friend brought me from India. We enjoyed playing with it, draping the silk folds this way and that. I looked in the mirror and thought, I'll never be a bride. It seemed as though a doomsday pronouncement had been made." Or, "I was suddenly uneasy about things related to marriage as I hadn't been before. My roomie got married, and though I knew I liked Stan on a rational level, I felt angry—he wasn't good enough for her. I realized my feelings were jealous and competitive—I 'deserved' to get married—look at all I had been through—and I predicted to myself the relationship couldn't last." Or, "She got a silver pitcher at the shower from a mutual friend who had introduced the couple. For some unknown reason I just resented it, that's all." Or, "I was hit by the heavy mention of couples at a conference. I felt like a third wheel around my married friends. When they touched or exchanged affection, I felt like a beggar who had been invited to a banquet to only look."

Single life both before and after age thirty is flecked with incidences like these; now they are fleshed with a new pain and color. Valentine's Day isn't a joke anymore. The age thirty crisis is about to begin.

II

THE AGE THIRTY CRISIS

"When I was twenty-eight, I took a teaching job in a rural school district in downstate Illinois. It was part of my back-to-the-earth phase; I wanted to buy and renovate a little farmhouse, become part of a small community." She paused. "I had no idea I was headed for an absolute disaster."

Lynn Harrington sat on her couch and folded her legs beneath her. A tall, fair woman of thirty-four, she is now an assistant principal of an elementary school in a Chicago suburb. She spoke thoughtfully of her concerns: something about her appearance and manner seemed particularly youthful, an appealing quality I have sometimes noted before in other women who teach or work with young children.

"I was, for sure, one of those shot-out-of-a-gun types who fairly lived to teach. I had my master's degree within three years after I graduated, and was well on my way to administrative credentialing. Everything else in life came after that, my social life included, but I thought little of it; several of my friends were the same way. I dated some and had been seriously involved with several men, and was briefly engaged once. I figured in time I'd probably marry. In fact, I used to tell myself that if I were still single by the time I was thirty, I'd be in real trouble. But I felt I was in control and would probably be able to work things out, just as I had worked out many other problems before.

"I don't know what triggered it, but suddenly I was caught up in a real crisis. Every night the moon came up over the prairie and every

50

night I sat there, all alone. I felt terribly lonely and cut off. A sort of panic mixed with depression set in. I felt as though I had overlooked one of the most important things for my life, and now must go back and find it. I longed to find a man and marry him and have a family.

"I fantasized the joy that would fill my life if only I could find this great love. I had ingested all those sticky-sweet Rodgers-and-Hammerstein-type songs as a teenager, and now I clung to these very romanticized ideas of an overpowering love that could transform my life.

"The disastrous thing about this crisis was that I turned on myself, trashing myself for all the shortcomings I now perceived. I had sometimes had an uneasy sense that the way I was developing my life was dangerous to my chances for marriage: all the emphasis on education and success in my career. Most of the men I had been involved with were similarly well educated and very ambitious. Certainly, they were overtly sympathetic to what I was into; I didn't hang around with slobs. But your gut sense tells you something else: that at some point career goals become a turnoff to men.

"I had sometimes sensed a yellow warning light flashing on and off: Too much emphasis on smartness and success is like throwing down a gauntlet into a relationship—it's not man-pleasing, it's threatening. So you face a dilemma and I tell you, it's a painful one. Either you're going to be up-front and own who you are, how you see yourself, what you want; or you're going to play the classic and eternal female game: Hide your light, represent yourself as being something less than you are (I feared I might well *become* something less than I was), don't challenge him, for God's sake, but support him, *take your place.*

"Well, now I don't see some of these things in such black-and-white terms anymore—supporting somebody else doesn't have to take away from supporting yourself. It can, but I've seen otherwise. I have a friend whose husband is in a very competitive advertising agency, she's in a demanding job herself, and I note she manages to give him a lot of encouragement and support through his ups and downs—and no doubt gets some back, though I don't see that part of it.

"As far as threatening men—I continue to think most men are fairly easily threatened, but you can find a few heartening exceptions."

She stopped and sighed. "I mean, yes, I know of such marriages, I see them. And I think: *That's what I'd like.* But some part of me just despairs. It just seems like such a long shot to find a man that secure, and then be able to develop a really wonderful relationship with him." She brushed the hair off her forehead and looked away.

"No doubt some women, maybe myself included, do come off as threatening, often without knowing it. But where's the fine line? It's a question of degree, I guess, and I don't know to this day that I've really found where that fine line runs.

"But going back to my crisis—at the time I saw it as a moral issue: Do I co-opt myself or not? Sell out, or not? I saw it as a matter of being true to myself. I couldn't be two selves, more or less live a lie. So I didn't cover or underplay my background, my ambitions; I didn't 'play it smart.'

"Now I had a sense that all this was catching up with me. I was being punished, and God, it hurt. I seriously questioned whether I had done the right thing: The price seemed so terribly high. I had to reexamine the whole premise which I had previously accepted at face value: Would developing a career bring me happiness if its price was a life alone?

"And I thought of all the relationships I'd had with men that hadn't worked out— 'worked out' now meant 'ended in marriage' which was all that counted at the moment. Obviously, this was every relationship I'd ever had, since I was still single. All those relationships contained some kind of problem that reflected a shortcoming on my part, I fantasized, and I began to believe I had this dreadful flaw which must be perfectly obvious to everyone else but was hidden to me. As I got deeper into my shortcomings and failures, I saw myself as not only inadequate but incomplete, lacking something, not whole. I had read or picked up somewhere the idea of an incomplete feminine personality. That was it! This great void I was feeling could only be filled by fusion with a masculine identity: A man was necessary to fill my life, make me whole.

"I imagined myself as a middle-aged spinster. By the time I was forty I would be ugly and dried up and alone, alone, alone, marked forever as a freak and a failure. I could only save myself by pouring everything I had into an effort to end my aloneness: I had to find a man, a man I could marry.

"I sensed that another woman teacher in our district felt as I did, though there was no way on earth I could have owned up to my feelings. I was terrified I might appear desperate and tried to avoid that at all costs. I felt I had to rein in my emotions for fear they would get out of control altogether. I hinted to her that we ought to sort of join forces to improve our social lives; it turned out she was in a 'single panic-fever' as bad or worse than mine. Although we helped each other in a practical sense, it was like two drowning swimmers clutching at each other. The anxiety and fear of one fed the anxiety and fear of the other in sort of a vicious cycle.

"Well, we tried to figure out every conceivable way to find and meet eligible men, but a small town has few single men. Most men marry by the time they're twenty and we weren't interested in truck drivers, hardware salesmen, and the like. Men with more prospects had left for St. Louis or the West Coast long ago. Gail joined the country club and I guess it was there she met Hal; you can count on it, into a situation like this *inevitably* walks a married man.

"Hal was as attractive as any man could be; God knows I could understand how she could fall for him. He was a retired military officer and was terribly self-assured. I could just smell the military polish, the medals, the glamour. He was managing the local paper and lived with his wife and teenaged children outside of town. Gail fell hard for him and they carried out their affair in a very public manner; they were oblivious to anyone's opinion about their behavior. Actually, I don't think anybody minded much; in a small town episodes like this provide a lot of interest and entertainment; nobody likes to seem to spoil the fun.

"I saw a lot less of Gail once this got started. She may have sensed that I, at least, wasn't so shot down about the arrangement; I doubted Hal would marry her, as she implied he would. My guess was that he was a skirt-chaser from the old school, that Gail was probably only one of a series of extramarital adventures. I thought this because he had rather casually made a pass at me once, when I was working with him on the United Way Fund. I couldn't imagine a fortyish wife with teenaged children suddenly giving him his freedom; he probably knew he was safe, and was enjoying the relationship for whatever it was worth to him, and for the points he was scoring around town.

"This relationship continued for several years, long after I left. I never knew how Gail made her peace with it; she apparently accepted it at face value and masked her real feelings. About four years later Hal was killed in a car accident, and at that point Gail quit her job and returned to her home.

"But I'm getting away from my own story. I began to realize I'd pulled a real bummer in coming here and should get out. So I plotted my next move. I'd go to Chicago, reestablish my career in some suburban area, and find a man I could marry. I subscribed to the Sunday *Chicago Tribune* and the local magazine, spending my weekends boning up on the places to go, organizations to join where I would surely meet the kind of men who interested me.

"I leased an apartment at a smart North Shore address, checking carefully to see that there were many single male tenants, and a large pool and recreation area. I well remember the night I arrived in town; I attended a mixer put on by the Northwestern Bachelor's Club and was taken home by the president. I took that as a good omen for my new future. That same weekend I attended a lecture on international affairs and joined a sailing club. I was in control; the city seemed to be full of handsome faces, potential situations. I was sure to succeed; I was so smart to have come.

"I must say I was very successful in developing my new life. My homework and planning paid off well, and I was very good at devising new and even cleverer ways of meeting men. I belonged to a host of community organizations. I had friends and even my landlord fix me up with men they knew. But I drew the line at anything that smacked of the organized single scene—those pay-at-the-door meat-market hotel dances, those pathetic church groups, the Friday-night singles-bar scene. There was a constant conflict between doing what I was doing yet not appearing too open about it. Above all, I had to keep my cool, because I didn't want anyone to think I was desperate!"

Lynn paused at this point, then excused herself to get us some coffee. I sensed she was pushing herself to tell an unpleasant story. I fiddled with my tapes and notes; I was aware I felt uncomfortable, too. Her story reminded me of some of my own experiences; the tense competitiveness of these situations, the cruel evaluations made on the basis of a finely tuned scale assessing sharpness by dress, occupation, mannerisms, and background; the appraising, synthetic quality of it all. Conversations in the powder room: brief, telegraphic exchanges measuring probable success of chance encounters; makeup being applied as if the success of the venture depended on it. Lynn returned and resumed her story.

"My life was a whirl of dates and social activities. At my peak I went out two or three times during the week and usually twice on the weekend. I was in a real hurry. I had to find the love of my life before it was too late.

"I got involved with Bob, an engineer in an international construction company whom I met at a reception at the International Affairs Club. The relationship got off the ground rather fast—by occupation, age, and background he seemed like a 'possible.' He was a terrific cook and invited me over for dinners for two. He was quick with nice entertainment—tickets to pro football games with brunch beforehand, and a big party afterward, long weekends at a private club along the Lake Michigan dunes. Never mind that I didn't like his friends, who seemed shallow and superficial and only interested in fun, fun, fun, or the fact that he spent an undue amount of time at the neighborhood watering hole. Nobody was perfect, I told myself.

"He painted and had marked artistic interests—that somehow

seemed good. He didn't have a lot to say, in fact he was rather taciturn, but in my great enthusiasm for these quests, I put that aside. Strong and silent—like my father, I thought. What came through was that he seemed interested in me and my goings-on, an unruffled type I didn't seem to threaten, always a sensitive point with me. I was very interested in him.

"So one night about three months after we met he rather casually proposed, mentioning something he'd somehow managed to overlook before—he'd been married and divorced twice. I felt like the floor had been pulled out under me. I asked him a little about his marriages, and he treated them quite lightly. Apparently they had been rather short-term affairs, and he spoke of them as incidences of no real or further importance.

"Well, I could imagine somebody in and out of an unfortunate marriage once, but twice? And treated as hardly worth mentioning? What did that say about his proposal to me? Such a casual proposal too—as if it were something to be gotten over with. Nothing about what I meant to him, no 'I love you so much, marry me.'

"Now I had to focus on things about him I had been able to sweep under the rug before. And immediately things began to go downhill. I felt betrayed, like he had suspected I wouldn't take this too well, and had hidden an important part of his background—a background I now realized I didn't really know much about—until he couldn't avoid telling me any longer. What else was he hiding from me? Maybe I overreacted, but that was the end of the relationship.

"And there was a stockbroker, Neil, who I met through a computer dating service, the only time I've tried something like that. Neil was just such a pleasure to be around, had a nice personality, so bright, and was just a good all-round companion. He took it upon himself to teach me quite a bit about investing in the market from an insider's view—I'm still grateful to him for that. He had a very close relationship with his younger sister Ann, a very brotherly and supportive role, and I liked him for that. But a couple of things about him bothered me. He was so tight with his money—not just thrifty or conservative, which I sort of admire in a man as a sign of trustworthiness or responsibility, but a real squeeze-the-nickel-till-it-screams variety, beyond all reason for a man of his income. He drove a very old car and lived in a walk-up I'd be afraid of after dark. He spent his Saturdays servicing a series of jukeboxes and laundromats he'd inherited from his father, risking his neck on the South Side for a couple of dollars from each machine.

"Well, it turned out that he was saving every cent he could make and investing it various ways so he could retire when he was forty. Actually,

what he was doing was buying himself out of his whole way of living—
he said he really hated his job and about any other kind of employment
he could qualify for, hated Chicago, and just generally wanted to
escape. That struck me as dumb—he just wasn't dealing with the
problem and I thought he should come to terms with making a more
satisfying life for himself. I guess he thought more of the possibilities of
money buying happiness than I do. But I didn't say much—I sort of
imagined using my money to buy a house and having a nice life
together. I was pretty seriously interested in him.

"Remembering my haste in my relationship with Bob, I encouraged
him to talk about his background. From what he said of his other
relationships, he apparently was attracted to and had dated a number
of strong women. Good. One of the things that touched me about Neil
was his openness, his willingness to show his vulnerabilities, his
sensitivities. He often talked about his childhood and some really
upsetting things that went on in his family—he encouraged me to be
more open, too, more willing to show my vulnerable side, share fears I
might ordinarily conceal.

"Well, on the surface of it, I guess that sounds good—sharing your
deepest feelings, being real self-revealing with someone you like a lot.
Actually, it wasn't so good. Because I guess when you do that, you're
looking for the other person to respond to whatever need you're
expressing, maybe to come through and shore you up in whatever is
bothering you. And that didn't happen. We just sort of kept confessing
to all our problems and pains, getting in deeper and deeper. We
listened to each other sympathetically, but nobody was meeting anybody's needs, so it was kind of futile.

"The stories Neil told me were beginning to scare me. Piece by piece a
picture emerged that sounded like a Charles Addams cartoon. I don't
remember all the details, but his parents had had a very disturbed
relationship, with an absentee father, now dead, and a very spacy
mother. Neil and his sister, Ann, had gone through childhood sort of
clinging to each other, like two survivors, helping each other as best
they could. That's why they were still so close.

"My first thought was certainly not to hold anyone's family background against him, but I'm psychologically enough oriented to know
that if you're interested in someone, you have to consider what kind of
a background they're coming out of and how it's influenced them. As I
continued to be involved with Neil, I began to understand he was a
rather insecure guy. He seemed to need support, and I wasn't very sure
I could give it to him—and it was clear my own needs weren't being
met.

"I decided I should meet his mother. He resisted—he rather openly said he didn't want me to. His reticence made me more uneasy, and I pressed the matter. So he set up a meeting with her one Saturday morning and I'll tell you—it wasn't real. The first thing out of this woman's mouth was her psychosexual history, how she'd had a hysterectomy and all the weird, *totally* inappropriate tales somehow related to that and other sexual things—she seemed rational enough, just didn't know how to respond to the situation. Poor Neil sat there and died. God, I felt for him. Nobody should be held responsible for his parents, but this meeting crystallized my fears about Neil and our possible relationship, a fact I'm sure he sensed.

"Maybe in both cases, Bob and Neil, it took sort of a confrontation which shook me up before I'd focus on things in the relationship I wanted to ignore. I see now that because I wanted them to work out so badly I had probably developed a pretty selective way of looking at things—seeing what I wanted to see.

"Neil and I continued to go together a while after that but it was mostly downhill—we were sort of bogged down in these unhappy feelings, and neither of us seemed to be able really to support the other. I began to see Neil as a more and more shaky guy—I didn't know what I could do for him, and it was obvious he couldn't be a strong partner for me. There was a sense in which we turned away from each other in quiet futility, though actually he removed himself from the relationship more than I did. I wish I could say we're still friends, but he wanted out, and got out.

"I don't mean to give the impression that all these relationships were total washouts—there were certainly some pretty nice ones. I found there are relationships with men that sort of defy definition—they aren't love-in-bloom romantic encounters, and they aren't just friend-ship or platonic encounters—they fall into an undefinable middle.

"At one point two brothers moved into the apartment next door to me. The older one, John, was about my age, and from the beginning there was a mutual attraction between us. The younger brother, Nick, was about ten years younger than I and I liked him as just a real pleasant guy. The three of us would spend evenings together, eat together, and just generally run around. But sometimes Nick wouldn't be there and it would be just John and me.

"I'm positive John wanted to get this relationship moving as much as I did—but we got stuck in dead center and just couldn't get it going! I used to think of different little strategies—different settings, topics of conversation, whatever—that would sort of change the vibes between us. I know John was thinking along the same lines, but so help me neither of us could make it happen. My old fears about coming on too strong and being threatened were kindled, but I don't think that was it. So we just continued as we were—friends who basically wanted to be more. To this day, the only thing I can make of that was that the basic male/female dynamics were somehow off—whatever that means! Eventually they moved, and John got involved with another woman.

"I was certainly aware that women sometimes remain unmarried because their standards are unrealistic, and I warned myself not to be unduly picky. I thought these relationships over and figured that probably wasn't the problem. I had always known it would be hard to find Mr. Right and I continued to feel pretty optimistic and confident of my ability to handle almost any situation. I dated literally dozens of men, slept with some of them, and saw myself as worldly and 'with it.'

"But after this continued for some time, I began to have second thoughts. Most of these relationships were fairly superficial. I felt like Marie Curie going through the pitchblende, looking for what-I-wasn't-sure-but-I'd-know-by-God-when-I-found-it. In a sense I was using these men, although God knows most of them were as caught up in the whole gamy aspect of it as I. When I was honest with myself, I had to admit this glorious whirl of activity was very stressful, and not always fun. It required an enormous amount of energy to keep this scenario going. Oh, well, I thought, all this will pay off in the end; I'll find somebody.

"The whole thing came to a head one night in a restaurant. My date was an air traffic controller at O'Hare, and he was describing his work. He dwelt at length on the ins and outs of signaling pilots, of directing takeoffs and landings, of avoiding collisions. Suddenly, I began to imagine that he was somehow talking about me and my life with men; that the course I was now on was somehow a collision course, and I was headed for a disaster of major proportions. I fled from the table with hurried excuses of not feeling well and sat in the cigarette smoke of the women's lounge, trying somehow to reconcile what I now recognized as the larger issue: the conflict I felt between my frantic overt behavior, designed to find someone to meet and marry, and my deeper feelings, which manifested themselves as strain, tension, shallow relationships, and now illusions which frightened me. Something was seriously wrong. I realized I couldn't resolve the painful ambiguity I felt and decided I should seek professional help. I would find a therapist who might be able to help me understand my painful confusion.

"A friend referred me to Dr. K., a psychiatrist she felt was especially supportive. I felt a little foolish in owning up to all this, but managed to choke out my story—the goal I was so sure I wanted, the great effort I had put into meeting and dating men, the relationships which never really went anywhere. He was indeed supportive, and very kind. I struggled to tell him about my deepest feelings, my most intimate desires. We talked about my problems for an hour and made an appointment for next week. I went home relieved that I had at least had the courage to begin resolving my dilemma.

"About seven-thirty that evening the telephone rang. It was Dr. K. He was in the neighborhood, he said, and I had seemed so upset this afternoon—he wondered if he could come by.

"I told him no, that wouldn't be necessary, and politely ended the conversation. I hung up, shocked that the trust and confidence I had invested in him in his professional capacity had been used so he might approach me in a personal way. My attempts at professional therapy ended with that call.

"I'm not entirely certain how I passed through my stormy crisis. I'd credit the women's movement as much as anything. I began to read feminist literature and joined a group which centered on relations between women and men. Little by little I began to understand that the conflict I felt came from a clashing of the messages I had been receiving all my life—on one hand were the traditional messages of how I and other women were supposed to lead our lives, and on the other hand was the picture I valued of myself—seeking self-realization, valuing autonomy, being independent.

"I remember our group discussing the socialization of women and the roles we are supposed to assume—we would go on and on, half the night. We talked about how thoroughly women are taught to accept a secondary role in every institution and part of society. Being a wife is an excellent example of a secondary role. Marriage is held out as being virtually obligatory for every woman. Marriage is supposed to be our major commitment in life; it even redefines us by changing our very name, labeling us with a distinctive title. Yet within marriage wives are surely in the secondary role—and sure enough, once married, a woman finds her main responsibility is to care for a man, nurture him, satisfy him sexually, and give him the support he needs to carry on his dominant role. From there, of course, her role is carried on to the needs of their children—to support, nurture, and subordinate herself to their needs. What's rich about all this is that she's supposed to realize herself through these endlessly subordinate positions. It's crazy.

"In one of the sessions, a friend pointed out my strong desire to be successful. I know I'm very achievement oriented. How hard it seemed for me not to succeed in achieving this much-touted role! And we talked about the 'success paradox.' While women are not supposed to succeed, when we do succeed at something, we are still said to have failed if we don't succeed at everything! I know the struggles of some married women to be superwives, supermothers, and super-career women. Now I understood that the same pressures, to do everything and do it extraordinarily well, could be brought against me, too.

"I don't mean to say that I sat through a couple of consciousness-raising sessions and read a few books and zip, zip, zip, just like that, it all fell into place. It was a hard, painful process that proceeded in sort of piecemeal fashion over several years' time. It was coupled with other factors, too. I think as you grow older you get more realistic. My more romantic side, those starry visions I had, got a little hardened by reality. The scales of a perfect love largely fell from my eyes. And I observed married women's lives a little more closely, and I know things are not what they are made to seem.

"Let me digress a moment and say something about communication between married and unmarried women. All through this time I was close to several married women who had some idea, at least, of what was going on with me, who must have had some sense of the illusions which fed into my dilemma. They hadn't given me a realistic feedback about the nature of marriage and they didn't gently puncture my illusions. The women's movement has opened a more open and honest dialogue about the reality of marriage for women, but I find this openness is mostly in literature; face-to-face, there is a great tendency to admit to no flaws, to make one's marriage look as good as possible, until the marriage fails, and then it all comes out.

"It would have been so helpful if the women nearest me would have been more straightforward. Maybe I should have been more self-revealing than I was. But I think there would be a real value if both married and single women could share the realities we find in our respective marital statuses, even to try to assess honestly the benefits and costs, the gains and the losses we find in singleness and in marriage. That would be a valuable dialogue.

"Eventually, my self-esteem reappeared. I took heart from my many accomplishments; a woman who could do all that I did should feel very good about herself, I knew, and I sensed, that in terms of my career, the future held a lot to look forward to.

"And I came to realize the problem wasn't all of my own making, that values and beliefs well beyond my control—ideas that were outdated and superficial—worked against me. The environment of which I was a part makes it damn tough for women who move toward autonomy and self-realization. I quit dumping on myself for my alleged many shortcomings. The world around me was a harsh enough place; why add to my own troubles through self-abasement? I should support myself through all this, rather than add to pressures that were beyond my control.

"And those feelings of needing a man to make me whole? Well, I came to realize I had come into the world alone. I would leave it alone also. And traversing those two points was basically for me to do."

She spoke more slowly.

"I came to realize there wasn't anyone who could assume a basic part of me, nor could I or would I want to surrender any part of myself. There is no one who can complete me, make me whole—no more than I can complete someone else. *There are no others.*

"I felt that I was therefore all I had, but I was everything I had, and my sense of my selfhood was whole, precious, and very sweet.

"And in the end I realized I would hold that selfhood, I would keep me for myself.

"I'd like to believe some other way might be possible, but in my heart of hearts, I don't see it. I just don't believe it. And that's basically where I am."

The marital imperative. How constant, how close to us it is, how it demands to be answered! Sooner or later women who don't marry are called to reckoning and come face-to-face with the paradox of their position. The Age Thirty Crisis is the term we shall use to describe this encounter: this conflicting and clashing of feelings and values held about marriage, followed by a working-through process which brings one to terms with singleness. This is not to say that a conflict over marital status hasn't occurred before thirty, or won't again. But the Age Thirty Crisis is characterized by its sense of resolution, however tenuous; it results in a changed self-concept, a revision of life expectations.

Age thirty is widely understood as the age by which women are supposed to be married. Indeed, many single women told me they expected to be married much earlier; for them, thirty was not only a cutoff point, but a late one at that. This view of thirty as Doomsday is further reinforced by literature dealing with women's lives, by various "official" criteria such as the census and academic studies on marital status. It is recognized in the popular culture, by parents and friends, by the media.

Not all Age Thirty Crises are as dramatic and as clear cut as Lynn's. Hers shows in a heightened way the major aspects of the Crisis: coming to terms with the reality of her own life vis-à-vis the prescription of obligatory wifehood and motherhood she knew society held for her, and she, in a rather unexamined way, held for herself.

Other women faced the issue in other ways. Rosemary Poulos, thirty-eight, a warm and gracious woman who is a high-level administrator in a small Rocky Mountain state, tells her story.

"I guess my hard time began when I ran into old high school friends downtown one afternoon and realized how much we had grown away from each other. We had coffee together, and I found myself straining to find a common ground. It wasn't that I wanted to change places with them, but I began to envy the security, the warmth and support in their lives. My love life was pretty bleak at the time and felt as though it might be that way forever. Having baby pictures pushed under my nose was something I didn't need. That afternoon started me on sort of a downward spiral.

"It was as though the most vulnerable parts of my psyche had been exposed. I did such a number on myself—dumping, feeling inadequate and socially gauche. I knew I looked okay, but I thought there must be something wrong with the way I related to people. So I buried myself in work, which has always been a source of positive strokes for me.

"Relations with men haven't come easily for me. My father was an invalid and my high school days were socially restricted because I was needed at home to help care for him. I dated some, and went to some of the proms, but I felt ill at ease around boys and didn't learn the social skills, the boy-girl things I should have learned then. Greek families tend to be very self-contained and I didn't know many people from outside the family and had few ways of becoming more socially aware. It led me to doubt my ability to judge men—whether they are trustworthy, someone to know better or develop a relationship with.

"When I first started working, the men I preferred had gone off to college, and there weren't a lot of desirables around. After all, your options in a town this size are never great. I had a couple of steady relationships with guys at work, reserved, intelligent, solid types I probably chose because they didn't seem too threatening. We'd go out a few times, but no real flame developed and that was that. Actually, Dan Grew meant the most to me. He had lived in the neighborhood and left the state, but came back occasionally on weekends to visit. He was high-spirited and liked a good time. We had friends who owned a ranch and we'd go riding, or take off for Denver to catch a show. We liked each other a lot, but it was just that—no blazing thing beyond good friendship.

"In all honesty, my major energies weren't in men. I saw myself as a late bloomer and figured 'someday' and told myself there was always plenty of time.

"I was caught up in work. I sensed I had a good thing started career-wise. My father's precarious health had taught me plenty about the value of secure employment, an adequate paycheck. He was gone; my mother depended on me. And I liked my job; it was easy to put it at the center of things, to knock myself out for long hours, come home, collapse, do it again the next day, run into the office a few hours on weekends if I wanted to. I felt pretty self-sufficient and was a little cut off from other people, except at work. I remember that I took a few classes and read a lot.

"Then my late twenties began to creep up on me, with the panicky feelings I described and the vague sense that I was losing out. I just didn't know how to cope with it. I'd be irritable and upset and catch myself yelling at my mother, and our usual disagreements would get magnified out of all proportion. I was restless, wanted out. However much I had wanted to believe that I could find happiness in work and accomplishment-oriented things, now there was a real crack in that veneer. I couldn't sweep the issue of men in my life under the rug any longer.

"I had always held them in a sort of awe; I was always concerned with what will they think of me. At work, I had to struggle to respond, speak up, listen, articulate—'why, what will they think of me, a mere woman?' Gradually and with great effort I struggled to overcome this.

"Work helped me develop confidence in other ways. About that time my supervisor began sending me to conferences. The experience of flying to other states, meeting other people in my own line of work was good for me. I was lucky to be working with people who probably saw something in me I didn't see in myself, and who nudged me a little, and encouraged and supported me. Sometimes they put me in work situations which terrified me, but I'm a risk-taker and the stress and challenge were what I needed.

"Then I took another risk—a trip that calmed a flare-up of my panic about getting married. I'd always lived at home, carrying rather heavy responsibilities for my mother, and my aunts and cousins too sort of clung to me for advice and support. I wanted to prove I was as independent as I liked to think I was; the whole arrangement was getting stifling, and I had to have a break.

"I'd always dreamed of going to Europe, so I got on a plane to Athens—just jumped on, had no real plans, didn't even have a hotel reservation. I know a little Greek from home—three words of Greek mixed with two of English—so I plunged in and stayed for a month. Well, it was one of the best things I ever did. I wandered around and met some great people on trains and buses. There was one elderly couple with a small pension on the coast and they took me home for a couple of days. I had the experiences everyone has with Greek person flirtations and silly encounters. I'd meet men on a tour bus or in a café; we'd go see the sights, maybe take off on a picnic or something afterwards, end up dancing and drinking in some little place. Or I'd meet American men staying in my hotel, and we'd have dinner and go explore the city by night, and have a couple of nice days together. Not a lot came of it, except that it was liberating and fun for me. By the time I got home I was speaking rather good Greek, which just amazed my family. I'd had a great time and I thought, They think I'm okay.

"My awe of men began to ease. In fact, in my thirties my self-confidence has really just taken off in so many directions—maybe it's a spill-over from job success, but I think in general I've just learned to fit the pieces together better. I still work damned hard but I try not to be so compulsive about it. Right now a couple of other women and I are trying to get a networking thing going for women in the capital; I'm closer to other women than I was and in fact the whole social side of my life is just much richer than it was when I was in my twenties. I date some, as much as I like; it still isn't what you'd call a heavy or constant involvement, but it's satisfying to me, and that's what's important. People say I seem to have become a different person. Maybe that's a stage beyond the Age Thirty Crisis.

"I have a cousin I would say went through the same situation. She's thirty now, very good-looking but not terribly bright. She had a breakdown that had a lot to do with the fact that she's growing older and is still single. It's true she's afraid of her own shadow, and that may have had something to do with her feelings of inadequacy, but she always had a number of boyfriends in high school and college and since she's been working. I have no idea why one of those guys didn't work out for her. She was unhappy with her job and restless living at home. All she could see was that she wasn't getting married and had nothing to compensate for it.

"I suggested she move out from her family, get an apartment, and begin doing things on her own. She pretty largely followed my advice; she got some additional secretarial training and found a job she liked better, and rented a nice place. Not long afterward she fell in love with someone she obviously wanted to marry, but he made it plain he was not interested and broke it off. I expected her to be shattered, but she took it fairly well. She found the apartment pretty draining financially and recently moved back home, but I think the experience was good for her—she seems to be over her crisis now.

"As for me, I'd be interested in marriage if I met the right person someone I'd respect and admire and have all those qualities anyone would want in a partner—but it's clearly okay by me if it doesn't happen. I think the sharing would be a wonderful experience. When I was approaching thirty, I was panicked about it: What's wrong with me because no one wants to marry me? Now I'm happy with my life as it is; it's fine, but if the right situation came along so that life would be enriched by sharing with someone else, that would be great too."

Gail Hoffburg, thirty-eight, a practitioner in the holistic health movement, remembered the time in terms of pain and described a crisis which isn't fully resolved yet.

"Actually, I think I've blocked a lot of it and just remember the high spots, which is to say the worst spots. I know it was my twenty-ninth birthday which seemed especially unbearable—I wasn't in my mid-twenties anymore so I'd lost my excuse as to why I hadn't done the marriage thing. I knew I was bright, and I sometimes thought I was attractive, but underneath it all I was terribly unhappy and saw myself as a failure. I mean, I had failed myself and my expectations this far in life, though I didn't accept that I had failed forever.

"It was so painful for me that by the time I was twenty-nine and a half, I was telling people I was thirty, just to get away from that awful number. I went so far as to cancel a charter flight just in case I might be able to go with a man next year! I was constantly perplexed, mixed up, and didn't know what to do next. I was then working for a very WASPish corporation, and the work setting did nothing to help my confusion. I am Jewish and I figured I couldn't find a man there, which made the whole scene all the more alien.

"I talked and talked and talked to my friend about it—until I got tired of the subject. I remember saying that all at once there seemed to be very few single men around and she commented, 'People should start getting divorced anytime now.'

"Once in a while someone would fix me up, but not as often as I liked, and not always with someone as good as I thought I deserved. That bothered me. Maybe because of my age I was already a sort of discard. I was ready to lay that on myself.

"I just continued to be as confused then as I am now because I didn't know what to change then anymore than I do now."

Another woman said, "My Age Thirty Crisis coincided with my coming west. I had been in my job six years and I thought: Life is not a dress rehearsal, I want to experience the real thing. I felt I had grown up emotionally very slowly. When I was in my mid-twenties my brother was killed, and that had been a terrible blow. I had stayed single by choice several times and was then enmeshed in an affair with a married man I loved but the affair was plainly going nowhere. I visited San Francisco and I loved it, so everything indicated I should leave home and go west.

"My father was against it, but Mother encouraged me. Five days after I arrived he died, and I went home and more or less had to make the decision to come all over again. The age thing loomed suddenly. 'God, I'm still single and it's getting harder and harder to meet people here.' One of the things that entered my mind was that I might be becoming one of those rigid old maids and I wanted to see if I were really flexible and could really go through with it. Being thirty was horrible—sixteen meant nothing, twenty-one, nothing, but thirty was like a magic number—it was the first time I'd thought of myself as having *an age*, in the negative sense. All of my friends were married, and I began to wonder if I had completely blown it, if it was all over by now. And I said, 'I might be looking for a man for the rest of my life. Do I really like what I'm doing meanwhile?' I was totally programmed to get married and have babies. All these fears prompted me to try the move again.

"And partly it was the positive pull of the region. San Francisco held such a strong attraction for me. It was the era when everyone was into his psyche, his feelings, that whole thing, and I thought I'd bloom a little.

"My father's death had made Mother and me so aware of the passing quality of life. I really credit my mother who, despite her new widowhood, insisted I return. 'My dear, if you don't go now, you'll never know. You've got to go back and give it a try.' I'll always be grateful to her for that final encouragement."

Linda Nelson, thirty-one, of San Francisco, focused on her experience in a more general way.

"A lot of things hit me when I was coming up on my thirtieth birthday. The major thing was that thirty was *definitely grown up*. I felt I should have some sort of a base or accomplishment to show for it.

"It wasn't that I felt over the hill, but it was a new decade, and the focus was different. I began to think about settling down; I thought of leaving San Francisco and going to Dallas to settle down with a guy I knew there. . . . I wanted to change where I lived, where I worked, my whole style.

"I realized that I was in transition and I felt a bit down about it. I asked myself what I was going to do with the rest of my life, instead of just hopscotching around, living a day at a time, not thinking too much about anything.

"I think almost everyone goes through an 'Oh, My God! I'm Turning Thirty!' syndrome with some dread. I was talking to a man at a party the other night, and he kept referring to 'we.' I asked what happened to the other half of 'we.' 'Well, she came of age.' I said, 'What's that?' 'Well, she was getting along to thirty and beginning to think of kids and wanting to settle down, and I didn't!' And there it is, the biological clock saying it's time to have kids or not to have them. Your style changes a little bit. You don't want a live-in boyfriend, you want a marriage, so you can start looking forward to having kids. That seems to be a major factor in marriage, a major reason for it."

Coming of Age

In an unpublished Ph.D. dissertation, *The Twenty-Nine-Year-Old Never-Married Woman: Response to a Deviant Social Status,* Ruth E. White focused on stresses experienced by thirteen single women twenty-nine years of age. These women, too, found the period difficult; the time between twenty-five and twenty-eight was especially important in forming an identity as a single woman. White described three stages of the crisis; the examples which follow are from women I talked with.

1. *Life by Script.* Like women everywhere, these women grew up expecting to get married. They graduated from college, traveled some, went to graduate school, and/or found jobs. By the time they were twenty-five most of their friends were married, and they began to focus on the fact that they, indeed, were still single.

2. *Identity Crisis.* As time passed and it became increasingly clear that their identity and fulfillment might not come from marriage and motherhood, the women began to realize they might have to find success and attainment in other ways. An upsetting discovery! Self-esteem dropped and their confidence shriveled.

Six months away from a Ph.D. Janice wondered if her degree would mark her forever as a professional woman unsuited for marriage and seriously considered dropping her program; Ruth abandoned a promising career in the foreign service as "not worth the price in aloneness." Michelle vented her feelings by going on a buying spree of extravagant clothes, expensive sports equipment, and a Porsche she couldn't afford and had to resell.

The women often drew closer to other women, valuing old relations more deeply, actively seeking new ones. Pat moved out of a studio apartment, now preferring what she and two other friends referred to as extended family living in a rented house; Cathy sought out old high school and college friends, wondering what had happened in their lives since they last met. Some women said they stopped regarding friend-ships with women as second best.

They were often influenced by the women's movement and various feminist ideas. They saw that women's roles were subordinate to men's, and that they had been taught to play down their initiative and aspirations. They began to understand that so-called feminine behavior had little to do with gender, but had a lot to do with powerlessness. They began to separate themselves from the roles they were supposed to play and became more aware of dreams and hopes they had long ago buried.

White found relationships with parents changed significantly during this period. The old parent-child dichotomy shifted to adult-adult, which for a while made relations more tense. Denise reported, "Mother used to feel fairly free to sort of involve herself in how I lived in my apartment; she'd even shop for me, picking up household goods I didn't especially like. It annoyed me, it was like buying panties and socks for some little kid. I finally made it clear this was my real home, I could afford life's necessities and wanted to pick out things *I* liked. I guess what was really bugging me deep down was that I know she doesn't do this to my married sister."

But in time parents come to accept the new relationship. It may well be that single women find it harder to get parents to recognize their adult status and independence, since one function of marriage is to initiate couples into the adult world.

Work activities and educational accomplishments helped the women feel more competent and contributed to their growing self-esteem. By the end of the crisis, the women's perception of themselves and their life situation had become much more positive.

3. *Self-Definition.* By this stage the women had developed a distinct consciousness of themselves as individuals and were moving toward meaningful goals, generally in employment and educational areas. They continued to be rather optimistic about getting married, although their focus had shifted from looking to relationships with men to make their lives complete to concentrating on leading a rich and full life with or without such relationships. They did not wish to have their lives defined by a spouse or children and stressed the importance of maintaining an independent self. Their increased self-esteem enabled them to possess a positive self-concept, though they realized society in general regarded their singleness in a rather negative way.

As I traveled around the country and talked with never-married women in their late twenties and early thirties, I heard themes of the Age Thirty Crisis over and over again. "I suddenly realized I should be thinking in terms of grad school and a real career; working wasn't going to be such a temporary thing after all." "I worried more about financial security; hand-to-mouth living was becoming a drag. I wanted stability, something to show for all the years I'd now been working. I thought about starting an investment plan, putting away something for a rainy day." "I noticed my interest in frenetic, running-around weekends stopped; I became more interested in being a more *together* person and entered a meditation class and paid more attention to my health." "I took a new look at my whole life situation."

I saw the pain and the turmoil; giving up plans and dreams is never easy. And the struggle: "My biggest regret is that I had to put so much of my life energy into coping with being single. For three years I was just drained."

Women who did not speak about a crisis directly nonetheless seemed to have entered a down period, as though a nameless something were going bump in the night. The bright high flyers of the early and mid-twenties come in to rest and brood during the last part of this decade.

But hope and confidence persist. These women are sometimes bent, but rarely bowed.

Looking at the Age Thirty Crisis

There is a sense in which the Age Thirty Crisis is a too-typical example of the kind of social lag which often affects women today. Women begin to act in ways which have only recently been validated: They develop their lives, they forge ahead independently, they get on with the tasks of adult development. And then the past catches up with them: They are attacked from behind by traditional ideas of women's lives they have learned earlier, and by the roles society still demands of women. Deeper and more emotionally held values of the past rise up to war against newer and more rationally held attainments of the present.

Women's lives are changing very rapidly now; new generations form very quickly, perhaps as often as a school generation, every four years. The women in this book, chapter by chapter, age group by age group, form portraits in time, snapshots along a continuum of growth and change. We see and we will see again how clearly the social ideas of their early years influence each generation. The women of the Age Thirty Crisis are different from the women of Chapter I; by dint of their few extra years, they are products of an environment which was changing (and which they themselves sometimes played a part in changing) and to which they must respond and change as well.

It seems likely that in the future the incidence and perhaps the intensity of the Age Thirty Crisis will decline. It is hard to imagine that Marty and Dorothy and Julia and Randy and Susan will be as thrown by the Crisis as Lynn and her peers were. Less affected by old standards, their values will be more closely examined and their awareness of women's roles will be much more sophisticated. They may well have to make some painful changes, but their foundations for growth as single women seem more firmly entrenched and more broadly based.

Before we continue to the next life stage, let's look at a few factors relating to the childhood and background of never-married women. The following material is not taken from any one group of women, but forms a composite of all the women I came to know.

Childhood and Family Background

Parents   Because little is actually known about the reasons women don't marry, a rich folklore of suppositions has grown up. Some of it is about the influence of home and family upon her never-married status.

One theory goes that her home background was so secure and therefore she is so perfectly well adjusted that she has no need for marriage. This, at least, is a refreshing reversal of the more frequent idea of the maladjusted spinster. Another story has it that for various reasons her family background has convinced her that marriage is bad, and motherhood should be avoided. (Note, not for the first time, the confusion and mixing together of these two different statuses, marriage and motherhood.) A variation on this theme is that personality defects springing from her home setting cause her to avoid marriage and family. But the matter is not as simple as any of these theories suggests.

I found that these parental marriages and home lives of never-married women were very diverse. They were children of the happiest of marriages and the worst of marriages. Sue Ann was born the cherished "only child of two only children" in a New York suburb which offered every advantage. Dixie came from an abusive family which dissolved when she had to be placed in protective foster care. Judy's family moved seventeen times with the Army, but her home life was secure and warm. Mary mentioned the life of a businessman's family in Dayton—"ups and downs, just average, pretty normal." They recalled their childhoods as happy, repressed, secure, stable, so-so, miserable, traditional, and okay. Economically, they were wealthy, middle-income, and dirt poor. Most rated parental marriage and home life somewhere in the middle and reported the usual ups and downs, conflicts, and contradictions.

Although a more scientific answer could be found by comparing parental marriages and home life of these women with women in general, there seems to be little clustering, no sense of a trend, among the women I interviewed.

Family Size, Structures, and Birth Rank Social scientists often speak of the size of the family, its structure (whether nuclear or extended), and in recent years have stressed birth rank (first-born, middle-born, or youngest) as significant in personality development. The women I interviewed came from families of every size, from every birth rank. They were only children and the youngest of nine; they were raised by fathers alone or in a family whose interconnectedness would rival the Waltons.

Presence of Other Never-Married People in the Extended Family Does never-marriedness run in families? Are there some extended families whose members perhaps influence each other to stay single? We don't know for sure. Never-married women did report some bachelor uncles, maiden aunts, and unmarried cousins, especially in older generations. But never-marriedness was far from uncommon in the Victorian age; perhaps one-third of all adults stayed single. So most families today have spinsters and bachelors somewhere in the family tree, not just the families of single women. We would have to do a more complete correlation than is possible here to discover if never-marriedness runs in families, if somehow the presence of older unmarried family members tends to influence younger members to remain single.

Permission-givers One fact that *did* appear with a high degree of frequency was that *many never-married women have permission-givers in their immediate backgrounds.* A permission-giver is someone close to them who has said in effect, "It's okay to remain single."

Permission comes in two forms: overt and covert. Overt permission, usually verbalized, is direct and clear; the speaker tells the hearer that singleness is acceptable, that it's all right to remain unmarried. Covert permission is communicated indirectly. It is "said between the lines"; it may be "heard with a third ear." Even though it is less clearly conveyed, the hearer nonetheless understands the message.

There are four kinds of permission-givers. All are emotionally close to the recipient. All are female, except for a few fathers of women whose mothers had died and who assumed the role of permission-giver. (In the discussion which follows, the term single is used generically. It is unclear whether permission-givers may be never-married, divorced, or widowed, except as stated.)

1. *Permission-givers who are single themselves and feel positive about their singleness.* Usually this is a close family member (an unmarried aunt or cousin) who communicates the "okayness" of her singleness to her niece

or cousin, implying that this may be a desirable situation for her, too.

Marian remembered, "My mother's sister, Aunt Elena, used to visit us every so often. She lived in Seattle, dressed well, and drove a nice car. Her life seemed interesting and exciting; she was full of tales of dangerous excursions into Alaska, trips to Hawaii, and adventures with a flying club she belonged to. Mother envied her, I know, and gave us little hints and signs that Elena was better off than she. I know they both influenced me to stay single."

Liz's older cousin Bertha lived across town. "She was a respected teacher, the president of the teacher's association, and often had a prominent voice in educational and other decisions around town. Our family was proud of her. I liked to hang around her; she took a special interest in me and was always generous in material ways, partially supporting me through college. It was clear she was happy in her life, and sometimes pointed out the advantages of being single."

But family friends, relatives, teachers, or others in the community function as permission-givers only occasionally; emotional closeness seems to be an important factor. These women also serve as role models, but their permission-giving quality seems to be their most important function.

Happily single women constitute only a small proportion of permission-givers.

2. *Happily married mothers who give their daughters permission to remain single.* The largest category of permission-givers, these women do not prescribe marriage as a condition for their daughter's happiness. Quite often, they may be identified by their "no strings attached—whatever's right for you" attitude. Included in this category are mothers who seem neutral or noncommittal about their daughter's marital status but are concerned for her best interests. Given the overwhelming norm for marriage in this society, I count their neutrality as permission-giving; their message is more covert than others.

Linda reported, "For some reason in my household, getting married wasn't brought up, it wasn't hammered home. My mother never said, 'You go to college, and you find a man,' which was the message an awful lot of other girls got. It's 'You go to college and learn how to support yourself when you get out.' When I was growing up, more than push me towards a relationship with a fellow, my mother resisted my getting really involved with any one guy, but preferred to see me out with lots of boys. There were sexual overtones to that; she didn't want me to get intimate with anyone.

"Her own marriage is sort of separate but equal. Yes, my folks are happy together but she has a large element of doing her own thing."

Connie told me, "My mother has two points which mean a lot to her; her role as an academic—she teaches French literature—and her humanistic values, shaped by the fact that she is a Unitarian. I'm sure her own self-concept turns more around her academic role than the fact that she's a wife and mother. She tends to see people in terms of what they do in work, or contribute to the community, what their values are, rather than in all these categories, like married or single, rich or poor, family background, or something like that. She values freedom highly and avoids telling me what to do with my life, especially around issues like getting married."

Georgia's mother emphasized, "School first, friends second—boys after that. There's plenty of time for men." This is a typical theme: value placed first on education, the ability to be self-supporting. Men and marriage may or may not follow.

Yet given the happiness these same women are seen as having in their own marriages, what might prompt this paradoxical message?

Perhaps it springs from mature impulse: mother realizes happiness is not dependent on marital status; she knows of fully realized single women. She sees her daughter is doing well as she is; she generally manages her life in a way which meets her approval; all is well.

On another level, it may be a response to the conflict and ambiguity inherent in any marital status: even the most happily married among us experience degrees of marital stress, and have our fantasies of "what if" we had remained single. Vicarious identification is by no means rare. Permission-giving may be a release, a manifestation of this conflict, an acting out of something otherwise suppressed.

3. *Divorced or unhappily married mothers who give their daughters permission to remain unmarried.* The message of divorced mothers is apt to be unequivocal, clear, and overt: Don't be like me, don't repeat the mistakes of my life. Their motives are straightforward and understandable enough: They do not wish to see their daughters relive their own misfortune. Julia Hawkins' mother, who emphasized that she should "get out there and *do,*" is a clear example of this.

Having become single women again, the divorced permission-givers have a clear and pragmatic understanding of the strengths of single life, a trait they share in common with the permission-givers of the first category.

For the unhappily married, the message may be more covert: There is lots of face-saving in marriage. But the evidences of unhappy marriage are usually clear enough to daughters, and the essential message comes through.

4. *Single fathers may serve as permission-givers, too.* Three women in my group had mothers who died when they were young. They had been raised primarily by their fathers, who served as clear permission-givers.

"I was the most active and rebellious child, and my father said I caused him more problems than the rest of his children put together," Louise commented. "But on the bottom line our relationship was really very good because he came to understand my aspirations were more like a boy's than a girl's. He never pressured me to marry and was happy I was job-oriented in a serious way. He said not a word when I entered graduate school, though he didn't want me to leave home."

Joan said, "The one thing I got over and over again was the necessity of being able to take care of myself—in case there was another Depression, an event which had really burned Dad. And spin-offs of that idea—that I don't need anything from anybody; that intellectual attainment was good, because it led to success. I don't remember that the question of marriage was ever discussed."

Although this sample is too small to be conclusive, it is interesting to note that fathers can function as permission-givers too.

This is not to say that parents do not sometimes express a desire for marriage and offspring from their daughters; they do. Parents, after all, live with social norms and expectations; they themselves have married and had children. But often such messages are conveyed in a contradictory way, or in some other sense convey the impression that the desire for marriage is not really their bottom-line wish.

Says one of these women, "My mother sometimes says she wishes I'd get married, but I know she likes to glory it up around the other teachers at school, telling them about the celebrities I've interviewed or the book I have coming out." Mother was a frustrated writer herself. Daughter knows Mother's identification with her career carries more weight than her interest in a possible marriage.

Ann told me, "I remember asking my mother as a very small child about school. She explained about grade school, high school, and college, adding that boys went to college, and girls got married, sort of with the implication that the higher things in life were denied women. I decided I wanted to go to college right then and there—and in fact, I went; my brother never made it.

"But talk about mixed messages—I'd describe my mother as a frustrated housewife with an enormous amount of energy who was held back by her traditional New England farm background. She talked—

she urged—marriage and family to me, yet never let me touch a dish or help with anything around the house. I was twenty-five years old and had a master's degree before I learned how to boil water, literally."

The most extreme example of a mixed message I heard concerned a friend of mine who came home once to find a wedding dress draped across her bed. "My mother has always been clothes crazy and her choices were always unorthodox, but this was something else. I asked her why she bought it. 'In case you ever need it,' she told me. Well, actually, I didn't care that much for the style. I put it back in the box and I still have it." A message most women would find devastating was not for Marie. I knew her relationship with her mother to be unusually strong, more cordial than most mother-daughter relationships. There was no doubt of the "no strings attached—you know what's best for you" attitude of her mother. Marie had long loved to cite stories of her mother's latest acquisitions, her more outlandish choices. Even a wedding dress on a bed didn't override the real message: You're okay as you are. And Marie knew it.

I think with appreciation of my own mother, a happily married permission-giver, whose message was not mixed, but very straight. About the time I was thirteen, she began giving me pieces of sterling silverware as birthday and Christmas gifts. How easy it would have been for her to speculate on the circumstances under which they might be used, to comment on the husband's hand which might one day hold the carving set! But she never did. She was careful to say, "This is for when you have a home of your own some day"; more often, she said nothing.

I heard a story showing the other side of the coin from a very-married friend of mine. As a teenager, she went to an antique store with her mother. They came across a beautiful old lace handkerchief, with her initial outlined in pale blue. "Look," her mother exclaimed, "something old, and something borrowed and blue—with your initial." At no small expense, the mother purchased it as a special gift for her daughter, to be carefully put away for her wedding day.

I sometimes hear this same woman make predictive comments to her own young daughter: *"When* you are married, *when* you have a family. . . ."￼ Her daughter is strong and free, an independent spirit who can reasonably aspire to anything in life. I want to cry out, "Don't say that, don't put her in a slot, don't script her before she's even begun, let her go free!" But restrained by social convention, I say nothing.

Another woman told me, "It's hard to sort out—an assumption was built into things that I'd marry—like it's a natural part of a woman's life in some unquestioned way. I remember a sort of tension, an importance around men and dating that was different from other things. I could get away with spending more on clothes if I said they were also clothes for dates. My father had not very gracious ways of indicating he didn't expect to support me forever—that some younger man should take this responsibility from him, though maybe I could get a job in the meantime. Family weddings were always whipped into big, heavy occasions. Oh, parents can have dozens—hundreds—of ways of laying this expectation on you." Married at twenty-two, she was divorced nine years later.

Single women do receive pressure for marriage, but they cite the sources of it as distant relatives, family friends, "society in general." They rarely mention parents, siblings, close friends, or people at work.

So what about the cliché of the mother who sits down with her single daughter and says, "Dear, now that you're getting older, don't you think it's about time . . .?"

I didn't hear many stories like that.

Maybe all those women are married.

Role Models and Expectations of the Future

When I asked single women to name persons who served as role models when they were growing up, they rarely mentioned any single women. Could they think of any single women who *might* have served as role models? Almost never.

If pressed, they could name single women they had admired: an older woman at the office, a teacher, a fictionalized character. But these women did not seem to loom large enough to be true models; they seemed to be seen as good examples.

I met several women who commented on the positive changes they had noted in women coming out of marriage. We have already seen that Randy Howard perceived her mother as growing and taking hold in widowhood, that Marty Cardenas admired the career progress her mother made as a single woman. Rosemary's Poulos' grandmother held her husband's coat, brushed his boots, and let him make all the family decisions. After his death she became a dynamo. These examples must influence thinking about marriage in some way.

Nor did any of these women have a preconception of themselves as single women; their childhood dreams of the future seemed quite traditional. They would perhaps go to college, almost always get married and raise a family. Some thought of jobs: teacher, nurse, secretary, seen as pursuits secondary to being a wife and mother. Most did not recall being especially motivated toward careers or other attainment. None imagined themselves remaining as single adults.

No role models, highly traditional expectations. No wonder the Age Thirty Crisis is and has been so hard on women. There is so little preparation, so little help in establishing an identity as a single person. In the years ahead, it will be fascinating to observe the experiences of the New Generation, which seems to have a somewhat different set of expectations.

III

INTO THE THIRTIES AND EARLY MIDLIFE
Confronting a Biological Imperative

Whatever else can be said about a confrontation like the Age Thirty Crisis, it will eventually pass, to be replaced, one hopes, by a new understanding, new insights. As one woman, Marian, described her sense of getting clear and coming into her own: "I simply realized that the box I lived in was unlike other people's boxes—by the word box I don't mean anything weird or psychotic, but the way I live, my interior house and how it's furnished and peopled—my long-term friends, my full social life, the number of good sexual relationships and good intellectual relationships I have with men. I had felt nervous about the difference about what I had, and what other people had, or wished they had. But recently I realized my box wasn't going to change and be any different, so I might just as well feel good about it.

"I look at what I have and I'm satisfied with it—I can live on a number of different levels. I'm happy living alone. I can create my own hours and my own conveniences and I can have it perfectly quiet when I want to and I don't have to deal with anybody unless I want to. I have a dog, and that's important to me. And I like the sensation of being able to be free. I don't know that I'd be able to tolerate having that any different.

"I don't see myself restricting myself sexually at all, none of the men I spend time with expect a monogamous relationship, there's no way I could do that. I'm satisfied with the idea of turning up at parties alone,

78

I've been doing that since I was sixteen and I'm glad I've had the experience, for now it's no trouble for me whatsoever. I walk into a party alone and I can always pick up on some of the available men. I'm very happy about that.

"Always before there was this feeling that I should be part of a couple even though having sampled it, I knew I didn't want to be half a couple. There was always a lot of conflict about conforming to the socialized norm. It was easier if you did and you felt you should. There was this cultural fiat that said: 'We hold these things to be good and dear and you ought to think so too.' And I was saying, 'Look, I don't care for any of the concepts I've been offered and I've been offered a few and they're totally and utterly unacceptable.'

"I was able to raise up from the Imperative Should—things I should, should feel about traditional couple arrangements. Then I thought, 'That's okay by me but how's that going to play in Peoria?' There's still that consideration, that pressure, though I feel it a lot less now."

I asked if she could put her finger on just how she crossed over that threshold. "Well, I entered therapy and that no doubt helped but I think more importantly—the last relationship I had helped. Maybe one of the reasons I got involved with Hal was me saying to myself, 'Let's give it one last try. Pick a man that passes all of the tests of middle-American culture for a suitable husband and potential father and get to know him and see what happens.'

"Any mother would love to have Hal as a son-in-law. There were admirable things about him, but on a close personal level, not much. He dominated everything—that hand! He never actually used his hand to wave off my words, but it seemed he did. He simply interrupted me when I attempted to get a point across. He couldn't listen, couldn't hear. My job was to conform and do things his way. He brought me back to everything I don't like about typical 'coupleness'—his value to me was to tell me I didn't fit the mold. I needed that relationship to tell me once again what the problem is between the sexes.

"I had been involved in a marriagelike arrangement when I was in my early twenties. I found I just got swallowed up—his friends became my friends—being together became a lot more important than maintaining myself. I put up with a lot of 'second in importance'-type stuff. Typically men overrule women in conversations and arguments—they overcome women with words or if they can't do it fairly and logically, then they do it unfairly and illogically. That's almost the middle-class American standard of marital behavior.

"As far as women friends go, with a handful of exceptions, it's like there's some component missing. There's not a whole lot of intellect running there—it's not that they're not bright, I don't know any stupid women—it has more to do with the fact that they're unlikely to be in tune with that subgroup unoriented to the notion of marriage, and they potentially want children, and if not that, at least presenting themselves as half a couple—they feel very involved in that. Most of them are still more than happy to be paired off. I don't feel I've had a peer anywhere along the line, which is sad, because I think a number of them will eventually take a position similar to mine. But now they're still wishing there was this relationship they could rely on. My interest is in forging very strong relationships with people who don't require any of that of me—male or female."

Not all women move out of their conflicts and irresolutions as firmly and finally as Marian did. More often, the process is more gradual—there are more shades of gray. Linda Nelson talks about the issues of men and marriage as they appear to her in her early thirties.

Linda Nelson

"I see myself currently on the verge of putting a career together. It has taken me a long time to get to this point. I think I'm going to go places in film production—if the job doesn't eat me alive in the process. Still, the future for me is sort of blank; I'm not sure what is going to be coming up next. Whether I settle with someone is really quite open. It's not something I've determined is going to happen. I feel fairly confident of myself; at the same time, there are times I'm unsure of my direction, unsure of what I'm going to do with my life. But I'm not real anxious about any of that."

Thirty-one-year-old Linda Nelson surveyed her world from a small apartment above a garage in San Francisco. A production assistant in a film company of worldwide recognition, she described her work.

"What you have to understand is that the film industry is just this whole other world that will gladly consume you if you let it—just as it consumes most people who are in it in any major way. I'm first assistant, a sort of Girl Friday to the producer. I do a lot of logistics work, like when you send a film crew on location, you have to get them all there, and have a room and everything arranged for them, and sort of work to keep the wheels turning on the set. My administrative stuff is just shuffling papers and taking care of very personal demands of the man I work for. Plus miscellaneous problem solving, like renting a piano overnight, or finding a seventy-five-pound riding double for a boy in a movie, or tracking down the whereabouts of a cinematographer somebody wants or any number of things. So it's always changing, it's always different. I mean it's the same kinds of things, but they vary from day to day.

"I came into this from advertising; fell into it, really. I had been an account coordinator and a glorified secretary/office manager in an advertising agency and wanted out. This job suits my particular strengths very well. I like the challenge, the essence of it."

I imagined people must find her work glamorous. "There is some aspect of that, but it's very minor. It's really not glamorous at all except that the people you are dealing with are 'name' people. But that glamour wears off after about the first hour. Marlon Brando called recently. I was handling a lot of calls for the president of the company; any number of people want to speak to him; he wants to speak to no one, basically. So there's this voice [imitating Brando], 'Is Norman there?' and I said, 'Who's calling?' and he said 'Marlon' and God, I almost said Marlon who, but caught myself in time. And I asked Robert Duvall to move out of a seat reserved for me at a premiere; my sister almost freaked out. But that stuff becomes minor.

"Basically you're dealing with a lot of very big egos and you have to tread lightly. People tend to scream at me when they really are mad at Norman or my boss; it's nerve-racking but you sort of back off and calm them down.

"Sometimes I go on location. We were in Oregon two weeks; we're working from seven A.M. to eleven P.M. every day; it's unbelievably tense. You get this diverse group of people: horse wranglers, makeup men, truck drivers, casting directors, caterers, local people who like to watch, production assistants driving cars around, stars, families, girl friends. I run around like mad, directing most of the behind-the-scenes setup work. I had to get the film that had been shot to Los Angeles every night by courier; I was racing around looking for a 1936 red Ford pickup truck. And not only find one, but convince the people to let you use it and for as little money as possible. And take care of all the hotel arrangements and per diem money—I was carrying around fifteen thousand dollars in cash for a while.

"When you throw people together in a very intense situation like this, cut off from the reality of the real world for a couple of weeks or months, people get to know each other and develop feelings about each other in a very short period of time. Because of this intensification, there's much more likelihood of relationships happening. A man who's a photographer or crew member on location for a long period of time takes his family with him. Because if he doesn't he'll have a lady on location—it's common for people to pair off for the duration. It's happened to me. You accept it. There's no moral overtone, like there might be in an office. What happens in this rarefied environment happens faster and burns out much quicker in most instances than what happens out here in the real world." She laughed.

"The thing with me, I guess, is while I see myself as having a real future in this industry, I'm trying to stave off being absolutely consumed by it all. I stake out little areas that have nothing to do with this, that give me a little recreation, some perspective.

"Right now, that more or less is sports. I play tennis at seven in the morning, three to four times a week. And I play on a ladies' softball team; I have for seven years. It's an advertising league, so their whole business is different, out of the film world. I enjoy the team endeavor; it may be even more fun after the game, sitting in the car, rehashing it, talking about somebody's line drive and the catch somebody else made and this play and that. We can go to a bar and have free beer and conversation, and we have two or three, maybe four parties a year.

"One of my coaches and I are affectionate friends. It's kind of funny, I've known him for five years and never really thought about him too much. Then I realized he was coming on to me and so we started seeing each other a little bit. I backed off because he was living with a woman and had for a long time. He claimed he was getting out of the relationship, but he never did. So anyway. . . ."

I asked her about the other men in her life. "Well, for some reason I have remained very largely independent and singular. I'm rarely at a loss for male interest—there are usually men out there who want to see me or take me out, or get to know me better. But I'm cautious— marriage has never been a real goal. It's still something I think I want to do, but I've always resisted it, resisted tying myself to one person. There's something about the compromise that has to be made, or I think has to be made. Something about the restriction that makes me squeamish—tailoring my activities to theirs that makes me uneasy.

"I've always thought that if I really wanted to be married, I could be by now. I could have picked one of a half dozen men, and really gone after them, married them and gotten what I wanted.

"I'm not always sure of where I'm getting my emotional intake. Sometimes I don't get it. Sometimes I'm very lonely. A lot of times I get it from other women, close friends.

"I've always had lots of female friends, at least one or two I will share a lot with. We spend evenings together, we might play on the weekend, we might go out with other friends, including men, or share each other's trials and tribulations.

"We share work frustrations a lot, successes and victories and failure and hassles. We talk about current relationships with men—how it's going, what to do about it. One friend had a boyfriend who would drink heavily and threaten her. We were really at a loss about what to do; we discussed it many times. Then she'd go out and have another relationship with someone who was pretty much the same type. I was sort of a listening post; she wasn't seeking advice, so I didn't give her any. Rather than try to bring in how I felt about her relationship, I would try to open it up so she could talk about it.

"I have another friend caught up in a real stormy marriage; she comes to see me every so often. I would have told her five years ago to get rid of that guy, but I'd never mention the word divorce. If she wants to bring it up she can; I'm not going to put my thought into her head. It seems men always come into these conversations. That's part of everyone's life.

"I discovered to my surprise the other day something that baffles me. I think some of my married friends' husbands see me as a threat. They don't really want their wives to hang around with me, and I'm really at a loss to understand why. I'm not going to revolutionize them in any way, or throw questions or doubts on the validity of their relationship. I wouldn't spout feminist hellfire and damnation on them. They must think I might do that, or might somehow make their wives less satisfied with their relationship.

"One friend who lives in another state comes to visit—her husband is always real worried when she comes. He thinks we're going to get into all sorts of trouble, which is about as far from the truth as you can get—we mostly sit here and chitchat. We certainly don't go out to bars or try to pick up men or anything, that's the farthest thing from our minds. But my singleness is what makes it a threat.

"How open are they? I find most of my friends who have gotten married become more and more remote. Partly, that's natural—they're centered in another relationship, and have less energy and time to be around me. By and large, it's rare for a friend to talk openly about her marriage, divulge highs and lows, unless I walk right into it. I found one friend crying on the couch one day, and then it all came out. Mostly it's a matter of pride—not wanting to have their relationship viewed too closely, perhaps seen as a failure, not wanting gossip about it.

"Maybe older women are more likely to be more open about their unhappiness in marriage. I shared a house once with a forty-five-year-old woman who had been married seventeen years and was splitting from her husband. And her friends would come over and they would talk and paint a pretty bleak picture of men and marriage. One woman's husband fooled around on her, another's was terribly remote—in fact, it began to upset me because I didn't think it was quite that bad. They seemed to group all men together and their perspective was extremely unflattering. No, there's sort of a veil around the whole subject, the good parts as well as the bad.

"We don't talk a lot about my singleness either. No one much asks about how I feel about being single. There are a few women with whom I share confidences on the pros and cons of being single. Some people seem to find it admirable that I stay single and seem to get on so well with it, that I don't seem to have terrible hangups or insecurities with it. It's something they admire; they can't imagine doing it themselves.

"I hear a lot that there aren't any good men around. And I don't think that's true—as hard as they are to find. What's difficult is to sustain a relationship, or even develop one. I think a lot of that has to do with the fact that our roles are not as clearly set out for us as they once were. So it's a lot easier to be unhappier with whatever role you're cast into, whether you cast yourself into it, or whether it's thrust upon you. Saying that there aren't any good men around is a way of focusing on these problems.

"Now here's a point that's difficult. I do think that in marriage one partner has to more or less dominate; the subordinate role is what men usually expect of women and women expect of themselves. That shows up most obviously in the household and I guess the household scene is where the catch-22 aspects of this shows up most for me.

"Like women are expected to be the hostess. Okay. I went to a party the coach gave a couple of weeks ago, and the girl friend with whom he lives did all the cooking—she did it all—she was in the kitchen almost the entire time. She's quiet anyway, but it was a very supportive role she was fulfilling so he could entertain.

"Now I feel uneasy in a couple of ways when I start picking up in a relationship that that might be expected of me. One, I feel like that's a role I *ought* to fulfill, and I know I enjoy some parts of that. I mean I enjoy the outcome—say, people having a nice time at my party. I *do* enjoy doing a lot of household-type things that bring that off. But at the same time I don't want to feel like I'm *obligated* to do them. And then I feel guilty if I don't, or if I make an issue of it, so there you have it, the double bind.

"On one hand you have their expectations, and on the other side you have your own expectations. And maybe they fight against what you consciously want—a lot of unconscious behavioral expectations and patterns fighting a more rational disregard for those things. I say I want one thing but deep down I may act out a different kind of role. I think this gets in the way of developing serious long-term intimate relationships."

Not the first time we have heard this scheme: shifting roles, women and men caught up in changes, expectations, and deeper feelings rooted in older and more familiar ways.

"But emotional intake—well, I do have nice relationships with men. I lived with a fellow when I wasn't working. We had a lighthearted, easygoing, fun relationship." She stopped. "He sold grass—marijuana."

I laughed in some surprise. "Yeah! right. He was sort of crazy, and our style was sort of crazy. He would keep late hours and zoom around in the day, driving up the coast to pick up the stuff. But it was pretty carefree too. I had a good time and found myself smiling and laughing a lot. I mean I wasn't into what he was doing, but by virtue of the fact that I was living with him, there was some involvement with the class of people he dealt with and I wasn't really too crazy about that. But I consider that an interlude; as soon as I went back to work we broke up. I think he felt uncomfortable, even threatened around my new associates. And there have been others.

"I think that with most men I get involved with I ask myself if this is someone I'd want to marry and spend the rest of my life with. Usually my reaction is no and I sort of put it out of my mind. I have a habit of running away from anything that gets real serious."

She hesitated and spoke more slowly. "Yes, I do that—I run away. I'm afraid of the commitment; I'm afraid of what it all means; I'm afraid of something being taken away from me.

"I'm afraid of somehow losing my own identity. It's just the idea of being an appendage of someone else . . . I sense they want to possess me, control me. That I will cease to be me and become Mrs. *Them.* And that any progress I may have made in my career will dissipate. That I am no longer important, *they* are important.

"I resist the idea of becoming someone's mother. I think a lot of men unwittingly want that. Someone to nurture them, and they don't necessarily want to nurture back. They say they like the free spirit in me; the carefree quality, the independence. That's all fine and good, but when push comes to shove, they want meat and potatoes on the table.

"I think marriage has a better chance of being successful if each person brings his own identity to it and his own interests, not all of which are necessarily shared with the other, so they can be apart as well as together. But I think married people feel guilty about doing that. There's pressure in marriage to be together, yet it's impossible to be with someone all the time. It drives you crazy. But, if the things you enjoy are different, what are you sharing? But if you stick to the same interests just to share, that puts a burden on the quality of it, the pleasure of it. That worries me about marriage—the pressure to be with your partner and share it all with him. I don't know how people deal with it successfully.

"I flash on a song I heard during the sixties that goes something like people grow up and get married and hate themselves for what they are, and their children hate them for what they are, but 'you say we'll marry, so we'll marry.' It sounds so empty and bleak.

"I don't know, I don't like what I've seen happen once people get married. Personalities sort of recede, they just sort of disappear behind the marriage front of this is us and we're doing what Jimmy says we're doing. There seems to be a loss of *who they are*."

She sighed, and we fell into a troubled silence. Linda studied her fingernails, then looked up.

"And yet . . . and yet there are times I'd like to be married. *Certainly! Certainly! Certainly!* I'd be the first to admit I lack a certain definition of what I want to do with my life. And that's because something very traditional in me sees marriage as something that should happen, something to be wished for. It would be *so nice* to have somebody to come home to, not to always face an empty house, the need to call someone in if you want to talk with someone. You'd love to share the problems of life with someone close to you who knows your whole story and will empathize. And to share your life with! And to share your life with! I think it's meant to be shared with someone more intimate than friends can be. I think of marriage as being with someone you can share goals with, and bringing a purpose to your life larger than just yourself.

"Still, I don't know that married couples necessarily do that—share goals. Maybe that was more true in our parents' generation. Maybe that was one of the things that kept them together in all their craziness. People my age seem to divorce rather easily; maybe that's one of the things they lack, a common goal, this common desire or vision of what their lives should be.

"These feelings of thinking how nice it would be to be married come most strongly when I'm frustrated, keyed up, and I want to share my excitement. It would be nice to have someone to really share it with me. And boost me up. I think what I miss is someone to pat me on the back, prop me up and tell me I'm grand, and send me back out there to do it. I think it's hard to generate self-esteem by yourself. You know, to self-generate it. It would be easier to have someone telling me I have fine qualities, that I am a good person, have a lot going for me.

"I do get elements of that from my girl friends, but there are more elements when you are sharing that with a man. There's more intimacy to it; it's nicer to have a man put his arms around you than having a woman do it. And there's a certain pleasure and strength that you get from being able to supply that to them. It makes me feel very womanly, to be able to charge up someone else; fulfill something for them.

"So there's a part of me that wants to share my life with someone; there's a part of me that wants to have children and a home; there's a part of me that would like to have someone support me—that would like to give in to this traditional role of being supported.

"Yes, that's one of the traditional ideas I can't quite let go of—that marriage will provide someone to provide for you as against providing for yourself. If I hadn't had an unconscious expectation of marriage, I would have planned for a career much more seriously much sooner.

"It would be easier to be single if I had more money to be single with. I have a few pleasures, but on the whole I live very modestly. I think with inflation and the way the economy's going it's a concern for most people, and it's a real concern to me. That I'm not able to afford much of a life-style, or many luxuries, to go off on a vacation without draining what few savings I have. When women's groups complain about women earning about sixty percent or something like that of what men earn, I see that crunch in my own life. I don't think the economic factor in itself is strong enough to move me toward marriage, but I do feel it would be nice to have more security. Really.

"And yet—I don't think marriage is a way out of *anything*. I think it's much harder in many ways than being single. To accommodate another person, to compromise with another person, to share that much of your life with another person without conflicting irrevocably. I think it requires more give and take, more patience, more struggle! It's not an easy institution.

"Maybe, in fact, there's something terribly wrong with the institution or our expectations of it—I think it's our expectations. It doesn't seem to suit many people anymore, or work for the long term. There's something about it that most people are unprepared to deal with—all of the relationships I think of as so solid just seem to fall apart. It may be the length of it and it may be the closeness of it—the very thing you desire about it is what gets you in the end—it becomes suffocating. That somehow it causes you so much guilt, guilt because you're not living up to what you think it should be. Or that you are and you hate it! Or just given the nature of life today, it's untenable."

I asked Linda if she thought she would eventually marry. "It still remains really vague to me. And I think as long as it remains vague, it won't happen."

Darcy McNaughton

She's usually busy fourteen hours a day, organizing political campaigns, leading community groups, giving legal advice, teaching, counseling, attending to her friends—in addition to her regular work. Her energy and her intelligence seem almost formidable, yet her immediate openness, her approachability, her likableness offset her disciplined assertiveness. Something in her appearance hints of New Left politics, neighborhood activism, a feminist orientation. At thirty-four, Darcy McNaughton is a woman behind the scenes who makes things happen.

"It's organizing that interests me, pulling the strings, bringing the private and public sectors together. Women's issues, government reform, consumer things. Working in coalitions around campaigns, trying to influence how Los Angeles functions."

She ticked off her current projects. "I spent Saturday morning trying to get an endorsement for a friend running for city council in this district. At work I'm involved in advising managers in EEO programs, so I'm running a training program for that. Right now I'm preparing a speech to give to a group on affirmative action. I'm teaching consumer law in a college paralegal program, and advising sixteen students. I chair a citizens action group on civil service reform; I have to write up some legislation and find a sponsor for that soon. I've been appointed by the governor to a state professional advisory board. And I'm part of a network of politically savvy women who use their influence on behalf of women's issues—calling in the chips, you might say, for favors we've done in the past.

"About a month ago I was in New York for a week looking for money for a proposal I want to do studying feminist women's organizations. I got a very favorable response from foundations, and an offer from a magazine to run a questionnaire. We're looking at women in leadership roles, how feminist organizations are perceived, things like that. Though actually, my primary purpose in going to New York was to go to the theater—four times—and visit my cousin. I spent a couple of days in the Village, bought a ton of books, went to the Metropolitan Museum of Art, and did a lot of walking around the city.

"It *was* a heavy month—my job is such that I can't pick up the phone and intertwine these things during the day. I tend to go on binges, working hard and then taking time off for a week to do nothing. I squeeze in some of my reading then."

Her schedule seemed overwhelming, with no time or space left for personal matters. "I blend work and play. I went to five or six political fund raisers and a benefit for a neighborhood community cultural center. I attended a boat party put on by Young Lawyers for the Arts. I took in a couple of films, played bridge, had out-of-town guests on and off. But no, there's not always a good balance between what I'm doing professionally and my need for personal space.

"Actually, my chief recreation—in the sense of 're-creating' myself—comes from Ed, the guy I live with. We tend to lie around, read, listen to music, watch TV; we hardly ever go out. We have so little time together we'd both rather stay home.

"I've known Ed five or six years and we've lived together the past two years. He's sort of my househusband—he takes care of the house, gets the groceries, and answers the phone, taking elaborate notes; nobody ever leaves me a simple note. He's part of the Venice black musicians group. He gets a check from the VA and sometimes works at the post office; he's not at all career oriented. Maybe that's why we get along so well; he's not competitive; my achievement drive doesn't tie into anything similar of his.

"I can't really explain the basis of it, what we're both getting out of it. Ed's not my, quote, ideal man—I don't really know what it is, where it could be. If he wasn't living with me he'd be in Venice where everybody shares everyone's money and living quarters, crashes in everyone's flat. We tease around about getting married for his VA loan to get a house, but that's about as unrealistic as anything you can imagine.

"He's very perceptive, very much able to respond to my moods on a very deep emotional level. I came in half dead the other night and fell asleep on his sofa bed. He cuddled up and hugged me and watched TV while I unwound. I had to get up early the next morning so I said, 'Just hug me,' and pretty soon I drifted off to sleep. When I was studying for the bar, I was a horror to be around. He'd complain to my friend Jill, 'My God, Darcy's been terrible, I can't sit down without being yelled at,' but he never let on to me. If I need him to come home I don't have to ask, he knows by the tone of my voice. He tolerates my weird hours; if I get up at three A.M. and write, it's okay by him.

"I've had relations with men who are as involved as I am—we almost had to put it on our calendars if we wanted to spend time together, which is ludicrous. Or we never saw each other until midnight and we were too tired to even have a conversation. Those relationships always broke up—we'd get subtly competitive. With Ed that doesn't happen.

"We have a certain amount of social life with other couples—our former neighbors were over last night—but it's mostly a mixed group of singles, parts-of-couples, whatever. We have mutual friends and we have separate friends. Our emphasis isn't on a social life. Ed meets my everyday needs to be close to someone. If I'm traveling and have to sleep alone for a couple of nights, I really miss him. He satisfies that need not to live alone, but is someone who is there for the little things in life. In a sense, it's like a marriage—there's someone you're kind of responsible to, accountable to.

"The black-white thing doesn't tie in with much, though there are some cultural differences. Ed relates as much to the white community as to the black; his close friends are white; he has close black friends too. I was involved with another black guy once but the relationship was much more volatile. He was involved in the South Africa movement and Zimbabwe and the same radical politics stuff I was in during the early seventies, but not now. I'm burned out on all that stuff; I couldn't see that I was making any real progress."

I asked her how her parents regarded her living arrangements. "Basically I think my mother is okay about it; with my dad, we've agreed that he doesn't know anything, but of course he does. He came out here a few years ago when I was sharing an apartment with two women and had a male roomie; he decided that was a hippie commune, so he hasn't come back. He's a retired military officer from the South, though I didn't realize he had feelings about racial things until I wanted to bring home a black friend from college.

"Ed is certainly the major person in my life. After that, it's my friend Jill. Our lives are totally different; she's divorced and has two kids, lives in Culver City, is trained as a teacher but became a street artist, and has always struggled financially to make it. We're good friends because we have some of the same instincts about life in general and because we share certain cultural and intellectual interests.

"She's my hangout-in-Venice friend; we go over to the bars, hear the poetry and music, go to the theater, discuss books. She's also a person to talk things over with when I'm depressed or down in the dumps and need to talk about my relationships and all those things.

"When I first met her, she was freshly divorced and just getting back into the single life. She had married when she was nineteen, had her two kids, and finished college after she married, and she and her husband seemed to be headed for a nice upper-middle-class existence when whoom! He told her it was all over. So some divorced friends in my group and I sort of took it on ourselves to say, 'Hey, these are the new rules of the game' and to help her over the experience gap—she was a reentry woman in a lot of ways.

"I've really seen her blossom—her divorce was a devastating thing. She didn't have much money and she had been trained as a teacher and there weren't any teaching jobs. So she was taking any old clerical job she could get and learning there is a lot of discrimination against women in that. Well, I have this friend who took an interest in her and helped her get started. They got some plants and colored sand and various glass containers and worked out these desert sand paintings. Now she's an independent businesswoman who's gained a lot of confidence in her abilities.

"Jill has a mentally retarded daughter who's very frustrating sometimes. Jill will call and say, 'Betsey's driving me nuts, I've got to get out of the house.' We'll sometimes take Betsey someplace, to the movies, and I'll have her sit with me for a while.

"When I was in law school and especially when I was studying for the bar, I was just an absolute terror and I could always say to Jill, "Hey, I'm a basket case, come and rescue me" and she would. So she's just a very accepting person; in fact she tends to be too accommodating to other people's needs. I think we've learned a lot from each other, recognizing differences, because in a lot of ways we're very different.

"And there's another man in my life too, a guy I see as sort of a mentor. Part of our relationship is that he has a strong physical attraction for me and I feel hey! I'm not ready for that. He's a writer on world environment and has several books and does a PBS show too. And he likes to bounce his problems and ideas off me—he lets me read his things, proofread his galleys, argue over titles. He's always pushing, prodding me—he thinks I should be in business for myself. That's an interesting idea, but I don't know how it could be accomplished, and neither does he. I prod him too—about making a decision he's cogitating about, whether he needs a publicist to promote him, if he wants this broader appeal for his ideas. So it's a very interesting relationship. We don't get to see each other a lot of late, but we talk on the phone.

"He'd like it to be an affair. I feel very close to him and each of us can put out our deepest feelings, and these feelings relate to the broader spectrum of human life which has always been an important thing to me. He's already married. If we had met twenty years ago, I would be very much attracted to him as a life mate, because he approaches most of the qualities I would seek. Now if he were single and twenty years younger. . . .

"I have three real good friends I play bridge with. We're like a women's group, though that wasn't our purpose in getting together. Anyone who has something on her mind can raise it and get feedback on what's bothering her. I think we've exhausted about all the topics of interest to single women through the years—in depth!

"One sort of perennial topic of ours has to do with finding men, and we were discussing the other night whether you could really get results from 'hunting' them directly. We used to think so, but now I don't think it works. I think that's why women get so unhappy sometimes—if they really make that into the primary thing in their lives, if they're seeking it on any level—they're not going to find it.

"Why not? Because if you're doing something you don't normally do, putting on particular characteristics you think make you more appealing, you sort of strain and distort yourself, and you set up a set of expectations that isn't real. Also you're struggling with yourself to keep it going and then if you do get into a relationship, you have to sort of straighten it out into the real you. Like if I went to these poetry readings to meet men, but didn't have any real interest in poetry, I'd pretty soon give myself away that I was operating out of false pretenses. And I'd feel uncomfortable and he'd pick up on the 'offness' of it. The best thing is just to go along in your regular way, men will sort of appear on the scene, you get interested and involved and it's all very happenstance. It works for me.

"Along this same line one woman in our group was particularly eager to get married but could not find a man who lived up to her idealistic standards, is what it amounts to. We weren't chiding her, but we were telling her that perhaps she ought to reexamine the way in which she relates to men. I've fixed her up twice with attorneys I know; she went out with one about two times and I asked him a couple of months later what happened. She just kind of put out vibes that indicated that—she probably scared him to death—she came on too strong, she was too appraising, so I told her that. I mean, that's my point about when you try too hard. That person he met wasn't entirely Bea, but she had distorted herself and she really didn't get anyplace.

"It's something unique, the unquestioning ability we have to fall back on one another. We recognize it as a new-style family that's come into being. Ellen's father died and we helped her through that, and later she got sick and had to go to the hospital. Backing her up just happened—it wasn't even a matter of asking. 'Well, let's see, she needs to have her plants and mail taken care of, when she comes home she won't be able to cook, all right, I'll go Monday, you go Tuesday.' Bea picked Ellen's mother up at the airport and we entertained her and took care of her in sort of a daughterly way. There was little planning, it just fell in place, and I know her mother was very impressed with the whole thing. I don't think parents from the old school realize the way we look out for each other—they probably think we're out here by ourselves, all alone.

"Recently we've started talking more about family life, and our futures. We like our lives and don't see ourselves getting married in the traditional sense, though we'd all enjoy some kind of permanent relationship with a man. We kid around about what we're going to do in our old age and think about an extended family kind of situation, a continuation of the support group that already exists.

"But the heaviest question we're all trying to deal with is do we want children, and how would we survive if we had them. If I were to have a child, I don't think I'd have it based on any kind of a relation with a man that I was definitely expecting to continue as part of that support for the child—I'd have to know I could support it myself for twenty years or more. By support I mean both financial support and emotional support. We kid around about the notion of having a large flat, a child co-op, with other people who could take partial responsibility for raising that child. Not a commune where you sign up on a chart, but parents and maybe others, mutually concerned.

"In a year or two or possibly more I'll make a child-having decision. If I should get pregnant again—I was once by Ed and had an abortion—I think I'd be inclined to go ahead with it because I'm more settled now than I was then. I have friends who would desperately love to get pregnant, but they don't have a man around to father the child and maybe take some responsibility for it, and haven't thought of other alternatives. I've thought about getting married to give the child a name but not necessarily counting on that relationship to last—do it for legitimization purposes. I don't see much point in getting married for economic or social reasons with no children involved."

I asked Darcy what she saw as her biggest problems. "Generally where I'm going and what I want to do with my life—I can't seem to lay my finger on what it is I really want to do for the next ten years.

"I'd be the first to admit to my contradictions. I know my feelings about some of these things shift around quite a bit. Take my relationship with Ed. Now I see it as sort of meeting my basic needs, but there are times I'm not so sure it's enough. Maybe I should move on, look for a guy with more of a future to offer. I'd like to get a house with somebody and not tie up so much in rent. Ed and I have our outs, like anybody else. I sometimes get real down on him and think maybe I should throw him out. I fantasize maybe someday he'll throw a Lee Marvin case at me.

"And really, I do think of having a child basically on my own, but I still haven't closed off the option of getting married and having one. God, I'm just tired to the bone sometimes and I think it would be great to have someone take care of me and get married and stay home and do all this community political stuff without thinking about having to support myself. Still the marriage fatality rate among my political friends—just nobody is married in the conventional sense. Their priorities are just focused differently, around the broader social areas, not so much on personal needs. So I'd have to feel I could bring a marriage off in some different way.

"And I think about the future in terms of my old age. Some of my activist friends have sort of stepped aside in favor of building up a more solid base, a hedge against the future. And when I think more about security, I also think maybe I should shift my work to capitalize on some things I could get pretty well paid for in the private sector, like becoming a lobbyist, or a government-relations type. So maybe I should be looking real seriously at some career changes.

"And running—rampaging!—through all this is the fact that I know I have to decide pretty soon about having a child. I have to come to a decision about if I'm going to do it based on a relationship with somebody or not. My bridge friends and I have talked that one absolutely to death.

"I guess part of my problem is that I have so many options, so many choices, it would almost seem easier if I had to operate around more constraints on what I can do. I compare myself with Jill, whose options are very limited by children and money. I've made myself only one limitation—I don't want to leave California. If I hadn't made that decision some of my other problems would be solved because there are ten thousand opportunities elsewhere. Or maybe I should say they'd make the picture even that more complicated!

"Certain things are fairly clear. It's reasonable to think my political career will grow, that I'll pick up some more appointments, maybe a plum assignment or two. It's very reasonable to think that I could eventually run for office myself someday. I've basically been struggling with these problems for a long time, and I'm having difficulty sifting it all out. I feel like I'm in control, but there are times I don't feel I'm in control, yet based on the history of my life I see I usually choose the right thing.

"There's a folk saying about the difficult decisions being the ones most worth making. I think maybe I should adopt that as my motto."

Rosemary Poulos

It would be misleading to suggest that all never-married women have a man in their lives, as the preceding women do. For some women, dates and male companions are a low-profile, back-burner issue, secondary in the scheme of things, maybe not even that.

We previously met Rosemary Poulos in the midst of her Age Thirty Crisis. Developing relations with men had been difficult for her, and in her twenties she struggled to learn social skills, "comfortableness" she hadn't learned as a teenager. A somewhat solitary woman, the issue of men flared in importance from time to time, especially around age thirty. But work meant more, and she gladly poured all she had towards achieving one goal: being successful in her career.

A study of highly successful women—corporate executives, high-level professionals, government leaders—suggests that around half of them never marry. Because I think Rosemary is representative of the fairly large number of never-married women who place great emphasis on career achievement and deemphasize men in their lives, we will look at her life, at age thirty-nine, more closely.

By any standards, she is a pro, a star performer. I first saw Rosemary at a session of the state legislature, presenting a section of the state budget for the coming year. Confidently she reviewed the complicated figures, adding references, humorous asides, making the figures come alive, seem important. "Rosemary could explain the backside of the moon and make you like it," a jeans-clad legislator remarked.

The seeming casualness of the rurally oriented legislature belies the magnitude of her responsibilities. As budget director, Rosemary oversees the planning and disbursement of millions of dollars, supervises a staff of thirty, negotiates sensitive political decisions with legislators, the governor, special interest groups. "This job is essentially political in nature and I wondered if I were crazy when I took it. But it seemed such an adventurous thing to do. I figured if you're going to pick roses, you'll have to take the thorns. Actually things have been going fine for three years now and I think more about what I'm going to do next than worrying about a disaster."

We walked from the capitol to her nearby home, a remodeled turn-of-the-century cottage. "You ask how I see myself—responsible, confident of my abilities, satisfied with my life but sometimes impatient for more challenge. I'm happy with what I am and what I'm doing. I'm not lonely, though I sometimes wish I had someone to share responsibilities with."

I asked her to tell me more about the women's network she was forming. "Well, the basic purpose is really to help women support other women. A small group of us feel strongly about this. We're forming an 'old girls' club'—of course we'd never call it that—a Rotary-type thing, a network of contacts, to establish a sense of having someone to turn to. We should have role models for younger women so they won't go through some of the things we've been through and didn't tell each other.

"We're just getting started. We're thinking of business luncheons with occasional programs, very brief, with something of practical value. We're mainly talking about professional women though we won't limit ourselves. There is a group of women accountants who are interested and we want to cross professional lines so the accountants can share with the women in government, the government women with bankers, the bankers with lawyers, and so on.

"There's no doubt that in my thirties I really have learned to tie into other women for emotional support. I was such a loner in my twenties! But in the last few years a group of us who work together have come to the realization that we're all struggling along, having to deal with the same things, so we share with each other more—it's an informal network maybe even more meaningful and powerful than this one we're trying to start.

"I learned something about the value of 'woman contact' when I bought this house. There's so much to know—someone has to appraise it, someone has to see that the foundations aren't rotting out—and somebody has to tell you to go out and shop for a mortgage. Well, I was at a get-together reciting my home purchase adventures. A woman banker said, 'Be sure to shop and compare various interest rates, down payments, points, prepayment penalties, and so forth.' I just said, 'Oh,' and let it go.

"Not much later I went into this little local bank where I had always banked, and my parents banked, and my grandparents before them banked. I went to the vice-president, a man who lives on our block. He said to me, 'What do you want to buy a house for? All you need is a room—spend your money on clothes and travel.' At the time, I couldn't think how to react but imagine it! Closing out every account to buy clothes! Well, if he hadn't said that, I'm sure I would have my mortgage with that bank, paid a point more, paid higher interest and a larger down payment—but I was really frosted and then I remembered the comment of the woman banker. So I shopped around and I ran into her. She heads a branch of a statewide bank, and she was just so helpful, and, you guessed it, she ended up with my business.

"I was one of the first women in our group to buy a house. Whatever I'd learn I'd pass along to someone else who was interested and whatever anyone else knew, they'd tell me. Soon I was directing all sorts of people to this bank and to this woman. Now she's vice-president of the bank and I think I'm responsible for that! Of course, I don't really mean it—she's responsible for her success, not me—but I like to think I helped it. Her branch has grown more than any other in the state—and it's really exciting.

"Owning this house means a lot to me. I love it. I first considered getting an acreage out of town and keeping horses and dogs—I know I tend to substitute animals for children—but it was out of my range financially and would have isolated my mother, who doesn't drive. It's not that I'm enamored with this house particularly, but I *do* love owning a house.

"I'm a putterer. I find it very relaxing to come home and pound nails. When we first moved in, the plumbing was constantly on the fritz. You always have trouble getting a plumber in this town, so I got myself a fixit book, and it's great what you can do with a couple of diagrams, some picture hanging wire, a wrench, and a screwdriver! Now I do most of the minor plumbing and electric work myself—I wouldn't try to rewire the house or replace a pipe or something like that, but I can replace switches, build my own cupboards, refinish furniture, and handle most of those decrating-type things.

"I'm not at all athletic. I don't enjoy tennis or golf or softball or any of those other things people do to work out their frustrations after a tough day on the job. I come home and pound my boards and fix my house.

"And it's an economic thing. My salary's getting up there, I have no dependents, no other investments. I pay high taxes and need a tax shelter, and something that builds equity. This was a smart, hard-headed investment. And when I think of all I've learned and can do, how much this property has been improved by my own efforts, I know it's one of the things that's added to my feeling of self-reliance, my sense that yes, I can do anything I want to do!"

I told Rosemary I was interested in knowing more about the relationships of single women who live with their mothers. "That's a difficult question. In our case, we have a good relationship which is sometimes very frustrating. I have a sense of responsibility that says it would be nice not to have to worry about her. We had a very difficult time of it when I first took this job. I travel frequently. If I were tied up in a meeting or testifying before the legislature, I would not call and say, 'I'm not going to be home at five-thirty for dinner' or whatever. I'd come home and catch hell. If we were married, we'd have had a divorce, I'm sure! She would scream and rant and rave about how inconsiderate I was. Partly, she was worried about her dinner being ruined and I can appreciate that, but underneath I felt it was an attempt to restrict and control me, and I couldn't take it. I finally reminded her that when I was applying for this job and wondering if I were going to take it she said, 'Of course! Of course, you're going to take it!' So now I could say, 'Look! You're the one who wanted me to take this job. It goes with the territory!'

"I know my family intervened and told her to try and be more understanding and not make a lot of demands. They never said so, but some of my close friends talked to her also and told her she'd better cut it out. Part of the time we were still in the apartment, so it was 'she's going to walk out on you' or after we got the house 'she's going to throw you out.' I told her when we moved here that I wanted her to come and to feel it's really her home. I told her I loved her very much but didn't want her to put constraints on me. I'm an adult person and I'll have to come and go when I want to. Once in a while we're still back to that—I feel I'm being manipulated and it infuriates me.

"It's funny. I deal with confrontation on the job all the time and it doesn't bother me. But when it came to confrontation with my mother, all my buttons get pressed and somehow I can't deal with it on the same rational level.

"I suppose the reason I live with my mother is largely ethnic in origin. A Greek girl who isn't married lives with her family and my family is my mother. The cliché about single women being somehow tied to their mothers' apron strings doesn't make me angry; I just don't think it applies to me, or other women I know who live with their parents. If anything it applies in reverse, to mothers who come to do whatever their daughter tells them to do. I can see it happening with Mother and me now. She's beginning not to do anything unless I tell her it's okay. Now that's becoming my frustration!

"Actually, I relate more to my eighty-six-year-old maternal grandmother. My personality is much like my father's, though I'm much more outgoing and able to take risks. I'd never hesitate to try something. My grandmother, on the other hand—I'd like to think she could have been a Golda Meir, an Eleanor Roosevelt.

"When her husband was still alive, she was a good Greek wife, docile and obedient. When he died, she just sort of rose up and became the strongest person I know—strong-willed and brilliant. She has *The New York Times* mailed in and reads the *Smithsonian* magazine cover to cover and is the only person in the family who can discuss international affairs or the space shot to Jupiter. She sold her apartment building when she was eighty-one years old with the proviso she'd keep her apartment. She gardens herself, she's physically and mentally active, and she's a risk-taker: 'What do you mean I can't do this or that; of course, I can.'

"Her family came to this country when she was sixteen; her father came first, then her mother and the baby, then she came with her three younger brothers. That was an awful lot of responsibility for a young girl. Maybe that was the kind of thing that affected her self-image; that's the kind of person I'd like to be."

What does she think of Rosemary's career? "I'm not sure she thinks about it. She would think more of it if I were a son; Greek grandmothers think an awful lot of their sons. I think she's proud of me but it's no big deal.

"She wishes I would get married. My mother says that too, but I'm not sure she means it. The minute I begin to get close to someone, she begins to count their faults. A couple of years ago I was seeing a guy from Cheyenne who would come down or I would go there—we were seeing a fair amount of each other. She'd start in that she didn't like him and how selfish he was because he wouldn't call when he said he would. It was just nitpicking—signaling her unhappiness or maybe her uneasiness that something might take me out of the picture. I tried not to let her influence me. In time the relationship sort of faded from a lack of mutual interests, I'd say.

"I go out occasionally, as much as I like, though its mostly a sometime thing. I've never been sexually intimate with anyone; I've just never been in a relationship where I felt that that was something I wanted to do. And I think getting this job has somewhat altered what men think of me. I've sometimes wondered at meetings of old friends or classmates who have been divorced or whatever that they're—I don't know quite how to describe it—that since I've gotten this job, they're a little intimidated, a little put off. I think it's a question of rank, or because I'm supervising people all day long—maybe I come off too strong! Some people can't handle it.

"I've also felt there were times I was asked out because of the job I have. That I was being paraded somewhat. I was introduced to someone's business associates with my full title pronounced very clearly plus 'She's an old friend'! It was like 'here's what her qualifications are' and I sort of thought I had been billed in advance and the people could think, 'Oh, yes, that's who she is.' It was a little strange.

"I think rank does get a little threatening. I have a feeling that in a metropolitan area where it's not that unusual to find women in high positions and there are also a good number of men in professional jobs, the women don't experience as much of a problem. Even though this is a state capital, the town is small enough that anyone who is an agency head stands out, and people are a bit intimidated by them—and a woman in that position, all the more so.

"I would marry if the right man in the right situation presented himself, but it's not a matter of much importance to me. Actually, none of the women in my generation in my family has married—though my grandmother doesn't lay a guilt trip on any of us about it. Her attitude is 'that's the way you are, but I sure wish you'd bring home some kids.'

"I nearly did—at one time I was very seriously considering single parent adoption. Yet she got very upset. I concluded that the reason was because it was likely to be a colored child or a handicapped child. For someone so intelligent, she is a little narrow-minded. I guess when you are so closely tied to your ethnic heritage, it's hard to think of bringing an outsider into the family.

"I sure wish I had some children—because I *like* them. But I've decided against adoption on the grounds of my own selfishness. I have a job where there is *no* security. Perhaps that's just an excuse, and I'm not really being very honest with myself. But I had to consider how very greatly I would have to inconvenience myself for a child, since the kind of child I was likely to get would quite likely be either physically handicapped or mentally retarded. While I don't think I'd have any real problem with a physically handicapped child, I don't think I could go with a mental disability. Because of the things I look for, one of the things I'd want to be proud of, is the child's scholastic achievement. Without it, I couldn't enjoy parenthood.

"I considered a Korean child. But was advised not to attempt it. Mary Ellen, my social worker friend, had strong feelings about bringing children of a distinctly different ethnic and cultural background into another setting. She thought the transfer from Korean to Greek-American was just too much.

"And another thing is that I'm crazy about boys. I just love them, and I didn't think it was appropriate to bring a boy into a household of two women.

"So I definitely ruled out a boy and professionally I didn't feel secure enough to consider it. Plus my family situation. It was a selfish decision."

I asked her about future plans. "I really think I need a little more challenge, and a new direction. I used to work for a budget director who was a woman—the first appointed in the state—who advised me to go back to school. And I thought, 'Why should I? I know all that stuff, why should I waste all that time going back to school'? And she said, 'For your career. You'll need that degree.' And I said I'd be damned if I'd do it, just to have a piece of paper. Judge me on what I know, rather than how I got it. Now I'm much more practical, and I see I need that piece of paper.

"A college in the East has a program that offers a master's in business administration without a bachelor's degree and I understand it's a super program, a really tough program. That's probably the next thing I want. One, because it's a means to an end, and two, I'm really interested in private-sector experience.

"I'd like to know more about merchandising, the administrative side of business. The economy is a fascinating thing. Not money itself, but how it works, what it can do, and the whole power syndrome it fuels. I'm interested in organizational dynamics, to see some of these psychologists and the work they're doing with motivation and improving productivity. Budget sheets, analytical graphs—I've had that, I want to do something different.

"I believe in being fully responsible to myself, that I can't not do something just because I might fail. Anyway, I don't think there's anything wrong with failure.

"If you're always afraid to try, always afraid to make a decision, you'll never make any very good decisions. And decisions, moving ahead, are what it's all about."

I think the early and mid-thirties come into the lives of many never-married women I met as "straightaway time"—solid times, good times—"my salad years" one woman said. The Age Thirty Crisis has diminished, releasing new energies for new directions.

The virtues of being thirty that were hoped for in the twenties—"having some time to settle down," of "being in a more sane space," of "getting a certain amount of legitimacy—the twenties aren't taken that seriously" can now be claimed. The excitement, the whirling pace of the twenties, subsides somewhat and a desire for more stability, more continuity and permanence comes to the fore. Wanting to become gives way to wanting to be.

New roots go down. The apartment-to-apartment frequent mover, the nomad who tries out living groups with the season, the careerist who easily exchanges Philadelphia for Phoenix or Portland, calls a stop. "I landscaped the atrium of my flat at no small trouble or expense," Brenda reported. "I knew I was acting out my desire to be rooted myself. I intended to stay around and see my work take hold." Ann told her employer that plans to send her to Boston would be acceptable only at a much higher salary offer; another woman ordered "five hundred pieces of embossed stationery—I mean to stay!"

Often the good feelings are rooted in career advancement. By now, career objectives are fairly settled and the training and education (and often, reeducation) they require are completed. For others, long years of steady, unbroken employment begin to pay off. Blue-collar women become foremen and officials of the union local; crack secretaries become administrative assistants. Academic women gain tenure and become associate professors; government women are detailed to Washington, to be looked over and do some looking themselves. Being chosen is exhilarating and feeds one's ambition. Rising job status is reflected in increased self-esteem and a heightened self-concept. One is making an impact on the world.

For some women, squeezing by from paycheck to paycheck, filling in with odd jobs becomes a thing of the past. "I used to write checks down to the last dollar in my account," sighed Mary, "and I could sprint across the bank lobby like a marathon runner at two fifty-five and save a check from bouncing. It doesn't happen as often now." Usually without dependents to support and not often indebted or carrying extraordinary financial obligations, discretionary income rises. Darcy told me, "After I pay my rent and my bills, my money supports my political habit. Lots of my social life masquerades in the form of benefits—twenty-five or fifty dollars a plate campaign fund raisers, mixers at fifteen dollars a head. I made two three-hundred dollar donations to a campaign I'm working on. Last year I bought some art—tempera prints—from a friend. And I decided to move up from bean-bag modern to a real, honest-to-goodness white couch—with a coffee table to go with it."

Jackie, a personnel director of a manufacturing concern, said, "I finally managed something I'd dreamed of since I left college—a first-class wardrobe, pulled together by an image consultant—if you can imagine that!" Another woman expanded a collection of jade left to her by her mother. Little luxuries become more available—being able to hire a cleaning lady and to eat out and entertain with less thought of the cost. Some women traded in a car every few years, others traveled abroad. And many reported increased gifts and donations to favorite causes.

In the past, when single women often lived at home, their incomes could be important sources of support to aging parents or other relatives. That pattern has largely ended, especially for younger women, although some will occasionally lend a financial helping hand to younger or especially needy family members. More often, single women help with extras. Ann took her newly widowed mother on a winter cruise; Phyllis and her sister bought their parents a color television for Christmas.

Not all women are affluent and secure, however. Barbara Weinstock said, "Sometimes I get really angry about the financial aspects of being single. I know a lot of people are suffering from inflation and the economy—my income is about the same as it was five years ago and I have *much* less real money to spend. It's getting increasingly difficult to live in this city, socially and economically, and I sometimes think of making a move.

"I talk with friends and we say, 'Do you realize if the inflation keeps up like this we may have to live together to survive?' I don't like that idea at all—I don't want to *have* to live with someone. I know there are things I used to do I can't do anymore because I don't have the money.

Drama lessons—I would just love them—or going back to school full time without the pressure of money problems.

"I let Visa and Master Card lead the way. I'm not going crazy over credit buying, but if I have to take two payments to cover a pair of sixty dollar shoes and a few books and theater tickets, I'll do it. Those aren't outlandish things—they're necessary for a well-balanced life; they make me happy, even if it's only for a short time.

"Sometimes I know that since I'm alone and there's nobody else but me, if the rent's going to be paid and the food bought—well, I get a little tired of the sole responsibility. I wish there was someone who'd say Listen! Don't worry about it! That's where my fantasy of a nice, rich husband fits in.

"My awareness of money and economics is definitely keener than it was. I'm thinking in terms of providing for my old age, making some investments that will pay off thirty years from now, so I can be an independent senior citizen.

"These times are real frightening—I haven't read one good thing about the 1980s! I just get kind of scared. If I had a lot more money, it wouldn't make me feel happier, though it sure might make me feel more secure."

Interestingly, few women in this age group had substantial savings or investment plans. Some had retirement funds as a fringe benefit of employment. Most carried moderate amounts of insurance. Many professed to be relatively uninterested in money, saying they "had enough," "could get by," and "didn't worry much about it."

However, many women spoke of buying housing for personal use—condominiums, co-ops, or a small house, often simultaneously acknowledging that the real estate boom was likely to push them out of the market. Real estate was often cited as a good investment and tax shelter. And its function in meeting permanency and stability needs is clear.

Perhaps the good vibes of the early and mid-thirties are best expressed in the generativity—a sense of one's part in the welfare of a larger world—that often comes to the fore. We have seen it expressed in a concern for supporting other women, in strengthening family and community ties. It may take the form of supporting social, cultural, and religious institutions once taken for granted. Alice explained: "I got interested in the city historical society when I first moved here. I saw it as a way of meeting people and finding out more about where I was. But it became my introduction to the whole area. I got so caught up in fund raising and passing the museum bond issue that the whole thing just became part of my reason for being.

"Later I volunteered for Planned Parenthood and worked nights at a clinic. A friend from there got me onto the YWCA board, making me part of a coalition then trying to involve the Y in supporting an emergent abortion clinic. I met a number of women who were useful to me in job-related contacts; I chaired a major committee and felt free to 'wheel and deal' and try out looser leadership styles than I could at work. I joined a group which entertained international visitors and met some fascinating people. I taught Sunday school; I began docent's training at the museum. When I was transferred, it was the hardest leave-taking ever, because I had put so much of myself into the community."

A director of a large volunteer agency told me, "In all honesty I haven't given a lot of thought to the marital status of our volunteers but now that you mention it, there are a good number of single women. Probably that's because they have more available time—their home commitments are less."

Looking around in organizations in which I myself have been active, I often noted the frequent and even heavy involvement of single women. The women's movement, especially, seems to be fueled by a con-centration of single women. A friend of mine once commented, "Of course there are many single women in feminist-type organizations. Those organizations back up what our lives are all about. We have the most to gain from supporting them. So we get in there and pitch away."

For heterosexual women, perhaps the most striking thing about their relationships with men is their variety: the kinds of men they involve themselves with, the various forms those relationships take. The interviews in the earlier part of this chapter show the ups and downs, the ins and outs of these multitudinous relationships. Chapter V, The Men in Their Lives, will show again, in larger form, how these relationships affect women's lives, how they come to terms with singleness, and the resolution women find in a life without marital attachments. But before we leave the women in their thirties, I want to emphasize something I think is characteristic of many women this age: the growing savvy, confidence, and self-valuation these women often feel in their relationships with men. One woman, Maria del Monte, expressed it particularly well.

Though she was educated in the United States, Maria had immigra-ted to Los Angeles from Nicaragua in her early twenties. A woman of classic Latin beauty, she soon found work as a high-fashion model in Beverly Hills. Like all young women, she faced a transition to adult life, but Maria's transition was made more difficult by her need to move from traditional Latin ideas about men and marriage and to adopt American norms and standards. It was a lengthy and not always easy process, but one which started her down a path which led to the security and self-worth she feels today at age thirty-eight.

"My first years here were marked by one very good relationship—a guy who was very sensitive sort of helped me bridge my way into American ways of doing things. But our affair soon ended, and I entered a period where I was very confused and torn between two cultures. I was job-hopping a lot, making changes for no good reason. I was insecure and very shaky. I seemed to put this exorbitant value in having a man around to lean on; if I wasn't involved, I felt terrible. I seemed to think a man would be the answer to every problem I might face. I mean, rationally, I knew I had to solve these problems myself, but emotionally I was always reaching for a man. By the time I was twenty-four, I realized I was very mixed up. I had to stop and examine what I was doing, so I entered therapy.

"That was one of the most valuable decisions I'd ever made; I continue to see the value of it in terms of the gradual but steady growth of my own security and worth. I've grown to the point where I'm not clinging desperately to any relationship to get a sense of my own self-worth. I see what I bring into a relationship now, how I can hold my own. Let me tell you about Rob.

"He was a man I met three years ago. He had a lot to offer, financially and emotionally, and I was pretty committed to him; I wasn't seeing anyone else, and I was the only person in his life. He was pretty wrapped up in his work. Well, he was pressing me for more of a commitment—sort of 'let's be engaged to be engaged.' He told me he couldn't possibly think of marriage for another five years. I questioned how many years this would take out of my life, and where was it going? My time is valuable too—I'm not getting any younger. As far as he was concerned, we could go on together and then decide, which was a little chauvinistic, to say the least.

"And I thought, well, what's this doing for me? I'm really cutting myself off and for what, to see if in five years this guy really wants to marry me? I decided to break it off. It was painful, but not as bad as other times. I think I did the right thing.

"It was a decision which showed faith in myself and independence and a sort of self-valuing I couldn't have dreamed of at twenty-two. I don't deny that at times I'm lonely—it would be nice to have someone special again. But I'm special. It will be nice to share it when the right person comes along. I'm willing to wait. Whereas before I don't think I could, I was more caught up in the two-is-necessary thing. And the thought that if you're not involved, life is drab. But now it's not that, not at all!

"I see this time—right now—as my best time. I'm very career oriented; I have a good job; I'm in international sales with a petroleum company. I have many women friends and some good men friends and I'm busy with them. For a while I ran a little secretarial service out of here; I do a little tutoring in Spanish with children of a Beverly Hills family.

"That's the difference between the twenties and the thirties. In the twenties you're trying so hard to get your own self established. I'm mellower now—I feel it's nice to touch back with my roots and my family. I'm stronger as an individual, and have the self-assurance of not having to prove who I am. And my family's become more understanding and accepting of me in my own right.

"Mother, for example, has *always* been interested in who I'm going with and *if* there's a special man in my life and when's the marriage taking place? She doesn't say that anymore, though I know she feels it's better to be married and settled than single and working. But she has slowly come around, and at least considered my way of living, and she sees it is productive and that I really do have a very good life, for someone of Latino background, who's an immigrant to the United States.

"In my thirties, I've found that middle ground between the pull of the old culture and new, between the demands of my family and my own ideas of self-realization."

I asked Maria about the future. "One thing I might regret later on is not having a child. It's something so basic, so deep-rooted in women. The thought of being a mother, of raising a child. I don't think I would consider having a child outside of marriage. Well, if I had a very substantial salary I might be tempted to do it on my own. But really, it's a great responsibility; you need financial and emotional support. And I'm used to living a certain way now.

"Actually, I feel my most meaningful relation is still to come. By reason of the nature of the person I am or am becoming, the relationship would just have to have so much more substance to it and therefore would be so much richer. I have more to bring into it."

I commented that that was a positive and optimistic viewpoint. Maria continued. "There's something about richness or quality, whether it's in a relationship—or a piece of cloth or a work of art—that comes from having weathered some, from having something substantial put into it or about it or with it or whatever. It just doesn't have quality unless you bring some of these elements to it.

"Like that painting over there—it's so gorgeous. I never get tired of looking at it. Never. I bought it five years ago and it's increased in value to me ever since. I would never sell it. I might have once, but I'd never part with it now. Its quality has become part of my life. It's something I struggled to have. I know the artist personally. And he's had quite a struggle, so there's so much meaning in the whole thing.

"So I'm saying in relation to my life, I've been through struggles, and through investment in life I've become a deeper, richer, more substantial person from a process that's come out of living over the last fifteen–twenty years.

"I think that if you're really growing and being constructive about your life, you have that outlook on life always. I mean I feel like I could be sixty right now and be telling you my best relation is yet to come. Do you know what I mean?"

In looking at women's close relationships we must also consider something commented upon time and time again by nearly every woman I met: women's close relationships with other women. The growing importance of close ties between women seems to be one of the major characteristics of women in their thirties. One woman put it this way:

"I find a lot of value in my relations with other women. They're usually more exciting than the men I know in terms of what's going on in their lives, what they're involved in, what they're doing. I know more interesting women than men—more women I'd rather spend time with because of what they're into. They don't seem to be stuck in the same rut, but are at a growth stage and I'm at a growth stage too. I'm changing a whole lot. They're starting families, making career changes, deciding whether to stay married or not, making other kinds of changes in their lives. Whereas the men are in the same place, same career path, same kinds of relations with the women they know, still married or still divorced or still single but they don't change a whole lot. The women are just much more stimulating."

Pat focused on emotional and affectional needs between women. "There's no question but what I feel my emotional needs are well met, and they're well met through my women friends. That real sustaining 'emotional food of life'—I can't think of anything better to call it— comes from my close girl friends, a couple of women I work with, and my old-time friends who I see maybe only occasionally.

"What I want to emphasize is the really wonderful quality of some parts of these relationships—it really goes to great depths. Like with Carol, a certain amount of what we talk about is our whole life strategy—not so much our philosophy of life, though maybe that ties in—but what we want our lives to become, how we're going to get there. We weigh the values we're operating out of, the hard issues, like, oh, career strategy, the importance of men in our lives or a particular man in our life, my struggles (and hers) with childlessness, the painful stuff, the contradictions we find in weighing all that up.

"The times in my life I've had that sharing, that emotional strength from men have been very few. At best, maybe five percent of my 'real stuff' in life has come from men—ninety-five percent from women. Sometimes I think I should be gay, because women meet most of my basic needs—except erotic ones. But women have no sexual attraction for me, though I honestly feel I can meet every other need I have through other women. That realization that women can really come through for me—and I for them too, of course—gives me a lot of hope as I see myself getting older alone."

Women often spoke of the practical value of woman-to-woman contact. We have already seen the value they find in networking and social and business contacts. One said, "I always feel I have all this help and backup assistance available from my friends, just for the asking. I'm a writer, and last year I was on the road gathering material for a book. One of my friends had lived in the area where I was working and she called her friends from high school and college and asked them to lend a hand—I was looking for families with special characteristics that weren't easy to find. They helped me find the families and took care of me—invited me to dinner, let me do my wash at their house—in just the nicest way. That was an example of 'friend of a friend' and I find it both typical—and wonderful!

"Later, I was to make a television appearance in connection with the book. Lucy and Joan rehearsed me. We tried to anticipate the questions that would be asked, and they gave them to me and critiqued my answers. It was so helpful. They had clipped and sent me articles related to my field while I was working on it, kept an eye out for people for me to know about or interview. Their support was really tangible.

"I guess that's where my real security in life against the worst that could happen—lose a job, get sick, need money, get caught in some sort of a catastrophe—I know my friends would stick by me. And of course it goes without saying that I'd do the same."

Janice spoke of one friend in particular. "I've been close friends with Lil for over ten years. Our lives are different. She's married, has two children, and works, and I guess our friendship is based not only on the personal element but also in seeing how our lives run along their parallel courses—she as a wife and mother, me as a single woman. Maybe we both want to see what we're missing—maybe we fill in each other's gaps!

"I share family living with them—take her children around, go to their birthday parties, entertain visiting parents. I know I've always got an invitation for the holidays if I need it. I get a feel for what motherhood is about and I feel it's a family setting I can join into when I want to.

"My life gives Lil a notion of what it is to be single—what goes on in my love life (and often, what doesn't), my more strenuous efforts at career building, my own interest in having children, too. I mean our whole relationship isn't as categorized as maybe this sounds, but there's a real balance in it and we both like the insight we can get into the other side."

"I get by with a little help from my friends"—it could be the theme song of many single women.

IV

MOTHERHOOD BY CONVICTION

As women progress through the thirties, another issue, already touched on and mentioned by nearly every woman I talked to, comes to the fore. The issue is childlessness and for many women it poses a dilemma—and sometimes a crisis—of major proportions.

Safely put off and often thought of synonymously with marriage in the twenties, in the thirties the question of children separates itself from the issue of marriage. Unlike marriage, it cannot be indefinitely postponed; time is running out for childbearing; the energy for raising children also begins to diminish. Both gynecologists and adoption agencies discourage women over forty, even though more women past that age are having their first child than ever before.

Until recently, the desire for children among never-married and other single women has been little recognized, or else discounted. The maternal instinct was thought to spring to life only with the signing of the marriage contract. The married couple with the Dick-Jane-and-Sally-type family was enthroned as a sanctified norm; the fact that divorced and widowed women successfully raised millions of children was largely overlooked. Single women were allowed children when the chips were down, as a last resort—if no other kind of parent was available.

Despite this attitude, we can find a small tracing of parenthood among mature and responsible single women. Single adoptive mothers on the frontier were not unknown. I remember a story from the

Navaho reservation where I worked about such a mother with six adopted Indian children. When her high-school-aged daughter was asked what she wanted to do when she grew up, legend has it she replied, "Be an old maid schoolteacher like my mother and have six kids."

Many minority communities view single parenthood more benignly and humanistically than our Anglo society does. In my own experience, I've observed never-married mothers who had had their own children in black, Indian, and Hawaiian cultures. Yet the single woman who considers having a child might consider that the greatest American literary masterpiece, Hawthorne's *The Scarlet Letter,* is about the devastation of a woman who bore a child out of wedlock. A sobering thought.

I spoke with Carmen Beaty, thirty-nine, a commercial real estate salesperson. She was at the point of decision, having long considered single motherhood, now feeling the press of time.

"My reasons for wanting to become a mother are as mature and good as anyone's; God knows my motivation level is high. I've been child-oriented all my life. I have this fantasy of someone coming to my door some Saturday morning with a pink bassinet with a baby girl inside, and a big card tied to the handle, 'For Carmen.' I think this dream reflects my difficulty in making a decision; I want my hand to be forced.

"Part of the reason I hesitate is because this is really the most irrevocable decision of my entire life. Jobs change, relationships change, even marriage isn't bathed in the foreverafterwardness it once was. But a child! Who ever heard of a mother and child going their separate ways? Whatever decision I make will be with me one way or another to the end of my life.

"Now is a good time for me to proceed. I've had a number of relations with men and enjoyed them, but I find I'm losing interest in dating and being involved with men in the way I used to be. My career is well established and I have a certain degree of financial stability. I own this house and I've been able to travel a lot. I know what rewards all those things bring, and something of their cost. But everything I have is at arm's length; my life lacks intimacy, the warmth of having someone close to love. I watch myself carrying on with my friendly pooch here, and I realize I'm doing a lot of displacing." She sighed.

"People argue against motherhood at thirty-nine on the grounds of being too old. But I honestly think I'm more ready for it now than I was when I was younger. I have my act together so much better now. My twenties were turbulent and I entered psychotherapy in my early thirties to get at the root of some of my problems. I got in touch with the fact that my parents tended to give me mostly cool, distant support and tended to be judgmental and never warmly satisfied with my attempts to please them. They're not much in touch with many of their own feelings and my father tends to be detached. Well, of course there's more to my therapy than just this, but it helped me get a handle on my problems and feel better about myself, and also to see some parenting behavior I'll be sure not to carry into my own motherhood. When your closer emotional relationships are with your mother, it makes single motherhood seem more plausible, though I'd sure prefer to have a father for my child.

"And physically, I'm just in fantastically good shape. Both sides of our family are extremely healthy and everyone lives into deep old age. My uncle is in his seventies and still actively farms; I have an eighty-four-year-old aunt who holds down three part-time jobs and painted the trim on her house last summer. She could raise a child herself if she wanted to! So by the physical standards of my family, at nearly forty, I'm a mere child! Does all this sound like a convincing case?" She smiled, and I grinned and nodded yes.

"I think I must be the only reasonably sophisticated single career woman in town who knocks over a can of Lincoln Logs and Tinker Toys everytime I get the sweeper out of the closet. They belong to my two very special kids. Actually, they're children of friends but I consider them my friends in their own right. Patty and Sean. I guess because the trust level between their parents and me is so high, I've been able to take on a special role with them, one that goes well beyond the range of usual family friends. Patty has always spent a lot of time with me. I've taken her to most of the children's recreation places around here, taught her all sorts of things—for a seven-year-old kid she's a pretty fair cook. I do those mothering-type jobs, like going to school plays when her mother is tied up, going to the beauty shop for haircuts. My role is an indulgent one, a friend who lavishes attention and affection and gives approval and latitude that parents, in their more restraining role, can't always give. I think all children can use extra love and attention, that it's good for them to grow up knowing someone outside their immediate family cares about them and is concerned about their needs."

She showed me a studio portrait of herself and Patty and Sean. It had a distinctly maternal air.

She continued, "Actually, it's not the goal I'm unclear about, it's the ways and means. I know I'd be a good parent, that I want to do it. I've considered adoption, but the fact of the matter is I'd rather have my own child. I think *any* woman starts from the premise of wanting her own child. We have no descendants on either side of our family. And I'd like to have my father's family especially—whom I strongly resemble and who have these wonderful physical attributes I mentioned—perpetuated.

"But God, it's a hard step to take. Unmarried pregnancy remains heavily stigmatized in many circles—don't I know it. And I absolutely reject marrying for the sake of having a child and I refuse to let myself get pregnant through a purposeful 'accident.' If I make the decision, I'm going to be fully responsible for it and do it with my eyes wide open. Nor would I trick some man into a conception—that's exploiting a man's body and sex, just the kind of thing we women object to.

"My love life is quite dormant right now; certainly none of the few men I see socially I'd care to ask such a favor of. I do have a couple of male friends I'd consider. I hinted around about this to one of them and he really shied away. The second lives halfway across the country so the logistics would be difficult, but in many ways, he's the man I'd really like. We've had an on-again, off-again affair for eight years; he's married but I know he's good to his children and I think he'd take some interest in a child he might have by me. He's really bright and I think he's very good-looking. I'd have a true love baby. But I don't know how many months it might take me to get pregnant and at $345 for a round-trip plane ticket, the logistics would make it prohibitively expensive.

"I've heard some single women have turned to artificial insemination, so I decided to investigate that. I was braced for a turndown, but the doctor I approached did not seem at all concerned about my being single, regarding that as my business, but instead asked about my thoughts and plans for parenting. I appreciated that. He felt that since I'm quite healthy, my age isn't really a factor, except that fertility declines with age and we'd have to do an amniocentesis to protect against a one-hundred-to-one risk of mongoloidism. However, he couldn't offer me any control over the characteristics of the donor except to say he would be Caucasian, so I looked further.

"The second doctor's office I contacted was also not interested in my marital status; they said they could offer donor selection in coloring and height, and seemed to do a more extensive genetic screening. That sounded better to me.

"So I've begun a process of talking it out with my friends. My peers feel marital status is hardly the issue anymore, but focus more on dealing with child care and the responsibilities and changes a baby will bring. I still struggle some with the idea of using artificial insemination. I mean, I feel okay about using it myself, but I feel rather sad about it for the sake of the child—just never having the slightest clue about half your inheritance, having an anonymous donor for a father. It seems a little Orwellian, a little test-tube-babyish to me. Still, I think it's better than being adopted and having no idea of who either of your natural parents would be.

"I guess in the long run my own feelings of okayness would come through. I mentioned the possibility of artificial insemination to an older woman friend and I sensed the idea upset her. In fact, she later wrote me and told me she didn't think it was a good idea. I know I've clearly transgressed on an important social norm in her mind, though she just stated her objections very generally and said it would be more admirable to adopt. She's the only dissenting vote I got. Yet I need the experience of running into that attitude too. Basically I think the situation is manageable.

"Who knows if I'd ever conceive, or if an adoption agency would find me a child? Yet I've got to decide, and do something. I read that Simone de Beauvoir once looked at all the books she had written and called them the children she never had. She went on to say that all her books and all her fame didn't fully take the place of her unborn children. That remark haunts me. Being childless is the only thing I fear I may come to regret about my life."

Although many never-married women consider motherhood, most relinquish their dream; surely less than ten percent of never-married women become mothers.

The obstacles are formidable enough. One woman listed them with a sigh. "Basically, it boils down to the fact that the life-style of a single woman doesn't mesh with the demands of being a mother. Earning a living and keeping afloat in this world pretty much takes care of me. My job is exhausting and I generally work ten hours a day, counting commute time. After that I just flop in front of the TV. I'm beat. I wouldn't have anything left to give a child."

Another said, "The idea of having a baby only to deposit it with a sitter or day-care center from the time it's three months old has no appeal for me. It seems very unfair to the child. I'd want to stay home with it and see that it had the best of care. I just couldn't hand over that responsibility to a stranger, cold.

"I hear so much about the lack of good child care and the difficulty my friends have in finding reliable sitters. Financially, it would be a drain. I'd be strapped to pay for all that child care and all the other expenses that would come along. And psychologically, I feel children need to have a father. I'd love to have a child, but I don't think motherhood quite fits into my life."

"Lack of fit"—the difficulties of combining single motherhood with work and career, the problems of obtaining good child care and being able to afford a child—these were the most commonly cited obstacles.

Another woman, thirty-four, spoke of timing. "I mentioned to a married woman friend of mine with three children that I hoped to adopt a child someday but now wasn't the time. I'm in a critical phase of my career; I'm finishing my M.B.A. and if I really pour it on, I should be in line for a good promotion within the next year or so. Then I can think about motherhood. But she was dubious about what I said and commented, 'The time is never quite right to have children: You're always too busy, something's always about to happen or something just did happen. You just have to make your mind up and do it!'"

The availability of children is a real obstacle. Today, Caucasian infants and children are almost totally unavailable to single women, with the exception of severely mentally, physically, or emotionally handicapped youngsters. Formerly, white single women might adopt children of other races, but now many minority communities frown on placing children outside their group. In many parts of the country there are fewer minority children available for adoption, even for applicants within their own community. Jean Symons, a black woman, adopted a black ten-year-old only after demonstrating very strong credentials to the agency (her income is high, and she has excellent child-care arrangements)—and waiting three years. The high abortion rate, and the tendency of teenage mothers of all races to keep children which once might have been put up for adoption, has considerably reduced the pool of adoptable children for all applicants—and single women are usually considered only in the absence of suitable married couples.

One alternative for some single women is international adoption, a process involving a thicket of red tape. One woman I know made a flying tour of child placement agencies in South America, only to get some very tentative leads to adoptable children. Others have worked more successfully with church-related and other private organizations in the Third World. There are very occasional private placements, arranged through physicians or lawyers. There is an underground black market in adoptable babies, but no single woman I met would consider it.

Many women who might consider giving birth themselves are deterred by the stigma of illegitimacy still associated with such births in this country. The old idea of going away and hiding and having a baby and then claiming to have adopted it has little appeal anymore; women want to be more up front in their behavior. Yet they fear labeling themselves or their child unfairly, don't want to be misunderstood, don't want to risk a scandal. They wonder what people would think; they don't want to upset their parents. "My mother would understand; my father would die a thousand deaths."

Yet it appears a somewhat larger number of mature unwed women are choosing to bear their own children. I think the trend is increasing, especially in the large cities of the East and West coasts. No doubt the lack of adoptable children influences some women; the changing sexual mores of our times makes a wider variety of reproductive behavior more permissible. Feminist ideas support the ideology of women's full control of their own bodies, being fully responsible for their own reproductive lives.

However, most single women don't become mothers but instead find outlets that replace that part of their lives. Camilla Stevens, now in her early forties, produces and directs Little Theatre. She describes the process of staging a theatrical production by saying, "I've been having babies for years—I'm in the process of hatching one right now. They come out and when the final curtain rings down, they die." Other forms of creative work—artistic creations, literary pursuits, social projects which caused growth and new life in the community—were likened to the process of birthing or raising a child.

So, many women relinquish their dream, and some, it must be said, are glad they did. One woman at a cocktail party told me, "I went into such a panic when I was thirty-nine. I applied for adoption, and thought I would die, just die, if they couldn't find me a child. I told them I'd take anything. Now I'm forty-three and that motherhood stuff is all behind me. I don't want a child anymore. I recently lost my job and all I could think was thank God I don't have to drag a child through the financial problems I'm having. Frankly, I don't know what I'd do with a little kid hanging on my skirt. Maybe it was a biological thing; all those hormones or whatever just welled up as my reproductive years ended."

Among all categories of single women, the ones who seem least affected by the desire to have a child are women who work with children—teachers, child welfare workers, child care providers, pediatricians, others. Apparently the contact provided by work provides enough "child" for most of them.

But a few women persist. Powered by strong drives, they become natural mothers, adoptive mothers, foster mothers. This chapter is about these women, included not because of the size of the group, but because the subject is so important to many single women, and because nearly every single woman has thought about it.

Sharon Swanson

When Sharon Swanson opened the door of her home, the love fairly spilled out.

She had made a special effort to contact me. "I would like to have my story known because I think it would be important to other single women. Seven years ago, I was the first single white woman in Ohio to adopt a child. Motherhood has been a deeply gratifying experience for me. I think I can say that I have everything in life now that's really important."

At forty-four, Sharon is a claims supervisor with a large insurance company. Her home is a modern ranch-style house in a subdivision of a large city. She introduced me to her mother, Florence, who lives with her, and to her daughter, Sherri, a thirteen-year-old blonde. Sherri was making Christmas decorations with friends in the rumpus room, so Sharon and I sat down at the kitchen table.

"My childhood was difficult. Our family was poor. My younger sister had osteomyelitis before penicillin was available to treat it, and was constantly in and out of the hospital. The bills kept our family strapped. Mother always worked, and I carried a lot of responsibility for caring for my younger sister and brother. I was a quiet child, something of a loner—I read a lot. As I got older, my father became an alcoholic. I didn't understand what was going on for a long time. My parents were divorced when I was an adult, and later my father died of alcoholism.

"Fortunately, my early adult years were cheerful and fun. It was like I was making up for my lost teenaged years. Four other young women and I rented a big house and had many good times together. We all belonged to a dance club. I dated a lot and got engaged when I was twenty-five. But I rather quickly realized I didn't love Ed enough to be married to him, though I remember thinking how nice it would be to have a family.

"But by the time I was about thirty, getting dressed up and running around a lot began to wear thin. Three of my friends had married, and the two of us who were left in the house rattled around a bit. We decided to break up, and I rented an apartment close to a married friend of mine who had a large family. I've always liked to feel I have a home base.

"The Jacksons had little money, but plenty of love for each other and their seven kids. The mother and I became den mothers and coached the girls' softball team. We'd take the kids to the fair, go to the movies, and have many good times at home. But I realized my involvement wasn't enough and began to think of having a child of my own. I felt I had a lot to offer. I was financially secure, mature, and settled. I wanted continuity in life, and I wanted to perpetuate my values. It seemed nice to think of being a grandmother some day. But I'm not an adventuresome type, and for a while I just didn't know how I could manage it. But when I thought about it, I realized I had gone through many problems with the Jacksons—something of everything—and I felt that with only one child and an adequate income, my problems would be small compared to theirs.

"I made anonymous test calls to the Bureau of Adoptions, and in two years it was settled in my mind. So I made an official application. The Bureau did everything they could to discourage me. I thought in terms of adopting an infant but they were practically unavailable to single women unless one was willing to take a biracial baby. That was all right with me, but it didn't please my family. Others felt the biracial factor would raise difficulties for both the child and myself. So I moved the age limit up to four, thinking that would still give me time to influence personality development.

"I was assigned to a caseworker with whom I had terrific rapport, and we finished the home study by June. She told me there would be a wait of a year to a year and a half, so I settled down to put in my time. In September she called and said she had a six-year-old girl who had been in a series of foster homes and then placed with a couple who later decided they wanted a boy. I agreed to take her home for a day's trial. Imagine my surprise when I was presented with a teeny Shirley Temple, with a head full of golden curls, dimples and all!

"We both decided we liked each other and the next day I called my caseworker and told her I'd keep her. I began unpacking her little suitcase. Suddenly I felt like I'd been struck by lightning. 'My God, what have I done?' I wondered. It was the strangest sensation—I've never felt it before or since."

Sharon's mother had agreed to move in to take care of Sherri during the day—it was part of the adoption arrangement. I asked her how she had come to that decision. "I was certainly aware Sharon's growing up years had not been easy. She had carried a big load for a youngster. I felt I had often neglected her interests in order to care for my other daughter." She paused and looked at Sharon. I felt as if some communication was being exchanged between them that had not been expressed before.

"I retired about that time and needed to find a new direction in life. But this adoption took some internal talking into. It's not easy for a woman of my age to think of assuming responsibilities for a young child. But I had given so much to Jeanie, I saw this as my chance to do something for Sharon." Sharon looked tenderly at her mother.

A pause, and Sharon continued. "There were many small traumas involved in becoming a mother. I see now I worked at it too hard—for the first two years I was all engrossed with Sherri, and put everything else aside except work. I used to give advice to others about child-raising—oh, the fantasies of the childless!—and I had created an imaginary world of perfection. I was very concerned about shaping.

But now I see Sherri will never be a perfect daughter, nor I a perfect mother, and we're all much happier!

"Sherri would get tense every time she got into the car, fearing she was being taken away. I could remember something similar in my own childhood. When I was in the first grade, someone turned in my name for the 'Clothes for a Child' program and I was turned over to two women to be outfitted for Christmas. I took this to mean I was being given away, a painful memory which helped me relate to some of Sherri's fears. She cried a lot at first and lunged at things. I didn't know that she had lived with mongoloid children and learned some of their behavior patterns. It would have helped if the social worker had mentioned this.

"One night in the tub Sherri announced she didn't want to be Swanson anymore, but wanted to use the name of a foster mother I knew she liked. My heart sank. I told her as comfortably as I could that she could discuss this with her caseworker, but if she wanted to live here, she would have to be Swanson. I left the room and struggled to regain my composure. Sherri called me back and said she wanted to be Swanson. Her use of other names and discussions of other homes was always difficult for me, though I realized she must talk about it.

"I've never had any qualms about my decision to adopt her, though I've had many qualms about decisions I've made in raising her.

"There was one major worry underlying her adoption. They changed our caseworker. We were reassigned to a Mrs. Davis, a woman whose judgment was, well, questionable at best. The agency was given to such unfortunate reminders as 'Sherri really isn't yours for a year, she's Mrs. Davis'' and I'd read stories in the paper about her taking children back. It just unnerved me. So I applied for the adoption after six months to give the judge legal jurisdiction over the caseworker though normally one would wait a full year. Mrs. Davis took this as a vote of no confidence (which it was) and we really walked on eggs after that.

"But the real blow came eleven months after I received Sherri. She was playing at a building construction site and a two hundred fifty-pound tile rolled over her head. By rights she should have been killed, but damp sand under the tile cushioned her head, and she suffered what is called an orbital blowout. The bones around her eyes were crushed. Part of her skull split and another part was fractured. She suffered brain and spinal damage and hemorrhaged profusely. We frantically called the agency for a release to give her medical care. At the worst point, I feared she would be blind and deaf in one ear. What I couldn't believe was that the agency reacted to this mostly in terms of concern with her scarring. They assumed I would relinquish her. But she recovered quickly, with no permanent damage, which I see to this day as a miraculous healing. The accident had the effect of totally binding me to Sherri. It turned a sense of responsibility to love.

"I formally adopted her a month later. In addition to the usual procedures, I signed without hesitation a special waiver saying I could not relinquish her or sign back any responsibilities for her." Sherri came in and showed us her work. I thought she had an uncanny resemblance to her mother.

"We've struggled to get a sense of balance around certain issues," Sharon continued. "Guilt and a very heavy 'sense of should'—I should be spending more time with her, I should be more involved with enrichment activities—are the frequent companions of single mothers. I mentioned that I was extremely preoccupied with her the first two years I had her. I finally realized I needed time and space for myself and got active in the Business and Professional Women's group. That was good. I began traveling with my work and while at first that made me feel guilty, I took hold of myself and realized I needed a break from parenting. Mother and I found ourselves in conflict. She was used to one hundred percent control during the day, and then I'd come home and expect to be completely in charge. We had to work on that one, too.

"I had been seriously concerned about the effect of the adoption on my job. I'm extremely career oriented. I found the novelty of the adoption interested people at work, since I was the first white woman in the state to take this step. In general, both management and my coworkers have been very supportive. On the day I adopted Sherri, I found my office full of gifts—even a bicycle—and well-wishers. Some people got very emotional about it, and others wondered why in the world I was doing it, but my friends supported me fully.

"I found a bonus I surely never expected in motherhood. It has broken down the wall around my emotions. I am the only woman supervisor on my level among fifteen men and I've always felt it necessary to be highly controlled and very objective. But now I'm more emotionally responsive to my coworkers, quicker to respond to their needs. It was scary at first, but now I feel emotional openness is a strength. My reactions—tears, whatever—are their problem to deal with, just as I have to deal with others' swearing and screaming.

"Church is a hard place to be a single parent. I'm a convert to the Episcopalian faith and religion is important to me. But the Church assumes everyone lives in a neat nuclear family and is unaware of single people. About four years ago I ran into a nice Episcopalian bachelor. Sherri brought us together and right away I felt he must be 'predestined by heaven.' I really worked on it—a daddy for Sherri, a whole family for all of us. But I came to see I was doing this mostly for

Sherri—I didn't really love him, not for myself. He was a very small-town type, uneducated, who would have worn out fast with me.

"I haven't been significantly involved with a man since then. Sherri has informed me she wants a dad and a granddad. I think about our all-female household—my sister Jeanie moved in with us last fall—yet I feel Sherri is well adjusted and secure. She has a family unit—one that's not always smooth, but one I feel adds up to a good all-round setting.

"I think I have a much stronger drive toward motherhood than marriage, though I admit marriage meant more to me when I was younger. Other than motherhood, work has been of overriding importance to me, though I can't say whether a commitment to a career has influenced my desire to stay single or not. I do feel I would have outgrown any man I might have married in my twenties—I see that in some of my long-term friends and I sense some of my friends at BPW don't want to go home after the meeting ends. It would be tough to marry now because my job responsibilities are so heavy, our all-female household so well established. Still, I miss not having someone who cares for me, the emotional male/female relationship.

"I feel I'm fortunate to be able to do whatever I want—as long as I can get a sitter. I do wonder about what I'll do when Sherri and Mother are gone. I'll adjust, but then I might want a companion. Maybe I'm selfish—I want my life controlled only by myself."

Sherri and her friends came into the kitchen, announcing plans to go to a movie matinee. They pulled on heavy coats, dickered for money, and left. Florence Swanson commented, "No one here is sacrificing. We have our own lives, my activities go on unlimited. We have few real problems—we're as normal as any family in the block."

Sharon paused and looked at me. "My daughter is such a joy to me. We were getting dressed for a party recently. She had just had her ears pierced, and had new clothes and a new hairdo. She looked into the mirror and said half to herself, 'My hair looks pretty, my earrings are pretty, my clothes look pretty—but it's what I *do* that makes me pretty.'

"The joys of single motherhood are in moments like that."

Catherine Johnson

Catherine Johnson must be unique among single mothers. Her story is about three kinds of motherhood—natural, foster, and adoptive. At twenty-nine, motherhood and her career came together in the interests of justice for children.

"You could say I didn't have much of a childhood and grew up too fast. I was raised in a modest neighborhood on the industrial side of Chicago. Like many other black girls in my neighborhood, I became pregnant in my teens and had Roland. None of us understood much about reproduction; having and keeping a baby was a normal part of our lives."

Catherine rested her head and looked at me. We were in her flat, part of a subdivided Victorian in a black neighborhood of a large city along the Ohio River. Her rounded features and soft flowered blouse conveyed a feeling of maternal warmth. She spoke without drama, yet the force of her convictions was evident.

"I moved here not long after Roland was born, to be near my grandmother and great-grandmother, who live on the next block. Working part-time and getting a little help from my grandmother, I started college and was in premed three years, wanting to be a pediatrician. But the fourth year I dropped it. I wanted to improve the world and switched to a Human Services major. One day I noticed a school ad asking for foster parents. It seemed like a natural for me, since I already had Roland and a large flat. It gave me an immediate chance to act on my feelings.

"The social worker had a special program she wanted me to try. The idea was to place teenagers with young but mature foster parents. It gives the kids a role model to follow and cuts down on their tendency to rebel against older, more authoritarian foster parents. Since I had a child and had been a teenage mother, they wanted me to take a sixteen-year-old with a baby. I said I'd try it, and Denise and Charles moved in.

"Denise had plenty of problems all right. I really did feel like a mother to her, although I was only nine years older. She had a mouth full of cavities and wet the bed. She cried easily and had no self-confidence; she clearly needed someone to care about her. I got her dental work started. I wanted her to have a sense of pride and taught her how to change the bed linens and night clothes when she wet them, and wash herself, so she wouldn't lie in her own soil. We found that medication could help the bedwetting. She was slightly mentally retarded and I worked with the school to adjust her classes. I taught her how to help around the house and talked with her. Her speaking really improved, and I felt she was beginning to feel better about herself.

"A situation like this brings a lot of good rewards, and plenty of pain. Denise was in touch with her natural mother and would run off to her when she was upset with me. Or she would disappear with her baby's father. When the attraction of going to them wore off, she'd come back to me. It was really a strain.

"I felt I was making good progress with Denise herself, but I simply couldn't do anything with Denise as a mother. She was still a baby herself. She regarded Charles as a doll. I had to tell her exactly when and how to feed and care for him; she never seemed able to do it by herself. So I ended up with two foster children.

"Well, the running-away and coming-back stuff continued. Denise turned eighteen, and I just couldn't take any more of it. I finally told her she couldn't come back. She went to live with her mother, leaving Charles here with me. She hasn't used many of the things I taught her and has slipped back to some of her old ways.

"I've kept Charles; he's officially my foster child, but I've filed papers to adopt him. He's typical of a lot of foster kids who are placed somewhere but are never really able to go home. The state changed the law to make kids like these more adoptable, so they wouldn't be betwixt and between all their lives.

"I decided to go on with foster parenting. I had graduated by now and was attempting to build something I could roughly call a professional career. The job market was miserable. I picked up a temporary job as a parole officer, then worked as a nursery aide, then as a CETA tutor. I tried to get a job with the state highway patrol but was turned down. Another woman and I filed a charge of sex discrimination which is still pending.

"Our finances were really tough. The state pays only $3.25 per day per child (and picks up the medical expenses) so money was a *big* problem. Especially the first year, the kids lacked toys and going anywhere that charged admission was out of the question. It occurred to me that two paychecks would make life a lot easier, but I'd never consider marrying for money. I explained to the children that I didn't have a good job but we'd live more comfortably when things got better. I felt ashamed that I couldn't get decent work with decent pay and what with the stresses at home, I needed and got psychological help. The psychologist helped me deal with some of the immediate problems I was facing. He asked me about the men in my life; there weren't many at the time. I told him I was interested in men, but had a real fear of marriage, just a real phobia. The psychologist says it even has a name— gamophobia. I don't know why I'm like this. Maybe it's because everyone, *everyone* in our family ends up divorced. Maybe it's a perfection complex I can't control. But it's real, that's for sure.

"I enjoy being a mother ninety-nine percent of the time, and I know I'm good at it. Despite my problems getting established, I never thought of giving up the children; I'd have no purpose without them. I don't want to be a mother without being a professional, or a professional without being a mother. I eventually picked up a job at an agency dealing with fair employment practices and then things smoothed out some.

"There's no normalcy with foster kids. They have deep emotional scars and problems. That's what a foster child is—a walking sore. I took in three girls of an alcoholic father—a fourteen-year-old rearing the two others. Despite his abusive behavior, the father had visitation rights. He would show up, take them out of school, and bribe them into bad behavior, the same thing he'd done to lose them in the first place. And I had a boy of about eleven who was beaten and retarded. He had learned to get attention by fighting and hitting. He struck me till I was black and blue, and once gave me a terrible bite.

"I try to take care of each of them as best I can. Every child gets time alone with me. We have family and activity time together, and take little trips around the area. *I* get time alone. There are few hard and fast rules. I believe in communication and talking things out.

"I don't feel my work and other activities shortchange the children. Even kids as disturbed as these don't need a mother on call constantly. I prefer to think of my value as a role model to them. And I expect each one to help around the household—and get whatever part-time jobs they can."

I found it difficult to imagine how a woman so involved with children and work could have time for anything else. Yet Catherine has finished her master's degree and works with community projects in Alpha Kappa Alpha, her sorority. I asked her about men.

"About a year ago I started seeing Howard. Actually, I've known him a long time: We go back to high school days. He liked me a lot then and I was interested in him. In fact, he talked about marriage then and I, for sure, wasn't interested. He was nice but my feelings for him weren't that strong, and the idea of marriage didn't fit—scared me, as always. So he married somebody else. They split up last winter, and he started calling me. He's already back to the marriage thing, but I just don't want to hear about that, even though I care a lot about him. So the plan is, he's coming in January and will move in with me. Even that is a very big step for me.

"Actually, I'm waiting to see if he does come down. He's never lived outside Chicago. He's close to his family and his own children.

"And then there's Edmond.

"I saw him in a restaurant and liked his looks. I sent over a note saying I thought he was attractive and if he were free and interested, please call. He did. That was five years ago. We date on and off. We have some basic differences in what I'd call women's place. He's four years younger than I. He says he admires my heavy motherhood—most

men do; there's no adverse reaction. I'd rate Edmond as a good friend.
"And there's someone in D.C. I see now and then.

"I don't entirely rule out marriage but I doubt that it will work out for me. It would take such a special person to be as liberated as I am—as comfortable with his masculinity as I am with my femininity—not limited by roles as I am not, and who wouldn't be threatened by my need to achieve professionally. He'd have to accept my kids and understand how important they are to me. My kids would have to have a good relationship with him. Parenthood is pretty much a full-time activity, and I view marriage as a twenty-four-hour-a-day proposition, very much like a job, an actual job that has to be worked at. It would add something more to my life—maybe one more burden.

"Yet, still, I see myself as a very much misunderstood segment of society. Take my mother. She says she's immensely proud of me in every respect *except* that I'm not married. She compares me to my cousin, who's in the middle of a messy, messy divorce. Her twenty-year marriage fell apart, and she had been so much a part of a couple that she couldn't see what she had contributed to the marriage, to her kids, to anything. Now that she's alone, she's terrified—*she has no her.* She should have had some time for herself before she got married; she got trapped into the role of wife and mother before she knew who she was. God, it burns me when I'm unfavorably compared to a woman in a situation like that."

I asked Catherine about her future. "Well, the biggest hurdle now is to finish Charles' adoption, which is mostly a matter of processing papers. I've applied to adopt a baby girl—I'll take any racial background or minor health problem, but it must be an infant girl. I already have the crib."

I asked her to explain further. "Well, I want a girl to go with the two boys I have. I want as many children as I can afford, and I'm dying for a little girl to dress up and play with and more or less balance off my boys. If I adopt, I can be sure of the sex, and I know the need of children around here for a home.

"I see all this sort of coming together for me in what I'd call the child advocacy movement. I work with a group around here called Youth Advocates, a private group that looks into issues like juvenile justice, foster care improvement, and the like. We were monitoring plans for a children's detention center and managed to get it built separately from a jail. And foster care! I've seen too many kids get hurt from the present system, which greatly overemphasizes the rights of the natural parents. Parenthood is created by loving, by caring—not so much by biology. Yet kids often end up on the short end of the stick. People easily identify with natural parents and fear that if 'they'—the state, the court, the foster care agency—can take away one parent's child, they could also take away their child.

"So the upshot of all this is that I'm trying to move my career around these issues. There's a deputy position at the new detention center I feel I'm well qualified for. Over the long run, I may want to pick up a Ph.D. in counseling and guidance, so that I'm so good and so well credentialed I can never be questioned on the basis of my sex or race.

"The job development opportunities for me here are fairly good, and I must stick around to wrap up these adoptions I've got going, but frankly, I'm getting bored with this town. Eventually, I'd like to go to Washington, aim for a job where I can make policy, head up an agency, really use the background I've developed—or intend to develop."

Catherine's two boys tussled in the hallway. The foster child she was then keeping, a little girl, came in and requested a Popsicle. Sounds of a neighbor's television came through the wall. Catherine sat back in her chair, looking not at all tired, not at all stressed.

Martha Coleman

"Having my daughter was the best thing that's ever happened to me, though it's nearly cost me my relationship with my folks. You could never predict all the things that happen when you unexpectedly become a mother."

Martha Coleman, thirty-three, looked at me and smiled. Outside, a warm Virginia rain soaked the earth, providing a cadence for her slow, softly accented speech. Thunder rumbled far away.

"I've felt very strongly about motherhood all my life. I've always wanted to have children. The birth of my brother when I was twelve was by far the biggest event of my childhood—he was *my* baby, all mine. As a child, I saw myself as barefoot and continually pregnant. I still mother the world.

"Lisa was conceived out of an act of love with a very dear friend of mine. We've known each other for ten years; we once worked for the same business. He lives in Chicago, married, and has two teenaged daughters. We're the dearest of friends and we both know where we stand in this relationship. Actually, we've only had sexual relations two or three times in all these years I've known him. The actual cause of the pregnancy was diaphragm failure, though a psychologist has suggested there may have been a subconscious desire for pregnancy as well. I knew I was pregnant the moment I conceived.

"It would be an understatement to say the pregnancy threw me into a state of turmoil. My God, the world turned upside down. I just couldn't bring my feelings into any kind of focus. I never told anyone—not a soul—I was carrying until it came time to go to the hospital. My weight concealed my pregnancy, and I was able to teach right up until the time of delivery.

"I was terribly, terribly conflicted about the pregnancy. I made appointments to have an abortion three times. The third time I was at the end of the second trimester and was ready to fly to New York to do it, and I stopped at the airport. Not that I'm opposed to abortion—far from it. But I just didn't want it for myself.

"Only two people suspected I might be pregnant. I called my best friend Leanne the Friday night I went into labor and asked her to drive me to the hospital. I told her not to say anything to anybody, but when I woke up Saturday afternoon, my dad was standing by the bed. He had flown up from Daytona Beach. My mother was too upset by the whole thing to come.

"Daddy sat down beside me and took my hand. He told me in the kindest way he could that he knew I couldn't possibly consider keeping the baby. I had shown that I could be a mother because I could conceive and bear a child, and that should be enough. He said I didn't need to raise a child to know I could be a mother.

"The next day he went out and began shopping around for condominiums. He was thinking in terms of moving me into a new house and distracting me with the need to move and fix it up until I was over the emotional shock of giving up the baby. But I didn't see it that way. I felt it was kind of a bribe, that he was trying to buy off my baby, though *he* didn't perceive it that way. It really made me angry. Meanwhile, Leanne had called and told others. There was some relief in my not having to do this, but it hurt too because I was proud of her, and I wanted to announce her myself. I realized that her birth meant that she was no longer just mine, that now I had to share her, and that other people could intervene and interfere.

"It turned out that everyone was quite supportive, except the people that mattered most—my parents and Leanne. My folks are originally from a rural background, the conservative, fundamentalist deep heart of Georgia. They don't say it's a moral issue, but I think they feel this way. My dad wondered if I could handle it financially. My mother was raised without a mother and didn't think a one-parent situation was fair to the child. And they're still dealing with hurt feelings that come from not being told, from learning from someone outside the family in the middle of the night that they'd just become grandparents.

"I confess I've been a spoiled rotten little girl. On top of that I'm a daddy's girl. At the time Lisa was born I was toting around twenty-two credit cards my father had sent me. If I needed money, I'd call Daddy's secretary and she'd put a check in the mail. He paid my insurance, bought my cars, whatever. Oh, he'd give me a lecture now and then about not spending so much, but he encouraged it. He liked the dependency and encouraged it subversively. It was a way of tying his daughter to him—I was still his baby. And I flew home nearly every holiday, and talked to my mother, long distance collect, at least twice a week.

"Well, friends started coming by the hospital to see us. Things were terribly upset, with my dad pressuring me and my own feelings were all upset and ambivalent. Someone suggested I talk to a psychologist. Dad was willing to do whatever would help, but he has that old view of that kind of help—you know, you should be strong and self-reliant, and solve your own problems, and not have to lean on anybody. The hospital social service counselors also got involved, and actually they got through to him better than the psychologist did. But both were very helpful. They helped me express my feelings, explain why I had done some of the things I did, how I felt and was reacting to what was going on.

"But my parents were really set on my giving up my baby. Mother flew up for the express purpose of making sure that I would give her up. But by now I knew that I really didn't want to leave the hospital without her. I let them push me into a middle way—I would at least *try* to give her up. I felt I owed them that much. I signed her over to foster care for what was acknowledged to be a trial period of several months.

"So I went home and went on without her, day by day, week by week. I knew I was at a good age for motherhood, I was not close to being married—when would I have another chance to have a child? The baby's life was very dear and important to me—I had loved carrying her and participating in her birth. I had to convince myself now that I *should* keep her, rather than that I *shouldn't* have her, as I had before. I wasn't concerned about stigmatizing myself, or the effects on my career, but I was concerned about the people around me.

"I thought I just had a lot of acquaintances but found I had many caring friends. People I wouldn't have expected came forth with support and advice. Women friends rallied behind me and told me whatever I decided, they'd support me. They'd say, 'Martha, you're okay no matter what.' They wanted it to be my decision. They thought I should go get her, yes, but they'd never tell me that—they were trying very hard *not* to help me make up my mind.

"But my men friends weren't afraid of whether they helped me make up my mind or not. They'd just say, 'Martha, go and get her.' A colleague of mine—a man I'd always thought of as being puritanical and negative, made a point of telling me not to let anyone pressure me or push me around. 'She needs to be with you. It doesn't matter what somebody else can give her.'

"The security guards said they were disappointed I hadn't let them drive me to the hospital—they'd be *glad* to be her grandpa. I notice now they come by the office and check on me more. I got lots of notes, people dropping by the office. Others didn't say much but just appeared.

"One friend brought baby clothes to the hospital but was mortified at what she'd done when she found there was a decision being made. It just never crossed her mind I wouldn't keep her. That showed support and meant a lot because it showed she expected that of course I'd keep her.

"I heard there was some negative comment at school as the word got around, but the only unfavorable comment I heard directly came from a male colleague, who had, incidentally, sent me flowers while I was in the hospital. He told me, 'It's not a professional thing to do, it's very unprofessional, but it's done and I still love you.' Unprofessional! I could imagine being criticized on almost any grounds, but never dreamed of that."

I asked her why a woman so tied to her parents hadn't found some way to tell them about her pregnancy. "Mostly because I was so ambivalent about continuing it for so long. You don't tell people you're pregnant—and you don't seek obstetrical care—if you're going to abort. I didn't have my brains together about continuing the pregnancy until almost the third trimester and then I had such a revision of feeling! I was so ashamed I'd even considered an abortion.

"Also, things were not good with my parents right then. Mother was in and out of the hospital and at one point Dad was hospitalized too. Then Mother's stepfather died and she had to close his home and sell his things. Then we all went on vacation—if I'd told them then it would have spoiled the trip for them and I just couldn't do it. Then my brother left for the army. Somehow I just could never work it in.

"And I didn't get any medical care because I was embarrassed I'd put it off so long, and I avoid doctors anyway. That was pure foolishness; such a risk to both Lisa and me."

I asked about Lisa's father. "I'm sorry to say he knew nothing of her conception and birth until the agency contacted him for release papers when I was placing her in foster care. Of course, he should have learned about it directly from me. I called and apologized to him. I explained what was going on, and added that if this ever happened to his girls, I hoped he would not pressure them as I was being pressured, but would accept their decision, whatever it was. He supported me and said he'd accept any decision about Lisa I'd make. He is a loyal man and dedicated to his family. I didn't know what his reaction would be in relation to his marriage and family.

"He called after Christmas and asked if I'd kept her. I didn't know if I wanted to hear from him again; the call shook me up. He said he'd like to stop by and see her. I felt he had that right. Later, he called and said he'd had a business emergency; there were tickets at the airport if I'd like to come up. So I went.

"It was a nice meeting. He commented over and over again about how pretty she was. He put us in his car and apologized for not having an infant seat—his youngest daughter is fourteen! He checked us into a motel and bustled around looking for a crib. He sat on the bed and watched her sleep and said, 'It's funny, contact makes you feel paternal. I don't feel toward her as I do my two other daughters. I have no doubt she's mine, but I don't have a fatherly feeling.' But the next morning he wanted to hold her, and when we left for the airport, he put her in her snowsuit and kissed her goodbye.

"He said that it might be troublesome when she wanted to know who her father was. I haven't decided what to tell her—I might tell her things about him, but perhaps not who he is. He asked that I warn him if she were ever trying to reach him. But then he asked if he could see her from time to time. Now I think that's fine; I don't know if my feelings will change.

"I would dearly love to marry and give Lisa a father; I've never really enjoyed being single. As for marrying Lisa's father—we're good friends, but I don't know if we'd mesh for the long run. It's not realistic to think about it. I do not want to destabilize his marriage.

"But marriage appeals to me. I'm a homebody who enjoys a settled relationship, who much prefers fixin' dinner and having someone in to having to go out. I was engaged once and he married someone else. Otherwise I haven't been asked. But I'm not worrying about it and I'm not actively seeking a partner, though I know it would be good for Lisa."

I asked Martha how her parents have come to terms with the matter.

"I gave the relinquishment period an honest try. Lisa was in foster care nine weeks. I simply realized I couldn't live with myself—in fact, there wasn't even much reason to be alive—if I gave her up. Dad told me I was a strong person and if I made my mind up to do something, I could. But he wasn't thinking about the other side—that if I made up my mind to keep her, I could do that too.

"Then they put it on the line and told me, it's her or us. Actually, it hasn't quite come to that. I get Christmas presents for myself, but none for her. We talk on the phone and I get notes, but Lisa is never mentioned. I do write about her and send photos—they haven't told me not to. And of course, I've assumed full financial responsibility for us both.

"Leanne, however, has accepted Lisa. Once she saw us together and understood what Lisa meant to me, she really backed me up. She's been my friend since childhood; she even wrote my folks and told them she'd changed her mind, and that they should change theirs too. Actually, it's just as well it worked out this way. My mother needed Leanne's support; if Leanne had supported me from the beginning, Mother wouldn't have had anyone to bridge this with her. I had support from all these other people; at least Leanne was on her side.

"Interestingly enough, I've grown closer to my father. In my mind, he used to be such a tower of strength; I was sure he didn't have clay feet like the rest of the world! Now I see he isn't always the most logical soul and can make mistakes too. I see his emotional vulnerability and that makes him more human, easier for me to accept. It's true that in rejecting my motherhood he's rejected an important part of me. But he is beginning to see and accept me as an adult. He may have rejected my decision, but he has accepted my right, my ability to make my own decisions.

"I'm sure Mother is thinking this will last for a little while and then it will be back to the way things used to be. 'Martha won't be able to deal with this child, won't be able to handle the finances, and will give her up.' She assumes they'd then buy me out, and it's back to the old dependency relationship.

"But Daddy accepts my actions, though he doesn't support my actually keeping Lisa. He's not threatened about losing me as a child; he's willing to accept me as an adult and that's why I feel closer. I can accept that he's come this far, although he hasn't gone all the way to accepting my daughter yet.

"I see it's *their* loss not to be around her, to play with her and see what a fine granddaughter they have. It's their loss that I'm not around like I used to be. Lisa and I get invitations for holidays and vacations from friends; those gaps are filled in for us. But my parents sit alone; they have disassociated themselves to where they don't have a daughter or a granddaugher, either one. I know what it's like to give up a child because I went through that. And they had me for thirty-three years and then basically gave me up and that's got to hurt more. I'm feeling like it's a loss to them that shouldn't be.

"I feel for their pain. But they made a decision they felt they had to, just as I did, and they have a right to make that decision, just as I did. A year ago I wouldn't have understood that.

"I've become emotionally more self-accepting. I've always set goals that were close to perfect because I thought that's what others expected of me. Probably I was trying to live up to my father's expectations. But I think seeing he has clay feet has helped me become more realistic—at least I don't have to live up to quite as much, or have a fear of falling as far, so my self-image is a good bit better.

"I'm more assertive now for myself and my daughter. Before, I could easily be imposed on. If extra work was requested by my department head, I would stay to all hours to do it. But now I set limits; I can say I need time for myself and extra time for Lisa. I'll help and occasionally carry more than my load, but I can tell people no—I must keep myself physically and emotionally healthy for her.

"I don't go out as much as I used to; now that I'm paying my own way, I can't run around and travel the way I used to. But I'm happy to stay around home more because I'm so preoccupied with her; I love being a mother; it's the neatest thing ever."

I asked how people accepted a baby in her life now. "It doesn't matter too much. You expect it will, you dread it will really make a difference. But usually people I meet now don't know or consider my marital status or what it was when she was born. If they do know, they figure it's over and done with. Mother and Daddy will find this too, that people won't hold them personally responsible for what their adult daughter did.

"I'd like a second child—I hated being an only child, though Lisa may not feel that way. I wouldn't consider bearing another illegitimate one, but if I don't marry I'd probably consider adopting an older child."

I asked her if bearing one's own child compared to adopting one would make a difference. "It's nice to carry a child, to talk to it, to know you are participating in its growth. The birth process is special and dear. But love comes from giving and involvement, not bearing. I would feel just as much love, dedication, and involvement if I had adopted Lisa. Her inherited physical relationship is of some importance to me, yes, but her personality, emotions, and values are much more important than the color of her eyes. I was really mad when Dad said I had proved I could be a mother because I had given birth. That isn't the motherhood! Motherhood is the taking care, the raising, the molding, helping that child become a self-sufficient person and happy with herself. It's much more important than the birthing.

"I have my worries, my problems, but they're mostly the ones all parents have. I worry about the nursery schools and if the quality of care they provide will be good; I think about paying for college with inflation and all. I can still give to society and participate, as I have always done. Parenthood hasn't dimmed my perspective of the future and has probably brightened it. It's amazing how much more interesting it is to look to the future when you've got someone to be doing it for.

"Actually, there's one thing I would change. I really want to create a support group for single mothers—both those who give up their children and those who keep them—so there'd be somebody there when you really need it. It's such a very, very important and emotional and trying time. Not to take the place of a psychologist or social worker of course, but to answer questions, solve practical problems—I didn't figure all the time involved with changing bedding and coping with laundry! I needed hints on things that work and things that don't work.

"Certainly I didn't handle my pregnancy and motherhood as well as I should have. So many problems would have been avoided if I had shared my pregnancy and not been so afraid for my parents. We would have had some bad times, but we could have worked together and the outcome would have been so much different.

"The coming of a baby brings an impact you just can't imagine until it happens—to yourself, of course, and everyone around you. It's an extension of your family and self in a way teaching and writing can never be. It's a breath of immortality—and God's gift for hope for this world."

Laura Winfield

"I love being a mother—it's my most favorite thing to be doing of anything I could possibly think of. I feel my child is just teaching me so much, and leading me so much. And I've found so much freedom in being able to be myself in being a mother—it's opened a whole new world for me.

"It's a fun thing, being a mother. Oh, it's frustrating at times, but when it comes right down to it, that's only the tiniest part of the whole. I like making a home for her, making her clothes, and I like doing the things with her that you can only do with a child—things you never think of without one, or things you don't take advantage of doing unless you have a little girl to consider."

In a modest cottage in La Puente, California, Laura Winfield discussed her daughter and her motherhood. An attractive thirty-nine-year-old brunette with warm brown eyes, Laura is a physical therapist at a nearby hospital. Her daughter, Jennifer, four, slept in the next room.

"I was the only daughter of four children in a military family; we moved around a lot. We had a warm family life—my mother was the strong figure since Dad was often away. I had a brother ten years younger than I, and Billy was my pet—I loved to take care of him and pretend he was my baby. I always liked children, and I babysat and worked as a camp counselor when I was a teenager. I went to college in Boston and partially supported myself as a live-in sitter.

"Near the end of my college days I got involved with Guy. Not long after we both graduated we left for New York and set up an apartment together. Those years were good ones for me. I really developed my career and had a good thing going as a physical therapist in a well-known hospital. If I had really put my heart into it, I would have gone straight to the top, but I felt I was largely marking time. My major goal was to become a wife and mother, and this was just an interim thing. I traveled a lot, went skiing weekends, and was active in sports. I spent a lot of time meeting people and defining what I wanted in life and deciding the things I wanted to do—that was important.

"I see how I tended to get involved in very long-term relationships, and my relationship with Guy was to last nearly eight years, though it was an on-and-off thing during much of that time. He was a CPA with a big accounting firm in the city—very bright and very ambitious. He wanted to be extremely free and have as many women and experiences as he could, and he liked to develop all kinds of relationships. I'm not the type who can take too much of that. Though our relationship had its strengths, his playing around finally got to me and about four years after we started going together, I decided I'd had it with him. Guy wasn't into living the way I wanted to live, my college debts were paid off, and I was thinking about the possibilities of developing a new life-style in California. So I told Guy this was it, quit my job, and started driving across the country to Los Angeles. When I got to Topeka I stopped to visit my brother. I walked in the living room and there sat Guy; he'd quit his job and wanted to get things together with me and go to California too.

"His sudden appearance wasn't good for me; I felt pretty upset about the split-up and the traveling heightened my sense of vulnerability. So I gave in, and we came out and got settled here and spent another few years together. It wasn't any better than it had been—he'd find somebody else and take off, and that was extremely painful. But I clung to the relationship because I felt he was all I had; all our friends were his friends and I didn't know a soul; that's why I put up with him for so long.

"Then I got pregnant, and that's what completely broke us up. That was the end. We thought of getting married, but my pregnancy forced the issue of his instability and basic unsuitability for such an undertaking. I had to sit down and define my goals. When you are single you can just float a lot, but now I had to ask myself what I really wanted. I knew I couldn't stand all his other women and leaving and if I had to count on him as a husband and father, well, forget it. I wasn't ready for parenthood by any means; I was too young and immature and certainly I didn't have what I thought it would take to do a socially disapproved thing. I had an abortion and faced the fact that Guy and I were finished for good.

"That cleared the air. I went into what I'd call my swinging-single stage. That's not really me either, but was something I tried out and it was a good thing I did, because it gave me a basis for judging a lot of things. I went out with many men, went skiing constantly, went to the bars. After about a year of this, I met Chuck, and eventually we moved in together. Chuck is Jenny's father.

"Well, I was starting another in-and-out relationship with a strong man with strong ideas. I would soon find that Chuck wasn't exactly the soul of reliability, either. But I was in a very fun-loving stage and wanted to do adventuresome-type things. I took up bobsledding and even made a couple of parachute jumps. I would meet more stable types, but they didn't seem that exciting. I was plenty independent and needed a man who could go along with that. As it turned out, I traded off those settling-down qualities for the other stuff, and when the time came than I was ready for a more stable life, I didn't have the right sort of guy.

"Chuck had his ideas of what he wanted as well. He was basically looking for a woman who would go along with him, who fit his various ideas—I still tended to be managed very well by that kind, instead of doing what I wanted to do. In many ways, he was moving on different values than I was. He was in sales with a large electronics company and was that stereotypical big-business type, very determined to make a lot of money and get far in the corporation. He wanted a woman who enjoyed a heavy social life, could dress in a certain way, and was good at entertaining his customers and business cronies. He was fitting an image, and for me to get along, I had to fit that image too. When you're single and running around you play lots of roles and though this one never really suited me, and wasn't what I wanted, I was pretty good at playing it.

"But the relationship did have a lot going for it. We were great physically—Chuck has a beautiful body and he's great in bed. I wanted to do all these different things, and as a single girl it's difficult to afford the sort of high life Chuck offered, though that was only a minor part of it. We did a lot of theater and attended many symphonies, always with the best seats. I bought a four-wheel-drive camper and we went backpacking and skiing. One winter we went skiing every single weekend. That was just really wild, and really great.

"About that time I started to have some health problems. My mother had had vaginal cancer, and since it's highly hereditary, they started monitoring me closely for it too. I was starting to have trouble with endometriosis, an inflammation of the uterine lining. I developed a tumor on one of my ovaries and because of the cancer scare, the doctor felt it should be removed. I signed a permit for a total hysterectomy, if necessary, but made a pact with the doctor that he would absolutely not take anything he didn't have to. I was freaked out about the whole thing—I knew I wanted to have a child someday. I had long crying spells with Chuck, but he wasn't very sympathetic and just told me I should go ahead and have everything out. When he saw that that wasn't what I wanted to hear and got even more upset, he did the typical Chuck thing—he disappeared. He couldn't take me leaning on him for that.

"It turned out that the tumor was benign, just enlarged and overgrown with this endometriosis. The doctor took the ovary out. Later we discovered that both my tubes were blocked. He tried to open them by blowing them and I fainted three times from the effort, but it didn't work. The doctor told me flat out that there was no chance I could ever conceive, period. No chance at all. I was devastated.

"I decided I'd better reassess the situation and make myself some other goals. The ones I had weren't working. Chuck had taken off and I didn't see him again until six months after I had the surgery. However, when I told him I definitely couldn't become pregnant I was acceptable again; his big problem was that he didn't want to be bothered by birth control which he had to tolerate when I went off the pill when the endometriosis first started. I felt I should concentrate on advancing my career. While making money per se has never been my big goal, I did decide I wanted to buy a house for myself. I had an opportunity to work in a hospital in Saudi Arabia for a year at a very high salary and that would pretty well take care of it. I also needed to get away and see things in a different light. Clearly, my relationship with Chuck was ending. I was seeing him only about once every three months.

"Well, shortly before I was to have my final interview for Saudi Arabia, a friend asked me to house-sit for her. She has a gorgeous place in Pacific Palisades over the ocean. I went out and thought, Gee, what a wonderful setting—the moon was shining over the ocean and it was a mellow night and she had this big double bed and I just thought I'd call Chuck to come over to enjoy it with me—and that's the night I got pregnant.

"When I started missing my periods again I thought it was a flare-up of my old problems. I told the doctor what was going on—just as a precaution, before we started doing X rays, he said he'd have to run a pregnancy test first. It came back positive. We both laughed and said how ridiculous that was, and did another. That was positive too. Then we tried a new test, and when it came back positive, we decided I must be pregnant.

"I started thinking, What do I want to do? I told Chuck that I was pregnant and that I was going to make my decision and then I'd tell him what I was going to do. I wanted him to know that; he could tell me what he wanted me to do, but I was going to be the one to make the decision. That really took him off guard, because he was usually more the leader in deciding what we were going to do. He told me immediately and very strongly that he wanted me to have an abortion. He thought that was the only, only thing. I told him I was going to think about it for two weeks and then I would let him know.

"I had to drive to Fresno to take some things to my brother and sister-in-law en route to my final interview in Las Vegas. As I drove, I thought about it all—what I was going to do. Marriage was out. Chuck and I were operating on different values in many ways, and he clearly wasn't stable and reliable or someone I could definitely count on through life's difficulties—I had arrived at that conclusion long before. I talked to my brother and sister-in-law about it, and called my parents. My father was totally shocked and couldn't talk to me about it at all. Mother thought that for my own good and for the sake of my health and career goals and so forth, I should just go ahead with my plans and go to Saudi Arabia and not go through with the pregnancy. But as I talked with my brother and sister-in-law, I told them what my goals had always been in life and this seemed like one was finally coming true—it seemed as though I was receiving a gift of some sort. Physically I knew my pregnancy was a medical fluke; I could hardly hope I'd ever be pregnant again. By the end of the visit I decided I wasn't going to Saudi Arabia and told my family I was going to stay and have my baby.

"After all, when I stopped and looked back over my entire life, that had been my number one goal. I had tried many things and I badly wanted to have the experience of having a pregnancy—in a basic sense, I had to know what that experience was, what it felt like to live through. And my motivation for motherhood was simply unquestionable. There wasn't a shadow of doubt in my mind that I wanted to make a full commitment to raising a child. I feel in life you've got to get out there and do what you must do. True, you might get hurt, but you've got to try your basic things. When I thought of having surgery I wondered what having a child felt like, and what I would lose if I never experienced it. I wondered about having my body change—the psychological thing, the emotional changes. It was one of those things I had this strong compulsion to do.

"And everything was just so positive, so marvelous. Being pregnant was great—the neatest thing I've ever done. The fact that my body produced this child—it was a miracle to me.

"True to form, Chuck got very upset and I did not hear from him for another six months. But before he left we had a meeting with a lawyer friend of his to draw up a paper saying he was never going to have to support the baby; this was all my idea. The lawyer was a woman, the wife of one of his duck-hunting friends. The paper wasn't really binding, I was not giving away my rights of support; there is no way any man can get out of that legally. And anyway, my idea was that this was my thing; I was deciding to do it and I was never in my life going to punish him for helping me conceive this child. If it really hurt him that much to have to think about supporting it, fine, I'd sign. But I always told Chuck I was going to acknowledge him as the father of the child and tell the child about him when he or she asked. I told him I would not ask for support; it was my decision, it was not the thing he wanted to do. I knew he was selfish with his money and his main thing was collecting it, certainly not giving it away. I assured him there would never be a demand for him to pay anything unless I got into some desperate situation. Then I'd put the baby's and my interests first and fight him in court if I had to. So that's what made him get this lawyer to write up this paper which he thought freed him of support obligations. But the lawyer was laughing up her sleeve. She repeatedly told me it didn't mean a damn thing.

"By the time I was seven months along, Chuck started coming over. He was getting curious—he wanted to see what I looked like. Then he started coming over more and more, and finally he was always around, but still with a negative attitude—this was never going to work, but he was curious, because he had never been through a pregnancy with someone before. When I was seven months along, he and all the guys from his duck-hunting cabin gave me a baby shower—an all-male shower. It was really neat. I think that was the point at which he finally accepted it, though he never told his parents or family, and of course it was not to be mentioned around any of his business friends or clients.

"First I had to tell my boss, a rather stuffy type who is the head orthopedist. The group of doctors I worked with called me in and told me they thought I should have an abortion. They offered to pay my way through medical school if I would do it. Going to medical school was something they had mentioned to me previously, but now they tried to use that as a lever to talk me into the fact that having a baby was not something I should do. But when they saw I was really determined, that this was something I really wanted to do, and after I told them that no, I very honestly didn't want to go to school now, then they were very supportive and backed me up to all the rest of the staff and everybody else. The head doctor even decided that he was going to become a grandfather!

"I went around telling other people about it with a positive attitude. I quickly found that if I clued people to what my feelings were—if I let them know immediately that I was happy and together about it—then they would respond in kind. And I never had a negative reaction the whole time from telling anybody. I just made it clear that 'I'm pregnant, I love it, it's neat and I'm having a super time.' And people were just more than positive: 'All right, then, if that's what you want, great, go to it!' There was no hassle anywhere.

"My father was the most negative, but the good thing that happened with him came when I was about four months along and had to go east to attend the funeral of a relative. All the older family members were there—the eighty-year-olds and the ninety-year-olds. They started tittering about whether or not I was pregnant, and was I married. My father stood up and said he had an announcement to make and told them they were going to be proud grandparents and no, I wasn't married. That was the first time my father showed any real support, though he now loves Jenny dearly. To this day, he feels I'm not getting the benefit out of life I should have—I should be able to be a mother without having to go through all the hassle I have working full time and all. He feels I deserve better—I should be getting better, I should have someone to support me. But fathers are protective like that, and I appreciate where he's coming from.

"When time came near for me to deliver, Chuck took a vacation— flew east to visit a girl friend. I worked all day Friday, and on the way home on the bus, I felt a mild cramping, though I was sure it wasn't labor. I got home and it didn't go away—the cramps started coming regularly, though there wasn't as much pain as I have with my period. Well, I fooled around and cleaned the house and finally called my pet sitter, and drove to the hospital. I parked my car a block away in the employees parking lot and walked into the emergency room feeling a little foolish. My faithful doctor who had helped me through all my problems wasn't on call that weekend, so I had another, a guy who turned out to be fabulous—did everything just the way I wanted. He put me on the table, examined me, and told me to get right upstairs—I was totally dilated and ready to go.

"My first worry was that I didn't have a Lamaze coach. I'm a little lax with myself and wasn't sure I could discipline myself to stick with the methods. In the next labor room was a fifteen-year-old girl screaming with labor pains. Well, that bothered me so I decided to go help her and coach her into doing some Lamaze with me. She'd have a contraction and I'd have a contraction and we'd time each other and that was my coach. I was having a real easy time of it and every so often I'd stop, go lie down and be measured, and come back to her. Finally I was ready to go into the delivery room. I went back and gave her one last coaching, walked into the delivery room, got on the table, and they told me to start pushing.

"I pushed and I pushed and I pushed and I got her head out. She woke up and was looking around. I could look down and see her head and she seemed quite comfortable; she just lay there looking all around. The doctor turned out the bright overhead light, got the warm water bath ready, and turned on the tape deck I'd asked him to bring up from his car. There was a lovely feeling of peacefulness in the room. I wasn't in pain, but I was tired and wanted to give up. I started to push her shoulders out but it was hard because she was a big baby and I was tired. I wanted to push her back in and go home and come back when I felt more up to it. I kept complaining that I'd worked all day and wanted to quit and take a nap and then start up again. But the doctor said there was no going back—what were we going to do about her head sticking out? It wasn't pain that I remember—I was fairly comfortable, but I was really pooped out and did *not* want to push. So after an hour longer, she was delivered, and that was just great.

"She wasn't really a person to me for a few days, but a wonderful little someone I didn't quite know yet. I didn't have a separation depression then, though I had a serious amount of depression when I stopped breast-feeding her—it really killed me to do that.

"Chuck called the day after Jenny was born and flew back immediately. From that time on, I set a new standard in my relationship with him. I started setting new goals for myself as far as not accepting things I didn't want her to pick up as values. I feel kids can't tell when you are playing roles, not being totally honest, not being a real person. I stopped being the partygoer. I wouldn't get a sitter and do that—I didn't want to be that to my child. I was never comfortable being a partygoer in the first place and was only doing it because of Chuck.

"That wasn't as important anymore. But he kept struggling to reestablish these old patterns and wanted to keep the old relationship patched together and be in the same kind of rhythm we had been before she was born. I was determined to be more honest with him and myself, and the relationship hadn't been built entirely on that. I shucked off the pretentious stuff and found the strength to stay with my own values.

"Nothing survived of the original relationship—we changed everything, and I mean everything. First of all, he wanted to resume the physical relationship right away. Well, I was weak and trying to get back on my feet and he has no patience with being denied anything physical. He got very angry about that and took off, but he didn't stay away long because he didn't want to be away from the baby.

"I later found he felt left out because of my relationship with the baby—my parents did too. But I was very happy to be single and alone with Jennifer when she very tiny, because I think in a relationship with two parents, there must be a huge ambivalence in the woman's having to decide what to do with her other relationships. I was happy to have my relationship with her all to myself, and I put all other relationships aside for a while. I could let her set her own schedule with me, and I didn't have to put a lot of things on her because I didn't have someone else pulling me in another direction. When I see the struggles my married friends go through with a new baby, I see it's very hard on a marriage. You have to figure out every communication with the baby and it takes a lot of concentration. You spend a lot of time on diaper changes, and all the feeding, and when they scream and carry on, it bothers two people. And there are many decisions to make. Chuck came around about every other day, never offered a penny of support, but he did give me space with her and let us work it out. Ultimately a very strong bond developed between them.

"The thing that was hard to get across to him was that in doing away with the relationship as it was, I wanted to replace it with something else. He kept resisting that and instead of getting into a discussion about it, he just kept pushing to go back to the same old patterns. We never really did get into a good discussion of how it should be.

"After she was about three months old, we resumed our sexual relationship. But when she was about a year old, I stopped it because it was threatening what I was trying to change. I didn't want Chuck as a lover anymore because we'd be pulled back into the same old patterns— three months up, four months down—up, down, up, down. Having a sexual relationship with him made me overly involved emotionally and I couldn't sort out the things in our relationship I wanted to solve. I do feel very emotionally drawn to Chuck, but by removing the sexuality I removed the spark plug that kept us in the old dynamic.

"We had a terrible time with this. He laid it on me that he was Jenny's father and he deserved it—that sex is his privilege as her father. Then I had to define that with her he's her father, but with me he had become a friend—maybe a deep friend, but a friend nonetheless. He couldn't believe I'd made this decision and decided to put Jen in the middle of it. Well, about that time he quit his job and went to work with another company in San Francisco. The break came at a good time, because he was giving me so much trouble. At that time, he started paying me fifty dollars a month support. I think he made that decision because he felt he really wanted to keep an in with her. Though I was turning him off in some ways, he still wanted to be there.

"He has always played the doting father to the hilt, as though he is always here and knows just what is going on. To hear him talk, you'd never realize we aren't an intact family. That's Chuck—great at playing roles.

"I invite him for all her events and every holiday. Jenny sees her daddy as sort of a charming Santa Claus who brings her presents and dresses. She puts a lot of pressure on him. Recently she said, 'Daddy, if you would only marry Mommy—Mommy says you don't love each other enough and that if you were together you'd be fighting.' He got very defensive—'I don't fight'—no, he takes off—but he wanted that clarified. Jenny replied, 'Mommy says she'd fight with you'—she straightened that out. Then she said, 'You know, Daddy, if you just loved Mommy a little bit more and would come and live with us, then you could take care of us and Mommy would not have to go to work and leave me with all these sitters.' She's been hitting him with this for the past six months or so and he can't handle it and never gives her an answer, so she keeps bringing it up.

"But we've discussed it, and when we go down to the beach, she looks for a man for me. She wants a complete house—when Chuck is here, she says, 'Well, now we're a whole family. It really feels good when we're a whole family—it doesn't feel good when one person in the family is not here.' I'm glad we're discussing it—though she's the daughter of a single parent, she still sees the whole family unit. I want her to recognize that model and think that's okay.

"I told her someday we may meet a man that I can get along with, and that she can get along with. I try to point out the differences Chuck and I have. She has seen us get into a very severe discussion of our value differences once, and it scared her. I told her if Daddy and I were together, we'd be doing that more often and that's one of the reasons we can't live together, that Mommy feels differently about things than Daddy does. It's very difficult to point that out to a child, but at the same time she needs to know.

"For example, it's typical of him to let her down by doing what he'd rather be doing instead of what she wants to. If someone pulls him in a different direction, then he goes—whatever rolls better, he'll do that at the time. He promised he'd come down for her Christmas program; he called from San Francisco the day before to say he'd be there, and then he didn't show up. To do that to a child is devastating, but at the same time I tell her Daddy does things like that, and it's one of the things I don't like. We also went through a whole bed episode. He promised to buy her a bed for her birthday, and though he spent well over three thousand dollars on household things for himself about then, he claimed he couldn't come up with money for her. So I pointed out that these are the reasons Mommy doesn't live with Daddy. I want her to get a realistic view.

"On the whole, my experiences with single motherhood are very highly positive—I can't imagine my life being any other way. But there are some problems in it here and there, though they're minimal. When she's sick, I need a good support system, because for her there isn't anybody else to be around except Mommy. I've always had a good attendance record at work and I always have these guilt feelings about not showing up because I need to be with her; on the other hand if I leave her when I feel she needs me, I work all day feeling guilty. I did set the priority. She always comes first. But that's the hard thing, when she's sick.

"And there's this matter of her preferring to be with me, and having to spend so much time at sitters and at school. I work full time and it bothers me because I do think it would be better to only work part time. Financially, we're not doing great but we're doing well enough. She has anything she really needs or wants and she's well fed. I spend money to have a lot of experiences with her but I've always done that for myself too. She's traveled. We're taking a houseboat trip this summer and we go see my folks in the East. Chuck helps with those things.

"I maintain these standards instead of working part time, though it was a hard decision to make. And I've decided to invest in a good private education—the public schools around here are so poor—so we'll do that at the price of me working full time and being separated from her more. Jenny and I can discuss these decisions about not staying home with her and some of the trade-off aspects of other decisions I must make—she now grasps that whole concept fairly well. Sometimes she can help me choose.

"But I feel all right because my priorities are clear. If I tried to handle each time with no plan of where we're going, I think it would be very difficult. And with some input from her into the decision-making process, it gets easier and easier. It was harder when she was too young for that. Now she's a part of it.

"Maybe the hardest thing is the fact that I make all the decisions that reflect so strongly upon her. We all like to think we do things because we want to or decide to but heck, it doesn't come from that. It comes from the values your parents instill or even impose on you. I don't mean that the responsibility for making these decisions is so overwhelming in itself—that's not my point; you just see the overwhelming impact that parental decisions have on a child. It's incredible! Absolutely incredible! And that's a humbling fear, because all my weaknesses as well as all my strengths shine right through, every one of them. She models herself so closely on me. I guess I wish there were some balancing off.

"But I think on the whole motherhood has been a lot of fun. I've loved every bit of it. I've learned just so much, and I don't think there's anything in life that's made me grow more."

V

THE MEN IN THEIR LIVES

Perhaps nothing characterizes single women's relationships with men more than their diversity, their endless variety—the range of these relationships is so great as to seem to defy description. Not only are two relationships almost never alike, it's difficult to find a common thread running between them.

The vignettes which follow illustrate this truth; they also show how women cope with and manage their relations with the men in their lives. Though sometimes painful, relationships with men can be ways women grow and learn.

Lisa

Lisa Schroeder's story takes us back to an earlier theme. Her story is about a diffused Age Thirty Crisis: less focused than some of the experiences we saw earlier, it spreads farther and wider and lasts longer than the examples we considered before.

"I come from a traditional German Catholic background and was well aware of my mother's belief that a well-brought-up girl was supposed to be married. But what I wanted was very different from the traditional scenario lurking in the back of her head.

"I won't claim to have always had a clear idea of what I did want, but for sure I wanted out—far away from the housewife's life she was leading. I always had plenty of interests and early on realized I'd never find what I wanted within the confines of a household. It was get out or smother.

"So I went to college—the first woman in my family to do so, and on a scholarship yet. My parents were shocked, but respectful, perhaps even slightly chipper about it. I'd bag a better husband this way.

"I had dated some in high school and college, but the man of my dreams didn't appear until I was in my middle twenties. I was working in an art gallery, and we'd put together a show of architectural drawings, some terrific twentieth-century stuff, and I had just been promoted to assistant-assistant instead of sub-assistant—something like that. Richard was a nephew of one of the architects. He came to the opening gala with his parents, who struck me right away as awfully stuffy, though Richard seemed to be nice. A few days later he returned to the gallery alone and started chatting with me. Then the next week he called and asked me out. Well, I was in seventh heaven—career and love life were coming together in fine shape, thank you.

"He seemed perfect. Tall, good-looking, and in the Social Register. He was a lawyer on Wall Street, in an old-line firm with obviously a great future ahead of him. He was interested in all those things—opera, art, literature, politics—I hungered to know more about when I was younger, and he clearly was able to move in the inner circle of some of these scenes himself. He was into all the 'better things in life'; I was hooked. This was definitely *it*. Most of the time the differences in our backgrounds didn't bother me; I was proud of my family, and I knew I more than made up for the so-called lack of hereditary luster by being funny and smart, certainly more interesting than those plastic debutantes he'd grown up with.

"We got into a routine where I'd see him once a week—usually on the weekend. It was like being rationed. We had those almost ritualized evenings; he'd arrive, I'd mix us a drink and have some hors d'oeuvres; we'd talk—usually the kind of talk I'd have with anybody at the gallery, nothing very personal or intimate. Then he'd look at his watch and say time to go; off we'd go to a restaurant he had chosen, then to a movie or play he wanted to see, me padding along completely happy. Sometimes we'd go to a party. His friends all liked me, and I liked them, and in truth I felt more relaxed with them than I did with Richard. I guess because I had so much invested in him, so much riding on this relationship, I couldn't afford for him to be human. He was up on some sort of pedestal and I kept him there—wanted him there. He was *so* handsome.

"I would watch the way other women looked at him and I would be both proud and afraid. Proud to have snagged him; afraid that someone else would snag him away. I bought more expensive clothes than I have before or since and went to a hairdresser regularly. I wanted to impress him *all* the time. He wasn't exactly reassuring in that regard. He'd admire other women extravagantly and then tell me I looked nice or something like that. It felt like a subtle put-down, but I ignored it. Sometimes a week or two would go by before he would call. I'd never call him. I didn't have the nerve, and besides it wasn't something a nice woman did—chase a man, that is. I guess the way I was behaving suited him just fine. I did whatever he suggested without so much as a murmur. I must have been very soothing.

"Sometimes we'd go to dinner at his parents'. His mother was a terror—she'd wanted him to marry some heiress but apparently he'd slipped the net, and his parents were still a little upset about it. His mother had arthritis, and she apparently felt this entitled her to be singularly unpleasant to the maid. His father, well, his father spent a lot of time talking about his cronies down on Wall Street, and about various social and business connections, clubs they'd been to where they hobnobbed with the eminently hobnobbable, etc. To them I was a real exotic, the daughter of upwardly mobile immigrants, a scholarship student in college. Certainly admirable enough but not quite what they'd envisioned for their darling boy. But Richard was already well into his thirties, and I guess they were beginning to wonder whether he'd marry at all, so in a sense they were both happy and not happy with my being in the picture. Do you remember the film *Love Story?* There were scenes in that that were pretty much like us—except that Richard was no Ryan O'Neal—and if I'm Ali McGraw, you'll have to judge that for yourself!" She laughed.

"Of course I wanted desperately to get married. This was true love. Never mind that I couldn't talk with him the way you would want to talk to someone you are contemplating spending the rest of your life with. Never mind that the sex wasn't very good. I was inexperienced, but even I knew that what we had physically wasn't very good, and behind my self-effacing manner there was enough ego left to realize it wasn't all my fault.

"Then things got more complicated. Richard and I sort of droned on, but a new factor crept into my life: I had terrible pains in my stomach, and it turned out to be a fibroid tumor. My gynecologist and internist both were treating me with drugs and between the two of them I was pretty much doped up all the time. They kept emphasizing I was much too young to operate on and perhaps the tumor would eventually dissolve and I wouldn't need surgery. In the meantime I was in pain almost constantly—not much pain, but it was always there, and after a while it and the drugs got on my nerves in subtle ways. I'd be a little shorter with people and Richard was beginning to annoy me.

"The condition got worse. I had to have one of those X rays where you swallow stuff and they watch how it spreads around your stomach cavity, and they could see that the fibroid was going to do nasty things to my ability to have a baby someday and after all I wanted to have children, didn't I? Oh, yes—one of my favorite dreams with Richard.

"The beginning of the end of our relationship came when I told Richard I had to have that operation. I was upset and very near tears. He was polite, concerned, but as always, distant. You'd have thought I was announcing an adverse weather forecast or something. I wanted him to sweep me in his arms and comfort me, tell me everything was going to be all right, maybe even hint that my reproductive future might be of a little concern to him, too. Emotionally, I got nothing from him except this pleasant stranger I thought myself in love with saying gosh that's too bad.

"I felt so many emotions, some of them quite contradictory at that moment. Rage, anxiety, fear—damn him, couldn't he just be a human being and show a little warmth and kindness? Maybe I should call in the janitor and see if he could do a little better! And a part of me had forgiven Richard for this kind of lapse so many times before that I was ready to make excuses for him again. Maybe he'd had an off day. Maybe he was tired. But no—I couldn't make those things stick this time.

"Up till then I had thought of Richard as strong and distant. After that I began to see him as weak and distant. I was marching to the drum of a weak man, not the stalwart silent type who haunted my fantasy life, who really did love me even though he was too bashful to say so. I realized I couldn't really rely on Richard, that I could never rely on him. I began to understand that you can't expect more from people than they are willing—and able—to give. Nobody can be everything for you. Obviously I wanted Richard to be, and when he so palpably wasn't, I found it impossible to forgive him.

"The operation was awful. They almost botched it up, and I was a long time recovering. Richard came to visit and sent tons of flowers; even his mother sent flowers. But I'd begun not to care anymore, and besides I was angry with him, not a big surface anger, but a slow-burning I've-been-had type of anger, though I knew the nature of our relationship was as much my responsibility as his. But he sensed he was in trouble and began to be very solicitous of me, visiting me often while I was hospitalized. It was the same old Richard, just trying a little harder. It occurred to me that it was entirely possible he might pop the question any moment. When that happened—and I remember the exact moment—I began to breathe faster and my heart fluttered a bit. I was *afraid*. I didn't want to get married—at least not to Richard. I'd be married to all that buried feeling and tepidness and distance and lack of real consideration—married to all that loneliness that Richard seemed to be. Marriage would put me in the same boat as my mother!

"I was over thirty now—thirty-one—and I seesawed back and forth with Richard for another year. It was as if the scales were gradually dropping from my eyes, and I was seeing Richard as he really was. A nice, good person, certainly, but limited, so limited in emotional ways that it froze whatever feeling I tried to summon up for whatever lay beneath. The poor man seemed to almost need a live-in therapist—that wasn't my role. I wanted a life for myself. Not a life by myself, just a life *for* myself.

"So we drifted apart. I discovered my career again. And I began to reach out to my friends more, and I developed many more friends than I had when I was with Richard. It was like he freed me from some emotional ice floe I'd been trapped on, though I didn't get involved with men again for another three years. But I am in a whole new life now, full of activities, full of friends, full of *warmth*.

"Any man I'd think of marrying now—well, he'd have to be my best friend as well as my lover. If I can't treat him as I would a dear friend, well, I'll never feel free to be his lover. I want everything to be open, free, connected, involved, warm. I want to enjoy the whole world, and I want to enjoy it *with* someone. But if he's not there, I'll enjoy it anyhow—by myself or with friends, close friends I can consider almost an extended family.

"I'm a lot kinder about and to men now than I was before. They're people too—something it was hard for me to realize when I only saw them in particular roles. I have a lot of men friends—some ex-lovers, some of them gay, some of them would-be-lovers I've turned into friends. I think women like me who want more from life than just a home and family have by definition a lot harder time finding men. One problem is logistics. Types like me gravitate toward the big cities because that's where all the jobs are, where all the high-powered careers are to be had. The men in the cities—well, the single ones tend to be less in number, and, as they get older, less appealing. A man over thirty-five who has never been married usually can be regarded as defective goods. I know that sounds cruel, but that's been my observation, and I *honestly* don't think the same is true of most single women—we're just an excess commodity. A man friend of mine who's newly divorced says he finds there are few worthwhile single men in the city. He's fond of me and would like to fix me up, but he says there isn't anyone in his circle of acquaintances he thinks is good enough for me. He says he constantly meets terrific single women, but almost zilch terrific single men. The dearth of eligible men is a fact of life that most women like me have to accept—that's just the way it is.

"Well, of course, there are always the married men—a presence as regular as the sun coming up every morning. They are often attractive and there's usually some lonely single woman around who will take them up on whatever they have to offer. I can't entirely condemn it— I've put myself in that situation a couple of times. Mostly, it's a younger woman's game. After a while, if you've got any sense, you get out of it because there's so little in it for you. They tell you they'll leave their spouse but few do—maybe one-tenth of one percent. Yes, it's a phase you go through—eventually you learn.

"And gay men—bless their hearts, often it seems that's all you can see for miles and miles and months and months. Many of them are sweethearts, though. Charming companions, the best friends and helpers you could ever want, sensitive, kind. As long as you respect the limitations inherent in their sexual orientation, it's fine. I think there's a large and natural alliance between many single women and gay men. Most of them understand where you're coming from and they aren't the least bit sexist.

"All in all, I think a lot of women like me are not married out of pure accident, or because 'the numbers' won't support us. Many of us are late bloomers, and lost out because our faster-developing sisters got there first. And often, we look for a situation on our own terms, and a lot of men are not up for negotiations.

"I do want to emphasize that I love my work. I'm organizing a new show at the gallery—choosing the artists, making all sorts of connections to make it a great show. One of the reasons I love my work is that the personal and professional spill into each other. I meet people in all areas of life who come into the gallery as clients and who become friends. I meet their friends in turn, and some of them become clients themselves! I love people and I love making connections, either introducing people to each other or to the right painting. In my life the intellectual and the emotional are intertwined, and that's the way I like it. I want to be fed on all levels. There's so much to enjoy, to experience in life. I want it all.

"I realized something the other day—I'm a free woman. It's taken me a long time to get there. I'm free to live, free to love, free to work. Free to make commitments or not make commitments. My life is where I want it to be: in my own hands."

Barbara

"You're interested in stories about men? I'll tell you two! I want to be clear about the first one—I'm not exactly proud of it, but I think it illustrates a certain truth about the way the dearth of men can sometimes affect us. I have a hunch I'm touching on a theme you'll find again and again. Let me tell you about Peter—a passing incident, but probably not an uncommon one.

"A friend fixed me up with a business analyst who called me one Saturday morning. He had a rather dead voice on the phone, as though he were doing me a favor—it was just shades of 'I'll meet you after class and see what you look like.' We went sailing and it turned out Peter was a good-looking guy, drove a nice car, was a little reserved but rather boyish in his manner. He told me he was thirty-three and had been divorced. I liked him and felt perhaps I was into a good thing.

"Sailing back he asked me if I wouldn't like to join him in some Mother's Day visits the next day. He was going to see his grandmother in a convalescent hospital and join his parents later. I didn't want to intrude, but he insisted my coming would make the day nicer for all of them. So I agreed.

"Early the next morning, the telephone rang. It was Peter. He said he couldn't sleep all night for thinking of me, and just wanted me to know that. I was a little flattered, yet a little bothered. It struck me as a rather forward thing to do. Anyway, we had a nice day with his family. His parents were in business together. I gathered someone else had raised him and I sensed there were some problems relating to that. His grandmother was a chipper little ninety-five-year-old woman, and I spoke a little Yiddish with her, which pleased her.

"We were home at nine-thirty, the end of a pleasant day. Peter came into my apartment, took off his coat, and asked me to marry him. I was flabbergasted and replied with whatever rationality I could muster, that no, I couldn't do that right now. And he said he would just continue to ask me until I said yes. And I said I would prefer he not do that, if he wanted to continue to see me. I looked at him and he was really serious. I certainly liked him. He was good company, bright, a nice guy I wanted to date. I'll fantasize about men I meet sometimes—sexually, wanting to be with them—but he didn't strike me in that way. I just felt gee, he's a nice guy.

"He pressed the matter, insisting I was just the sort of person he was looking for. 'How can you know that,' I asked, 'after knowing me just two days?' He insisted it was a matter of intuition, that I felt right to him. It was funny; I don't deny I was flattered; I couldn't help but be. He wasn't a creep. I said I would see him and we'd go out—that was reasonable.

"Well, we continued our relationship on what seemed to be a more normal basis. We dated for several months and things were pretty nice—sexually they weren't, for Peter was impotent, he could get a hard-on but he couldn't come. He could satisfy me in some ways, and he was just so wonderfully martyrish about it. 'It didn't matter,' he said. And I said that is not the name of the game. He then said it hadn't happened before and that I must be the cause of it. I didn't buy it, but I more or less overlooked the matter.

"Then we went to see his grandmother one Sunday. We were chatting along in Yiddish and she suddenly began talking about other women in Peter's life—Linda, Marj, Judy. 'Who were they?' I asked. 'Peter's wives,' she said quite clearly. Peter couldn't understand Yiddish but he understood those names, and he turned red. I knew her memory wandered a little and I wondered if she wasn't perhaps a little confused, and was maybe thinking of wives of other grandchildren. She wasn't telling tales on Peter deliberately, I thought, it was just that she loved him and was happy to see that he had a girl—again. But Peter's face gave him away and when I confronted him he confirmed he had been married three times 'But I wanted to tell you about them—I ended all the marriages, none of them left me.' I just looked at him in a state of shock. 'It seems as if you don't date, you just marry.' He proceeded to explain himself away—he could see I was bothered. I told him I thought this all said a lot about his maturity and who he really was. He said he wasn't trying to hide anything, but didn't think the time was ripe to talk about it. After all, he had told me he was divorced, which was true. He was also quite interested in whatever else Grandma had had to say. She didn't actually say anything else of great interest. I wondered what he was worrying about. I felt like I'd been hit over the head with a ball bat and told him to take me home, I didn't want to see him for awhile.

"One night I had a friend's car and was in Peter's neighborhood. He had had the flu and I thought I'd stop by and see how he was. A woman opened the door—at first I thought it was the wrong house. The woman turned out to be Wife Number Three who professed to be having car trouble as she was just passing through en route from Reno to Los Angeles so she was staying with him for a few days. And wouldn't I come in and have coffee. Well, if Peter got red when his grandmother whipped off those three names, you should have seen him then. 'What are you doing here?' I couldn't believe I was in this soap opera setting, but I stayed for coffee. Turns out Linda had left Peter to pursue a dancing career in Hollywood three years before—I didn't know people still did those things.

"I left feeling very strange—hurt, jealous, glad to be rid of him, everything. I called my girl friend and told her all about it. She went flat out on the floor. 'What's going on?' she asked. Well, I really didn't have any idea, nor did I care. Or so I thought.

"But actually, I think I hadn't entirely ruled out that something could come out of this, and I told myself to look at this in different ways. I cared for the guy, though I wasn't in love with him.

"Finally, Peter called me one night and insisted on coming over. We talked and talked and talked. I was brilliant—a real academy-award performance. Everything I said was right—I was hitting everything right about him. I told him I couldn't marry him. First of all I didn't love him, and he was professing love for me. The impotency thing had worried me enough that I had talked to my doctor about it, also describing Peter's background, and he very seriously warned me away from him. When we tried to talk about this, he just kept denying that it was any problem, that it hadn't happened before.

"So we broke up. I was down in the dumps, but not really in bad shape. I wasn't pleased with how I'd handled the whole thing. I don't know why I had put in so much time. What were my motives, what did I want out of this? Sometimes I guess I thought he would shape up and things would be fine and he could make me happy. Did I just want to get married? He offered me that. Was security all I wanted? Obviously not that much. I wasn't willing to make a commitment to him. Something about the relationship terrified me.

"The story doesn't end there. A few months later he called again with a new problem and insisted I was the only one who could understand. He was sterile! I couldn't understand how all of a sudden—it was weird. He went on about how he had to marry a woman who didn't want children, because now he couldn't give them to her. He continued to call but finally I told him to buzz off.

"A few weeks later I picked up the paper and for some reason I'll never know, I read the marriage license column. There was his name and the name of a woman I knew vaguely, a classmate of his in business school who was a good fifteen years older than he. My stomach fell right out, down to my toes, and I remember saying I can't believe what I'm reading. I went to dinner and couldn't eat a bite, I was that upset. I called and he answered the phone. I heard party noises in the background and said, 'Am I correct in assuming congratulations are in order?' And there was dead silence. And he said, 'How did you find out?' 'From the paper.' And he said, 'Only you would read the marriage license column.' 'It's certainly funny, I almost never do.' 'You know Joan is fifty and has had a hysterectomy.' And I said, 'That's a real good reason to get married.' 'Well, we had dinner the other night and we were talking about it. We've been good friends for years and we like each other.' And then I don't know if I said or just thought 'I really wish you lots of luck—you're going to need it' and then I added that I hoped I wasn't interrupting anything. 'Oh, that's okay, Linda (the third wife) is here and we're celebrating.'

"The p.s. to this story is that he has since divorced her and married another woman. His fifth wife. He's now thirty-eight or thereabouts."

Barbara paused and addressed a subject that seemed to be a theme with many women.

"I talk with a lot of lovely single women friends, good-looking, intelligent, and that's all I hear—that there's nothing satisfactory going on. The story I told you about Peter sort of illustrates that truth. I'm not exactly proud of it, the handwriting was on the wall almost from the beginning that he was real trouble, but an atmosphere like this tends to put an exaggerated value on almost any relationship that looks like it could even possibly go anywhere. Five women have been willing to marry Peter. Maybe some of them weren't screwed together quite right themselves, but I'll bet Wife Number Four, the woman I knew a little, just married him out of sheer desperation. I know in the last year and a half I haven't met one guy I'd like to really get to know well—put in a lot of time with, put effort into a relationship.

"I went through a stage of sleeping around and that doesn't sit well with me. Sex for sex's sake means nothing. I've also found a lot of poor performers in men, and I am not a ball-breaker! I feel very good about myself sexually, 'cause I had a good teacher, who has a very healthy attitude about sex.

"I've had relationships with men I've dated a lot and I've seen a lot of hung-up guys. I know when I talk with friends that good sexual experiences are rare. You may find somebody you get along with and feel comfortable with and all, but even those people have problems. It's terribly discouraging."

She stopped and sighed, raised her eyebrows and said, "Story number two.

"At the present time my social life with men here is really not much, though there's a man in Pittsburgh who means a lot. We've had a relationship—an affair—for over twelve years. We're just wonderful together, we're good friends who love each other and will probably go into old age together.

"I met Allan through a friend and literally fell in love with him ten minutes after we met. He's nice looking but—no—he's got something very important to me—fantastic humor, such sparkle, animation—and brains.

"He married when he was twenty and had a son, got divorced and then married again. The second marriage too has faltered. He's from a very provincial, conservative Jewish background that can maybe tolerate one mistake, but two, never! That is really frowned upon. I met him during one of his separations from his second wife and we saw each other constantly for a year and a half. But then he went back to her.

"When I was back there recently, we were together quite a bit. He's still with his wife and they have a child. It's a classic marriage of convenience—he does what he wants, she does her thing. She has gone back to school. She's got it made. He's paying for all this education. I'm sure it's guilt that keeps him with her. His mother is very sickly and he feels if they broke up he'd be handing her a second big failure. His wife is obviously an intelligent woman; she's busy with many things. He told me they hadn't had sex in almost a year. He just does what he likes, hangs around with his own circle of friends; he's not a womanizer.

"He'd love to have me back there but certainly will never ask me to come. At this point in time, to be perfectly honest with you, if he called and said, 'Look, I can't offer you marriage but will you come back?' I just might go. Because I've had enough of other relationships and I know a good one from a bad one and I know what I want and I know what I like. My friend asked, 'Do you think so little of yourself to live under such conditions?' But I don't think that's it. A good man is hard to find, married or unmarried.

"I hoped when I'd get back I'd see him in a different way and it wouldn't be quite so intense. Well, the magic is gone, it's not what it was. But it's still a special relationship, so it's kind of a shame. But at this point we're good friends, we really care about each other and as long as I'm here, and he's there, I can handle it.

"Yet, I think if I did go back and had nothing going on, I would probably put a lot of demands on him. He was primarily the reason I left Pittsburgh in the first place. And there's the theory that by tying myself up so much in an affair, I'd be closing the door to other kinds of relationships that might go further. Yet I think if I were to go back it would be very foolish, except that he's attractive and it's tempting to take up a relationship that's a tried-and-true love affair.

"I have a friend in an arrangement something like that—they've been together four years. Ron is a sweetheart, does well financially, and they're buying an apartment together but he refuses to marry her. They sent out invitations last spring and then he cancelled it. She left him for about six months, then went back to him—said she didn't want to be 'out there' again, alone, single, having to look for somebody. The condition she put on coming back was that they go for therapy. He went once and said it was too intimidating. So she went back on his terms and made peace with it. Later I asked her how she felt about Ronnie. 'It's all relative, Barbara. It hasn't been a great year but I'm back in school doing graduate work.' I think if she can turn this into better work, earn what she's worth, just maybe she'd reconsider. Ron doesn't put tremendous demands on her, he works six or seven days a week, and they both have a lot of freedom. Actually, he's writing the whole ticket and she's the passenger.

"Maybe I haven't gone back to Allan because he hasn't asked me. Really. Or at least said think about it—because I want it to come from him. I feel quite a bit of conflict about it, particularly right now. I'd get lots of flak from lots of areas if I'd do it. My mother would drown me— no, she just doesn't want me hurt. And everybody would tell me I'm a fool but that wouldn't stop me.

"If I go back, I'd have to go back doing something in my life I'm really into. Certainly not be wrapped up in him. If I were to make a move, I'd have to have my act together in my work. Yes, it would be much more palatable to go back there on my own terms and be established in my work, not really depending on Allan for a lot of things. And be involved and busy. I'd never go back just to sit around the house for him to call me and see him. I'd have to go prepared to do it all myself.

"A tempting idea—a very tempting idea. Times are tough, and you can only do what you can."

Camilla

Camilla Stephens' story shows something else—what the forces of tragedy can bring to women's lives, for hers is a complicated mix of love and death, friendship and service. It is also a regional story, a story about the South; it couldn't happen in Berkeley, near where I live.

Although Camilla is much involved in the theater, she would want least of all to be regarded as a tragic heroine. She is not; in her early forties, she finds her life rich and full. Her contributions to her family and community are many; she is high-spirited and animated. Yet hers is a story about resources women have and find, strengths we can call upon when we must.

I first met Camilla on her way to a theater opening. She was dressed in a black fox-tipped wraparound and drove a large sedan. I flashed on

Tennessee Williams' Maggie Pollitt. She swept into the festivities, one of the most attractive women in the room. Later we drove into the deep Alabama night to a gala party. I heard about fox hunts, debuts, hereditary societies. I learned to my surprise that balls (as in: to dance at) is pronounced: baw-alls.

"As a child—as a child I saw myself as Veronica Lake, with gorgeous blue eyes and blonde hair. Later I was a train conductor, or a lady doctor. But finally it was the glamor scene, like the heroine in *Cup of Gold*. And Scarlett O'Hara—oh, yes. Mother bought *Gone with the Wind* for me to read when I was ill. I read it day and night and then I was really sick—from envy!" She laughed.

"My family's been in the South for generations. Grannie was the state president of the Daughters of the American Revolution. She was always raisin' money to put up statues of George Washington and Thomas Jefferson. And scholarship money—the DAR had hundreds of students in school at one time. She enjoyed herself immensely, doing as she pleased. Her message to me was always be yourself.

"I went to Randolph-Macon before I entered the University of Alabama. That was the worst year ever—I've never been so bored in my entire life! I've always been involved in millions of clubs and activities, but at Macon you could join only one thing and I'd whip through my work and not have anything else to do. There were just six weekends a year when you could go off campus and when the nearest boys' school I wanted to visit is some distance away, it *limits* you! And I was homesick! I was *anywhere* sick!

"So I came home and joined a sorority at the University, and at twenty-two I made my debut. Once you are presented you go to all the balls, and there are twenty-nine of them, twenty-nine balls with dates. That same year, I was a provisional with the Junior League, so your friendship circle grows so. Suddenly you're really in the adult world, completely lifted out of the age-group thing from college. I'd have men in their thirties, men in their forties, even men in their seventies call me, invitin' me over to their house. And I was callin' them.

"That's how I met Charlton. He was captain of his ball and asked me to be queen of his ball, which unfortunately I couldn't do. He was dancin' with me one time and he said, 'When you're finished makin' your debut I'd like to go out with you.' So a couple of years later he did call and we started going out together constantly.

"It was one of those things where his friends were my friends and I just fell into his crowd. I was very naive and they just *adored* me because I was always making such ridiculous comments!

"I'd love it when someone would say, 'What do you do—are you a schoolteacher?' and I'd say, 'Oh, no. I work in a vinegar factory!' Well, I did! I was cost accountant for a big wholesale food producer and we made *lots* of vinegar!

"We started up a riding club to brush up on our horseback riding. We started with six couples—Charlton and I were still seeing other people then. All the girls dropped out when we started jumpin' so I had a date with all six of them on Thursday night and on Monday night they'd all get together and decide on who's going to have a date with me on what night. So I led a very full life and happy life. As a matter of fact, all of 'em proposed to me before it was over!

"But they were just my buddies. I really fell for Charlton. We were together more and more. He'd call and say, 'When you get home from work, dress, because we're going to such and such!' If we wanted to go to the picture show and hadn't seen all the picture shows in town, we'd catch 'em all on the same day!

"We bought horses and went hunting all over the South. We ran around with a crowd from Atlanta and had our own little local continental crowd. You know we loved each other and *liked* each other and were together constantly. Charlton did a lot toward forming my life because he brought me into the Community Players when he became an officer of the board. We saw that it needed help, and we'd better do something about it, so we jumped in.

"He was a wonderful dancer and a super cook. He taught me how to cook when he realized his friends *loved* for me to tend bar while he cooked. He got jealous, and figured he needed me to help him. That was the relationship.

"And he died. He had a heart attack when he was thirty-eight. I was twenty-eight. It was congenital—in his family—but still, it was very unexpected.

"It killed me. A big slice of my life *vanished.* I realized I'd just have to pick myself up and *do.* All the guys who'd asked to marry me from the horseback club started callin' again, but for what? I was in awful shape.

"We would have gotten married, definitely. Our motivation wasn't sexual as much as we were just *so* happy together. Or we could have just gone on like that for the next twenty-five years, because we were quite happy just as we were.

"It took me a couple of years to get myself back together, because everything I had, I had with Charlton. To keep doing the same things—like walking into the Community Players to do box office, even, bein' alone. I just *missed* him so, like part of me wasn't there."

In time, Camilla bought a house and became an officer in a family-owned business, working closely with her father. She continued to devote enormous amounts of time and energy to the theater group, serving on the board of directors and filling, at one time or another, "about every office, I'd guess." She was part of the production staff, raised funds (and supported the theater generously herself), and was available for the multitudinous miscellaneous tasks an organization like this requires. An historic building was purchased and renovated as a theater.

Another calamity descended a few years later. Jo, who had been Camilla's closest friend since third grade, developed cancer. "She failed for a number of years, and I watched her die. The family all leaned on me for support. There'd be calls at midnight, and hurried trips to Atlanta when she seemed to be worse, to support her parents and husband and children—but most of all to help Jo. She leaned on me; she was so desperate and upset. And I would come back from Atlanta just whipped." Camilla's duty of loving care to Jo's family was maintained long after Jo's death.

"One of the hard things I learned was the support I needed and didn't get when Charlton and Jo died. I mean because the relationship wasn't recognized—widows, parents, children, yes, but not friends and lovers. And I needed it so.

"That's one of the really hard parts of being single. You can't be sure you have support. If you lean too hard on others, they may get nervous. When I need to do some bleedin', I have a friend I call in New York, and she calls me if she's really down. But you basically have to be strong to handle it—and single women often are! Yet people think getting married is the answer to all of life's problems. That isn't so, but still you got to think about where you're going to get support, who's going to help you over life's hard spots."

Camilla maintains an almost frenetic pace of work: theater, friends, and community involvement. "I draw a deep breath in January and try to find a spot on my calendar in April to run up to New York and see some plays; that's about the only respite I get." She serves on an area council for mental health, raises money for a new art center, serves as an advisor to the Community Fund Drive. She was asked to produce Mardi Gras balls and from that developed a lively side business producing the state Junior Miss Pageant. She writes the scripts and designs the sets and oversees the production of the spectacle, "seein' that they're all standing in the right place at the right time."

She takes a wider role in the family business, and has developed an interest in family investments and "accumulations." She tends to her nephews and is a loving sister. Her first serious love from college reappeared several years after Charlton died; about eight years ago she began another long relationship with Bret, a divorced businessman who invited her to a ball "and moved right in on me. He was a gorgeous man—had a lovely house from the 1820s and loved to entertain. I was his hostess. I always get pulled into men's business lives as hostess for their affairs. We'd drive in the country, entertain artists and his clients. We liked to sit together by the fire and just read. Sounds funny, I know, but that's what we did.

"I loved him to death but it would never have worked as a marriage. He was looking for an ornament and a playmate; he couldn't tolerate being interrupted, as he put it, at the office. I adopted a wait-and-see attitude.

"About six months after we started going together he bought a business in Houston and left. We talked together on the phone nearly every night for years after that, and went back and forth. Then I began to sense he wasn't playin' straight, and last summer he announced he was plannin' to get married. I'd guess he'll go through a couple more wives." She is now seeing a stockbroker who commutes from Atlanta.

"I know myself rather well and I know I'm a strong person and I know my feelings and opinions. I enjoy life and I enjoy being who I am. I would not discount marriage but I think I'd be happier if I married somebody who traveled a lot—I'd never want to live with somebody seven days a week! I don't think I could stand his dirty socks and shorts on a full-time basis! I still want to be me—and there's so much to do, I never see how I could manage more.

"I pride myself in the *like* that precedes the *love* in these relationships and the fact that my close relationships remain that way. Once people come close, they don't go away."

The doorbell rang, and a group of theater people who had just wrapped up a Sunday afternoon children's workshop came in, talking excitedly. Camilla's six cats ran for cover. Wine flowed and the success of the afternoon was lived again. The smell of chowder and pecan pie wafted in from the kitchen.

It was evident there was a great deal of "like" and "love" in the room.

Carolyn

One of the most discussed kinds of relationships women have with men is living together without marriage. Carolyn Davidson describes her relationship with Ted, and how it came about.

In an office high above Manhattan's traffic Carolyn finishes her correspondence, returns some calls, clears her desk for the evening. Poised and smartly dressed, she looks like what she is: a highly paid management consultant, who flies around the country analyzing problems, advising corporate management. I asked her how she saw herself as a single woman of thirty-three. Her reply was direct:

"I like being single. I like the relationship I have with Ted. The way our arrangement is, by not being married there's no set assumptions about what our relationship is. We're constantly reworking, renegotiating things between us. Yesterday was New Year's Day, and we were talking about how we're going to be this year. Being able to be single makes us more creative, you know, just take it as it comes. I have always felt that Ted has been someone who has provided me with all the opportunities I would ever need to evolve and have the kind of career I've developed. He's given me a sense of independence both as a career person, and as a personal person, more than any other relationship I can imagine. Obviously, there'd be requirements if I were married. I can't see myself in that; I was engaged once, but that's not something I'm drawn to, being part of that kind of relationship."

I asked her to tell me her story. "We met about nine and a half years ago. He was separated at the time and was working in public relations for a Chicago research group. I was teaching high school at a private girl's school and had been un-engaged for about four months or so. So I was feeling very open to the universe of men. And I wanted to expand my options. I had lots of things in mind. I wanted to know that I was really making a free choice, that if and when I got engaged again, I was doing it based on plenty of insight and not just because I felt I hadn't been proposed to by more than one man. There's no freedom unless you have a lot of choices, so I wanted to make sure there would be. That was something I wanted to fix in my head or my gut. So I was out for being available."

I asked what had happened in her engagement. "Well, we were headed straight for a very traditional marriage. John's expectation of me was that I would be home chasing kids, and any kind of job I would have would be besides that. My contention about him was that he would be independent, emotionally solid, not dependent on me and at least in some respects smarter than I.

"What he had going for him was that he was very attentive, selfless, sensitive—a caring person. He and my mother loved each other. My mother was his mother. He worked for a large manufacturing corporation and was Young Management On The Way Up. He was a Methodist, family-loving, patriotic. He knew what he was going to do next, what would happen, where we would live and so on. And part of the attraction of being married was that I could be attached to someone else's long-range goals. You know, John would do it and I'd just hang out while he was doing this for forty years. It was a right-down-the-line relationship.

"It was a big risk to break the engagement. When I looked at why I had gotten engaged, I saw I was pretty much programmed to do it. My folks are devout Presbyterians, real scarred by the Depression and that whole trip that emphasizes stability and dependability and roots above everything.

"Well, then I met Ted. Talk about opposites—he was very hang-free. He cared a lot, but he also gave lots of freedom. He didn't make demands and didn't expect or give commitments. He picked up on me a lot; he understood I was quite the opposite of him, in many respects. He was sort of an unrooted guy, had lived many places, wasn't really dug into Chicago.

"So Ted presented very much of a risk, a real threat, a real different kind of person. I didn't understand how he could live on so many levels, have such a wide variety of interests. He fascinated me not only by his personality but because I didn't understand how it would be possible to be like that myself. My whole orientation was 'stay put!', 'Don't rock the boat!'

"We went together five months and would see each other maybe twice a week. He would always call me the last minute, like Thursday, and I would be available for the weekend. I liked him, matter of fact, I was smitten with him, but it was hard to tell where I stood with him. I was seeing other men, but Ted was the man I was most attracted to. And then one evening he announced he was going to New York to take a new job. There was no discussion whatsoever about me moving or going with him or anything like that. I was the only person he was seeing in Chicago, but given his worldliness, I thought he'd just move on. I figured his philosophy was that a relationship was really great while he was in the here and now, but when you move on, you move on and just cut ties. I felt that was his way and it wouldn't be fair for me to try and maintain a relationship, though that was hard for me to do. So Ted left and I thought 'Next!'

"However, he kept in touch, and that summer I went to New York and spent four weeks with him. We had a great time. I came home. I continued to date a lot of people and was proposed to by two men. Neither of them attracted me as much as Ted did; they made me feel claustrophobic. Part of that was because they set up this expectation that we'd have children. It was, 'Let's get married and have kids!', and though I didn't quite know it yet, I was getting more ready to hear, 'Let's be crazy and move with it,' and 'Let's be able to do a lot of different things.'

"Well, I went to New York again, to spend the Easter vacation. Ted had been with me at Christmas and said at that time, 'Did you ever think about moving to New York?' And I said, 'What does that mean?' and he said, 'It means, Did you ever think about moving to New York?' I said, 'What are you talking about?', and he said, 'Did you ever think about living in New York?'" She laughed at the memory of it. "I realize now that he was teasing me about the fact that my need for him to be specific was much higher than his need to be specific. All he was saying was, 'Did you ever think about living with me in New York for a while? I'm not making any promises, I'm not asking you to get married. If it doesn't work, I want you to feel perfectly free to split.'

"I of course was programmed to probe out if there was more of a commitment than there was. And Ted was not giving in at all. So I played with that, I thought about it for a while. I had to decide by Easter because I needed to renew my teaching contract about then. I realized moving to New York as a white woman with a degree in education and history and no teaching jobs available, those were four strikes against me. I thought it over and said no, I'd go back and teach in Chicago for another year. I was very attracted to him, I liked his life-style, but I wasn't quite ready to say 'I'm going to take this big open-ended whatever.' So I said no.

"I got on the plane. I was really upset. I understood how much I was attracted to Ted and committed to him. I asked myself how I could take such a risk. I was operating out of my intellect. I finally realized that I needed to pay attention to my intuition instead, and play down the intellect. I kicked around a lot of things and called him up on the phone as soon as I got home. We talked for two hours.

"Mostly, the next forty-eight hours were just a churning of emotions. A lot of emotions, and a lot of feelings, a lot of wanting to let go. . . . I wanted to do something for myself, actually. I didn't care how he lived, but I was going to do something else besides teach for a while. I could work at something in New York, maybe study, have some fun. I kept trying to rationalize, trying to provide some reasons for what my feelings were telling me. And then I said, 'Wait a minute!'

"I realized I had previously rationalized my way about my feelings in other relationships. I realized that was inappropriate. Why not let my feelings move me into a situation? Later, I could figure it out rationally! I hadn't previously taken many risks and this was a big risk. But I did it. I walked into the principal's office Monday morning and said, 'If you need to know, I'm not coming back to teach here next year.' It sounded as if my voice were coming from far away. I was in charge of the whole freshman program, and here it was, after Easter, and that would mean he'd have to get a replacement for me.

"And the other thing was that I was teaching at a girls' school. I could hardly be up front about the fact that I was leaving to go live with a guy in New York. So there was a lot of ambiguity about that, and with my parents and sister. They were upset that I was kicking over this wonderful job and couldn't understand what had gotten into me.

"One of my girl friends helped me quite a bit. She had heard my stories about Ted and she was really willing to support me. I had to tear myself away, and the more I asked for assurances from Ted, the less likely he was to give them to me. He said, 'I'm not going to support you emotionally, I'm not going to support you financially, I'm not going to . . . !' She laughed. "'You figure out what you're going to do. I'll do this for you. I'll go to the employment office and get a listing of all the school districts within commuting distance of Manhattan.' He did that, I wrote to them all, and it led to nothing. So, I arrived June ninth with no job. He had found an apartment and I wasn't familiar with Manhattan prices and I about died—my share was more than double what I had paid in Chicago. The first thing I did was start cleaning the apartment, and while I swept, I thought. I didn't know what I was going to do next.

"As a teacher, I was used to having the summer off, but the following Monday I was out looking for a job. I had a strong disinclination to get in the habit of hanging around the apartment. I looked in the classified ads under T for teaching and saw this super job in education, some sort of junior administrator for just as much money as I had been making. So I went to the placement bureau advertising it, and wouldn't you know it, it was gone. I'm sure it was a bait ad to get education people into the agency. Then came the inevitable question: Can you type. . . ?

"It so happens I can type like a whiz—ninety-five words per minute— so I got sent to a law firm for some underling position. And my fingers just froze—I didn't want that job at all, despite the fact I felt pressured to take something. I knew it was intuition telling my intellect what to do, or what not to do, in this case.

"Well, I won't go into the whole story of how I came to get my first job—again it had more to do with following my feelings about working for somebody I felt good with in a situation which felt right than it did with just following my brains. I sort of gravitated over to the work I now do through a series of job changes, by building on my talents, by trusting my gut instincts. If I had gone into it with a cold logic, an ex-teacher from the Midwest moving into New York into a business field, I don't think I could have gotten as far as I did by feeling my way."

I asked Carolyn what happened with her relationship with Ted.

"Well, we got settled in the apartment and we did a lot of exploring in the city that summer, took weekend trips out of town, and had fun. We were just doing a lot of playing around together. I didn't want to be domestic, but I had taken up cooking as a hobby. I was used to cooking for my old roomie, who'd trade off cooking for cleaning, so I just continued my habit. I liked to experiment and could make nice things. Ted was a really appreciative eater. I'd love to stick something under his nose and say, try that out. So he did and always liked what I made, and showed that he liked it. It created a nice feeling between us.

"I think in terms of our careers, we have been extremely good for each other. I needed a lot of space and time to develop my new line of work. Ted has never done exactly this kind of work, but he had worked in related fields and was savvy about what I was trying to do. He would sort of coach me. He said he wouldn't take on any responsibility for supporting me emotionally, but he did that, indirectly. He enabled me to move towards being more independent, developing my own interest areas. He was providing me with ego support and confidence I never had before, and it was that confidence that helped me go forward. Also, I would not be at home, I traveled a lot and belonged to many professional organizations that demanded my time. I always felt completely free to keep my own hours; I never felt I owed him time together, or that I should be home cooking or something. He was very understanding about time things.

"Sometimes I would describe something that was going on at work and he'd ask well what did you do? We talk stuff over. Sometimes he'd suggest maybe I was just looking at things at face value, maybe I should consider a different point of view and here's what that person might have really meant. Here's what you think but there's really much more—there's not just one message—there's more.

"I guess the major thing Ted gets from me is the personal relationship. He needed a lot of personal care he hadn't been getting, like this business of having me cook for him. Another thing he liked was that I was physically caring. I'm a toucher and a hanger-on. And Ted is just like a kitten, if you love him with these little attentions, he just laps it up.

"I set an example for him of talking about my feelings, talking about how I want our relationship to be better. I certainly don't pressure him for a commitment, but just say what more I would like from the relationship. And he's learned to express his caring to me and open up more. It's been good for him, good for me. Our communication ability grows and helps our relationship grow.

"Money has been a problem, and continues to be a problem. Ted decided about the time I moved in that he wanted to have a serious go of it as a writer—novels, plays, movie scripts. That takes a lot of concentrated writing time. It isn't really possible to try and hold a job and write at night. At best, it takes maybe three years of concentrated effort to get a writing career started. So he's living on a very reduced income, staying home most of the time in his scruffies while I tear out the door dressed to the nines en route to Cleveland or wherever. I didn't always perceive of that as hard work and it sometimes bothered me.

"Part of the problem was that we really didn't talk about it very clearly at first. I didn't have a very clear idea of what was going on, what it would entail in terms of time commitment and loss of income.

"Actually, the real problem was my perception about whoever has the money has the power, and how the major earner is the head of the household, and all that. It tied into my traditional values, too, about needing to know where the money's coming from long term, and Ted's need not to emphasize that.

"It was hard for me to get past my parents' ideas of what constitutes security and what's the right way to order things in a relationship, you might say. It took two or three years to realize that my financial future was based on me and was not going to be based on Ted, or his ability to bring in a hundred-thousand-dollar movie script. If I were waiting for him to make his fortune in the world, I might have to watch the world go by. If I wanted to have a fortune, I'd just have to figure out how to make it myself.

"Ted always had some money coming in, but I had more. So for about five years, I was partly supporting him. Two years ago he started picking up short-term stuff which paid fairly well but did nothing for his potential as a long-term writer. I felt better when our incomes became more equal, but I didn't like what it was doing for him, or to him. So yesterday we decided we'll quit that stuff; my income is more than adequate to support us both now; I feel Ted's long-term goal is more important.

"During the years we've been together we managed to make some investments in real estate. I would say the investment was seventy percent mine, maybe thirty percent his. Ted tends to compensate for this by doing more work on the buildings. He likes to work with his hands and he'll go out there and paint or sand or scrub—by hand, he won't use power tools—and ponder on his writing. He loves to do it; that stuff drives me crazy. So I've gone ahead and developed an interest in investments and estate planning. He's the real-estate expert; I understand the fiscal stuff. It seems to have balanced itself out.

"One thing that still leads to disagreements is that Ted gets pushed out of shape with me when he sees I'm giving more than I get businesswise—working fourteen hours a day when it's not entirely necessary or giving clients more than maybe they're actually paying for.

"We have our life together; Ted is my drama critic and we see many plays and movies; he knows the best ones to see. We have our friends together; he also has his personal friends and I have several good girl friends, though we have less social life now because my work is so demanding. We're great travelers and we love sports. We recently became legal financial partners; last year was the first time we drew a joint financial statement."

I asked Carolyn if she thought she and Ted would ever marry. "There's no reason to get married—I really don't see a need for it anymore. It would add nothing to our relationship. Marriage is a commitment two people make to each other and that commitment is there between Ted and me just as fully as if we had stood up in front of a church and said something. I remember from religion class that a couple makes vows to each other and marries themselves; it's not the minister who marries them; he's the witness. It's our commitment to each other that makes the bond. And it's the ongoing dialogue, the adjusting of roles, changing and growing through our work. In seven years we could have had the same relationship seven times over, or we could make the same relationship seven times as good—if you follow my thinking. I like to think we've made our relationship seven times better.

"I feel good about talking to you about Ted and me—better, the more I talk! Now we're into making five- and ten-year plans, helping each other make long-term goals possible. We're trying to figure something out so I can be financially free enough to only work four to six months a year, or take off a couple of years and not work.

"The commitment I have with Ted is the commitment I want: I can't imagine a better one. We have a relationship that makes me feel very free to become everything I can become."

Judy

Judy Heintz' relationship with Simon Taylor could be called Relationship as Catalyst. In ways she could have never predicted, it reached into nearly every part of her life, touched almost every relationship that is important to her, and indeed, changed a large part of her life.

Judy and Simon are physicians serving on a medical team in an Oakland, California, hospital. Their relationship began with the sudden death of Sy's wife.

"He was someone I had always liked and been able to talk to, though he was a little introverted. I learned his wife had become very, very ill with a terrible cancer that was spreading very rapidly. People around us seemed so afraid of talking to Simon because of this horrible subject. I knew he tended to keep things to himself; I felt the need to reach out to him, and we became very close. We ended up living together really much too soon after she died—I moved in three weeks after she was gone.

"It was an incredibly difficult time. Simon had a six-year-old son, Jeff, and of course both of them were in a state of severe depression and shock. The death took a great deal out of both of them. The trauma was such that I believe this became the first and only time that Sy let his guard down and became quite vulnerable, and really able to open himself up to another person. He showed me an incredible amount of feeling—in all sorts of ways.

"Right from the beginning he made it clear that he cared for me a great deal. He verbalized his fears and insecurities, his craziness about things related to the way his wife died, hallucinations he had of her coming back, and this horrible insecurity he felt about also maybe losing me. He related to me in just such a human way, rather than the way he does at the hospital, where he has to be in control and in charge. He was weak and vulnerable and he showed it, and didn't seem to mind being that way for quite a period of time. I found it deeply gratifying to have such a feelingful relationship with him.

"I hadn't been involved with many men before. My goal had always been to be a doctor and I guess, for various reasons of security, I hadn't often entertained the thought of getting involved with anybody. I'd been infatuated with various men over long periods of time, but usually they were men who were in some way unattainable, either by virtue of their character or by the fact that they were married. I lived with one man one summer, but it wasn't real like this. I never, ever dreamed of getting married, I think because of the miserable marriage my parents had, and I knew I was never going to become a mother, because I didn't want to be a mother like mine. So I was very leery of men and hadn't gotten involved with many. Except for Simon—for some reason I totally trusted him. Totally believed in him and he believed in me, too. It was a very serious thing, once it got going.

"Simon is not very sociable by nature and prefers family life. So we fell into a very domestic routine, which meant a great deal to him and was something novel to me, since my own family didn't function this way. We would go off to the parks and ride our bikes—Sy insisted I learn to ride, which terrified me at first, but was big with him and Jeff— and we'd go on picnics or down to the beach. Or just sit by the fire with both of us reading and Jeff lying quietly beside us reading a book and eating popcorn. I watched TV with Jeff—it was a real ritual. He was really into *The Six Million Dollar Man* and *The Incredible Hulk* and all that stuff and for him to have someone to share it with meant a lot. It was a fun, warm time, because we'd all be together, enjoying each other. Sy and I both love music and he can play instruments, which I can't. I loved listening to him play the guitar.

"I do want to point out that at first things were not good with Jeff. He's a really attractive, adorable child but he's very moody. He had a hearing problem that wasn't discovered until he was four and he just kind of lived in his own little world for a while. He was really quite spoiled. He never said please or thank you, or anything like that. There were all kinds of things that Jeff wouldn't do, and as I continued living in this household I started thinking 'This is crazy.' His father couldn't discipline him at all and his mother apparently hadn't either. I started disciplining him by getting him to say please and thank you. I told him to eat whatever he put on his plate and not to say, 'I hate you,' or 'shut up,' to people. Simon was terribly upset. He thought I was interfering with his child and his role as Jeff's father was being threatened. Basically, he wasn't very sure about discipline. Jeff got wise and started playing us against each other. I knew it was okay to discipline a child, and I told Simon to get out of the picture and let me do my thing with Jeff.

"He eventually did that, but first we had horrible arguments about it. It was a real threat to my relationship with him, to everything. But I knew if I was going to live there, I couldn't put up with that. Sy backed down when he saw what I was doing worked, though I think he nursed a little grudge because I had been the one to come up with it.

"Jeff and I ended up working things out very well. I always made it clear to him that I was disciplining him or punishing him or whatever because of his behavior, not because he was a bad kid or because I was trying to get even with him. And it was incredible, he loved the discipline. He'd come back five minutes after being punished and want to play. It brought us very, very close. And I think I really brought some sanity into the house—I allowed Jeff to know that it's okay to express himself too. While his mother was alive he was very quiet, but he became quite expressive while I was living there. His parents would withdraw when they were angry with him until they cooled off enough to be very rational with him. I can't deal with things that way—I have to deal directly with issues as they come up. And Jeff learned to do that. Sy eventually gave me credit for the changes in Jeff's behavior. He said I'd done a lot for him.

"This idyllic phase of Sy's and my relationship went on for about a year. And then, subtly, things began to change. Sy began to return to normalcy, and as he got stronger he saw he was being weak and vulnerable like a child again, and he sort of saw me as a mother figure. He began to withdraw. As things started turning around I had a lot of trouble seeing them for what they were, and I kept thinking it was just a phase of his depression and he would soon go back to being the open person I had known. But he never did. His walls began to go up and he became more threatened by me. He would sometimes say things about us being equal, but in his mind equality wasn't equality; he took it to mean I was superior—and threatening.

"I knew something about his relationship with his wife. He pretty well ran the show. He was very much in control. He was brighter, and he made the money, so he had the say-so. In return, she kept a nice peaceful domestic life for him.

"They had a really symbiotic relationship. They became one person with the same thoughts, the same activities. I remember seeing them at parties. They would stand right smack close together, moving the same, smiling the same. There was no individuality there at all. I think in the last few years of their marriage his wife was beginning to get a little tired of it and was starting to take art classes, trying to get away. But he would be a hard person to break away from, because he's very quiet, very passive/aggressive. He started getting more and more quiet and talked less and less. Initially, I would say, 'Oh, my God, what did I do? I must have done something wrong.' When he was unhappy I felt I had to do something to make him feel better, something I was very well trained to do at home. Then after a week or two it would dawn on me, it can't be me, and I would lash into him. I would become angry and start accusing him and asking him to talk to me. He would just back off and was always this stable, sane figure while I was the one out of control.

"So after the first year or so he wouldn't talk to me unless I approached him and said, 'Hey! I've got to talk this out!' Then he would sit down and talk. There's a very sensitive, beautiful side to him, but the anima in him—the female side of him which is such a beautiful part of a man—terrified him. And I kept trying to make him understand we all have different ways and it's normal to rely on different people and that was okay. He just couldn't accept that.

"And he would sulk—have real quiet moods when he would just button up over something I wouldn't know about, something only he was privy to. I found out three years later that he'd been very upset about the fact that I didn't think having children believe in Santa Claus was the greatest thing in the world. I had been brought up in a strict Lutheran church where such ideas were taboo, so the idea of foisting that onto a child seemed kind of stupid. I came to realize afterward that it's an okay thing for a kid to believe. But he held that against me and brought it up three years later.

"And I really loved the opera and started going to it with Simon's father, and Simon went along. For a long time I didn't notice he was always angry when he went. He didn't really want to go. When I finally confronted him with that, he said, 'No, I don't. Especially on Sunday afternoon when I could be outdoors doing something.'

"I said, 'Don't go! It doesn't matter—I can still enjoy it myself.' But he still had to go, to prove something—maybe that he was cultured or something. So here we are, going to the opera which I just love and this guy's coming along but he's really angry. I thought, 'What the hell are we doing here!' But he would insist on going.

"Then he would start bringing up my faults, gradually at first, then more and more. He started projecting his various problems on me. I'm not much of an athlete, and unfortunately that's one of the prime ways he related to people—physically, either through athletics, medicine, or sex.

"Then there was the matter of a house. When I first lived with him, we were living in a suburb where there were level sidewalks and we could ride our bikes. Then we moved into the Oakland Hills and I wasn't too crazy about riding a bicycle up there. So that was constantly my inadequacy. The house didn't have much of a lawn to cut or anything and it was a neighborhood with few children; it wasn't a perfect neighborhood for Jeff. And I was stupid enough to fall for all the complaints about that. So during our relationship I'd try to eliminate these things.

"Then we moved to another district: a big beautiful house—he has a big-house syndrome, he has to live in a big house—with level streets where you can ride a bike. There were tons of kids. I mean it was incredible. After we moved in it was so blissful, Sy outside puttering around the yard, Jeff outside playing with the other children, and I thought, 'By God, I've finally found the answer.' I still remember going to bed one Saturday night thinking 'Ah, this is just great! I've never felt so good!' And we got up the next morning and it was a beautiful Sunday and I thought I would surprise him and said, 'How about going for a bike ride?' Sy got this glum look on his face, and I could tell something wasn't right. But he insisted on going on the bike ride anyway except that I could tell he was really, really pissed about something. Several weeks later I found out the magic thing to have suggested would have been to go roller skating. And there was no single solitary way on earth I could have ever, ever guessed that.

"Well, our relationship clearly was in deep trouble. One day Sy announced, 'It's been two years since my wife died and I'm still not happy, so there must be something wrong with the relationship—with our relationship.' And he'd say, 'It's not working! It's not working,' and I kept trying to tell him it's not just an it, it's two people. I felt like I was losing the only real security I'd ever known—despite all those problems. Finally, I asked him to go into therapy and we started seeing someone.

"Unfortunately the person we saw split us up, rather than working with the two of us together. I stayed with him and Sy saw someone else. This went on for about a year, but it was obvious after a while that neither therapist had any real direction in what they were doing; they weren't working on our relationship together. Neither knew what was going on on the other side. I was in constant crisis over the relationship. So I got a recommendation to see a different guy and insisted we go together. We saw him once—this guy's really blunt and up front all the time, and after talking with us, he just said to me 'What are you hanging on to this guy for?' He said to Sy, 'You know she's interested in you, so if you want to see her, you contact her'—I had just moved out. And I guess the therapist threatened Sy because he almost bowed out of going the second time. He went, but he just sat there.

"Well, I had known for years that I needed to start in-depth therapy because of all the stuff I was carrying around from my home and family background. I liked this therapist and felt I could really work with him. I apparently needed a crisis—and this was a full-blown, gut-tearing crisis of the worst sort for me—to push me into getting some help.

"My family was very . . . sick, you know. Everybody in a nutty way degraded everyone else, just hated each other. I never felt part of any family, and I still don't. But living with Sy I did. In his way, he took care of me and allowed me to love him and he loved me in return, I think, for a good while. That's why it was so terrible to think of losing this relationship. And I'd come to see I really didn't know anything about relating to men. I realized after a while that I had taken on so much of the blame so readily for everything and that related back to my parents, who taught me to do that. I wanted to get myself straightened up so hopefully I'd be able to have a relationship with somebody else someday or at least know what to look for next time so I wouldn't fall into the same traps. I think I'm becoming wiser in psyching out men I might ordinarily back into trouble with, and for me, that's a lot. I've learned an incredible amount from my relationship with Sy and now through this therapy.

"I learned I sometimes related to Sy the way I related to my mother—the same pattern was operating there. That helped me understand both relationships. And it helped me understand how I could be a sucker for the same thing over and over again. I was never sure of whether my feelings were all right—normal, that is. My therapist gave me reassurance about that. The therapy goes into many aspects of my life.

"Well, Sy and I split up, though he kept dangling the possibility of us getting back together. For many years before I met Sy, there had been this incredible void in my life, so big that it was almost tangible. Splitting up brought it all back. The void was being alone, not so much being lonely, but being alone in a way I can't quite describe. It's this feeling of desertion, or rejection—I mean, total rejection! Of my entire entity! Which my mother did a lot of. I mean everything, every little thing I did was wrong and became a rejection of my whole being. Splitting up with Sy was just a confirmation that my mother was right, just as she always said. It proved I was bad and not worthy of anything. And so maybe aloneness meant that—a feeling of not being worthy. Not being accepted or acknowledged or whatever.

"I mean, my main goal in life is to rid myself of this pain that's been in my stomach forever and ever. And to feel comfortable and good about myself. To feel good about my life. If I can resolve that, I really think things will fall into place.

"Well, Sy and I went back and forth for a while. Then he got involved with another woman. When he really gets to doubting himself, it's me he turns to first thing: He calls me 'mother earth.' And it's still to me that he allows himself to express his doubts. He's capable at times of being very open with me on a level I can't have with many other people. It struck me the other day that he's very much like my mother even in the little games he plays with me. I've only recognized that lately.

"For a long time the possibility of our getting back together had driven me crazy, but I finally figured 'Fish or cut bait!' And when he finally decided to live with this other woman it was a relief to let him go. I'm not under any illusions; I don't think we could make it anymore now that I know what I know about him. The rational side of me is free of him, though in some ways my emotional side is still tied to him.

"So now he's involved with a woman who is very similar to his first wife, except that I doubt she has the same personal strength. My impression of her is that she's a princess who wants to marry a doctor—she's very impressed with the fact that he's a doctor. And he's impressed by the fact that she's impressed. She's very immature emotionally, more so than Sy, so he's in a good position to help her. And that makes him feel good.

"He rattles on about her bad qualities. He tells me he can't trust her, he can't talk to her about anything going on in this world, can't talk to her about his feelings, his insecurities. Their sex life isn't even that great—ours was fabulous. But she'll water ski with him. I would have done anything to make things work between us, but would I water ski with him? So he's got problems—I mean he's not just your average Joe Blow—he's *really* got problems.

"It's lost on me why women go off the deep end to marry a doctor. I think on the whole they make poor marriage material. I've been around male doctors for years, and first of all they are compulsive, controlled people who have spent years and years with their nose in a book and all these hours at the hospital. They tend to be immature emotionally, unaware of the working of the real world people live in. Their occupation puts them up on a pedestal and everyone looks up to them. But basically they doubt they're worthy of all this acclaim, yet they don't dare let anybody know they doubt it themselves. So they become even more controlled. I mean, it's an absolute imperative to be always feeding their egos, and I don't think they have very much to give— they're big takers."

I asked how being a physician affected her own relationship with men. "Well, it's a fact, it's threatening to most men, even fellow doctors. It's terribly threatening because people don't see you as a human being. They put you on this pedestal and think you don't want to have anything to do with anyone who isn't on your plane. So you often get rejected. That limits a lot of men who are available. I think men on the whole have weak egos, always needing to be superior people, so you know, it would take someone with a good ego to be willing to share his life with me. And I know for a fact there aren't very many men like that.

"I make it a habit never to use my title outside the hospital. And even in the hospital, if we're out of earshot of patients, I ask the nurses to call me by my first name. I don't like the idea of widening the gap between people who work closely together.

"If I meet a guy at a strictly social gathering I never introduce myself as being a doctor, I'm just Judy Heintz. If they ask me what I do, I tell them. At one time I went to some length to avoid saying I was a physician; I'd play games about it but that caught up with me and got embarrassing so I just tell them what I do. They get impressed and I tell them it's not nearly as impressive as they think. I don't put on airs. And often, the people I meet do very interesting things themselves and what they do seems to me to be just as overwhelming as what they think I do.

"The main thing for me in the future is getting myself emotionally straightened out and possibly restoring my relationship with my parents. I want to work on that and see what happens. I want to get to the point where I'm comfortable with myself and with them. I'm buying a house of my own and looking forward to fixing it up and really enjoying myself there. I was never able to enjoy those houses I lived in with Sy because he didn't enjoy them.

"And I would like to have a special relationship with someone. It would have to be somebody very special, someone who would accept me for what I am regardless of whether my qualities are good or bad. He must be willing to work on a relationship with me. Relationships take a lot of work. One big thing I learned from my experience with Sy is that they don't just happen.

"Something else I learned is that you can't make something happen without the other person putting work into it too. I thought I could make Sy into the type of person he has the potential of being, by waking him up, opening those barriers. You can't do it. I'll never again get into a relationship where things need to be changed unless that person's willing to work on it—it takes two people or you don't get anywhere.

"If I develop another relationship—oh, it's going to be hard work—it's going to have to have a totally honest, totally different basis. I'm still at the point where I'm pretty leery of having one. I don't have much faith. I hope that's just a passing stage I'm going through.

"Having experienced a relationship that was good for a while taught me to value relationships more than I did. I see now that it's wonderful to have someone to come home to, who cares whether you come home or not, who cares what you think and feel.

"I think it helps you understand yourself a little better too. Sometimes it's like living with a mirror of yourself. You see yourself so much better by being reflected off another person. You are bound to learn more and grow too, if that's what the relationship is like. Of course, it can also do just the opposite and become very stifling. Men have many wonderful qualities—being a lover, being a father figure, and all those roles the opposite sex fills. Whatever you need at the moment is right there in somebody you can trust.

"I've grown so much through this relationship and through this therapy. I feel very strongly about getting good professional help, because you just can't do it on your own; you can't see yourself correctly. For years I was just spinning my wheels, always trying with the best of intentions to understand myself better. I never really got anywhere until I had somebody who could point me in the right direction. I love my relationship with my therapist. It's incredible to talk with somebody you know is not going to reject you, who will not put you down unfairly or unjustly, you know, who's paid to sit back and listen and put out. Kind of like a parent I've never had, a substitute parent. I owe a lot to him and to the fact that I do want change and will work hard on doing it.

"Sy goes to therapy on and off but I don't think his therapist is very effective and Sy goes very haphazardly. He's usually too broke because he spends all his money traveling with this woman. And there again, I think that's a difference between women and men; women are so much more willing to face their feelings and look into themselves and I think therefore have a greater potential for growth. Whereas a man immediately after a separation looks for a replacement to fulfill his external needs, and all that. Men are very hesitant to look at themselves; it's very frightening to them. They don't even want to go through the process. To them it's an almost feminine, weak thing to do and they avoid it.

"But you can't grow without it. I really see this in Sy. He's really doing badly and all he does is sit there. So I think, for better or for worse, women are, you know, incredibly superior people; they are so much stronger than men in so many ways. And they have so much to offer, and yet men hold it against us. It's really a double bind, a catch-22. I know very well that the things Sy held against me were all good qualities.

"Besides all this growth and knowledge, there is one other wonderful thing I'm taking out of my relationship with Sy. My relationship with Jeff. I adore him. We get together about once every other week or so and do something fun. And he stays here, and we talk. We are really very close. I've made a point to stay with him, because so many women have left him. His mother died, and he has several live-in housekeepers who left and never had any more contact. He's known me four out of his ten years and I want him to know I'll never really fully leave him.

"His father used to hate my liking opera, but I've started taking Jeff to operas, *The Nutcracker* ballet, things like that. I was talking about Jeff to my therapist and he said somewhere along the line I must have had a fairly decent role model despite my parents' usual behavior. I guess what I'm trying to do is provide some sanity for him. Because he's not living a very normal life. He was living alone in a house with a father who's usually depressed and quiet and who then developed a relationship with a woman who basically ignores him, yet will do anything to keep the peace to win his father—the wonderful doctor, you know.

"So Jeff is really fending for himself. He really is. I've thought about him as I turn thirty-six, being single and all alone in this world. I don't really feel I have a family, but I've got Jeff, I really do. There's a strong mutual bond there that keeps the future from looking as bleak as if I didn't have anybody. If I'm in a bad mood Jeff understands and kind of takes it away. I'd like to find an adult relationship like that!" She laughed.

"Thirty-six is really a new time in life for me. I've had some terrible times in the past. Through therapy, I'm beginning to get at the core of some problems I've carried all my life, and get rid of them. So I really feel that I'm starting all over again, like a child would. I'm standing on sacred ground with a good solid foundation growing underneath. I'm feeling better, doing better than ever before. I'm on the right track—something I thought would never happen."

VI

MIDLIFE:
On Smoother Waters

Diane Harrison

I think Diane Harrison could generate enough energy to light a small town, if she wanted to. An itinerant journalist, she has lived in many large cities of the United States and Europe, plying her trade with major newspapers. Presently she lives in Los Angeles. She talked about turning forty one night in her apartment.

"My very best time is right now—this is just the best time in my whole life. I've never had that deep-down wish to be married. I've been with men I'm very fond of but I've never wanted to marry them, not really. And recently I've become more confident. I think I've always given the impression of being confident, but inwardly it wasn't so. You know the expression 'the older you get the better it gets'? I didn't used to exactly believe that, but now I do. When I was young I always thought that by the time you were twenty-five everything would be solved. Everything would be in place in my life. And I was thrown by my thirties because that hadn't happened and I thought 'What's wrong? All this should be taken care of by now.' But now I realize life is a matter of coping all the time, and I accept it.

"One of the good things I like about being forty is that old classic thing about not having to worry that much about other people's casual opinions and things like that. I've gained a lot of confidence on the job and with other people. It takes an awful lot to shake me now, and that's good.

"I remember a friend of mine saying no one is ever thirty-nine, because as soon as you're thirty-nine you start thinking forty. That was true for me; thirty-nine was the killer, 'cause I kept thinking nine months, eight months, and I'm going to be forty. And it hit me that it's hard to find attractive women over forty-five. That bothers me. I often think of that picture of Pablo Picasso on the beach striding along looking terrific in his eighties. But nobody ever takes a picture of Rose Kennedy striding along in her swimming suit. I think it's unfair, so when I was thirty-nine I kept thinking 'God, forty's going to be all downhill.'

"So I made plans. My birthday is in October, and in July I called my friends in the East and told them my birthday was going to be an event and I wanted to come out and celebrate it with them. I thought I was going to feel awfully depressed.

"I mean, it may sound trite, but I love life, I really do, and I was thinking there's not going to be a lot of time left. I started to realize I'm not going to read all the books I want or travel as much as I want or do the other things I think about. It hit me that time goes so fast. But I'll tell you, when I actually hit forty, everything was fine. I think I did it the right way; I've got wonderful friends. I plugged into my support network, and it was the greatest thing ever.

"One of my friends in Boston had a huge birthday party for me and invited forty people, people I once worked with at a paper there. They all came and threw their arms around me and it was this great big reunion. So it was a great birthday and after that I never thought of being forty.

"I realize, too, that at that milestone I was examining my life in relation to that of my friends. Like my friend Kitty, who owns her own home. She's my age, a lovely, lovely woman, one of the most loving and supportive people I could ever imagine. I wouldn't want her life, though! She's stuck! She's single but she's stuck! She has a beautiful home her father built for her and she's put everything into this home. But she seems to be acting awfully old—if she can't find her keys she gets fidgety and anxious like an older woman. She's gained a lot of weight. And things get to her a lot.

"I maintain part of her trouble is that she's been on the same job sixteen years, and I think people who stay on one job all their lives are just asking for trouble. If Kitty meets a man she likes she's so shook about it that it obsesses her. She doesn't have enough variety in her life to more or less balance things off so she really latches into any man that comes along. She ends up getting very depressed about herself.

"And she's so worried about being worried—and she *is* awfully nervous and tense. She's not as much fun as she used to be. And another thing, she bosses me around her house all the time and I can see she has gotten to be a bit of an old maid, very set in her ways— 'Diane, don't put your glass there, the coasters are right by you—'

"My friend Margie is just the opposite. A real live wire. She's one of the most talented people, a very talented writer, who was with *Life* magazine when she was twenty-three. But Margie will never be happy! She's married to a very dear man and has one child. She's very very conscious of being in stages and doing all the right things at the right time. Like being married by the time you are twenty-two or so and having a home that's a showplace by a certain age.

"I'm almost certain she got married for the sake of being married, though she's very fond of John. But I've never forgotten her sitting out in front of the house in the car talking, because she didn't want to go in to her husband and family. She used to do that eight years ago, and she still does it. She used to think, 'Poor Diane, you're not married,' but last time I saw her she actually said 'Hey! You know, you did it right. You've got so much freedom, so much freedom.'

"Actually she's married to the only kind of man she could be married to, one she really can't respect because he gives in to her all the time. If she's out seven nights a week it's okay. And I think she *is* out seven nights a week. She has plenty of freedom herself.

"Two other very good friends I visited were David and Marlene in Philadelphia, whom I knew at the paper. They were married about three years ago. They are just fantastic individually, though I couldn't take their marriage at all. They're not very relaxed when they're with each other and are on the go individually an awful lot. I don't think they eat together over twice a week. But they seem to make a point of demonstrating their affection in front of people by a lot of touching and hugging. I think they're trying to impress others with their affection for each other, and it's a little overdone. They must doubt it themselves.

"The ironic thing is that they are both writers for the newspaper, but she's much better than he, and if that were allowed to surface the marriage would snap like that! She doesn't want anyone to talk about how good a writer she really is. She gets angry and just turns you away. I don't know how women stay married or even very sane when they don't deal with things like that. The problem is less acute now because she's actually working as an editor in another section, so it's not an everyday issue.

"But her husband can't do a thing for himself and I swear, I wonder what it will be like ten years from now, because it's just getting worse all the time. He can't even find his own shoes! To me it's very tiring—and I think it's hostile behavior, playing like a baby to make her wait on him. It would drive me wild.

"I also visited a couple in New York who aren't married but have lived together eight years. Their interests are totally dissimilar. His activity is watching TV and hers is running all over the city. I think what keeps them together is probably the price of their apartment!

"But I do want to say I know one couple whom I would love to trade places with; they are in their late fifties and are just marvelous. They first met in seventh grade, got married when they were twenty, and have lived together for over thirty years. They share everything and are both so amusing and entertaining, so warm and lovely, both of them! You see how much they think of each other; he calls her a couple of times a day, and of course she has made her life fit his. He's a writer who gets up at four every morning and she makes sure they go to bed early at night, you know, the whole thing. But I couldn't do that now— I'm too old to go into a marriage like that, but it *is* a wonderful marriage. You just glow when you're around people like that.

"Well, I'm satisfied now, but it wasn't long ago that I was very dissatisfied! Before I came here I lived in Dallas and it wasn't a very satisfactory place for me. I felt like I was on a cultural desert; there isn't even a decent bookstore in that town. I felt scared and just developed an unreasoning fear I was going to be there for the rest of my life. I wasn't meeting many new friends, and I think I faced the reality of getting old for the first time, alone. I lived near an area where there were lots of poor retired people. And I had a rather unsatisfactory affair, though I learned something valuable from it.

"You see, I always form long-term relationships with whomever I'm seeing, that's always been my pattern. I attract a certain type of man— unattainable ones, not that they are married, but they are unmarried because they want to be. They love to have me around, and it's great. But this man was something else. I met him at a convention. He was from New York, in television, intelligent, a great sense of humor, confident. It was the first time in my life that I met somebody and went to bed with him the first night and I mean he was terrific, absolutely terrific. Then he came to visit me in Texas and didn't call again for four months afterward, and we had spent four days together.

"Well, anyway, I learned that if women could handle relationships like men do, we'd be better off. That's the wave of the future, for one person to be in one part of the city and the other in another and you get together on weekends. But see a lot of people. Don't get overinvolved.

Be a juggler. Don't be like Kitty who puts all her eggs in one basket and just latches onto one man—it's devastating for her. I mean that's the way one would like it to be, if all the conditions are right, and the man is right; that's the way I've always been. But I don't know if I want to be that way anymore. I've come to this conclusion because the kind of men we meet are maybe divorced and happy, or single and happy about that. And they date a lot of different women because they want to get around, and they don't want solid monogamous relationships that much. And the way to lose them is to zero in on them.

"So you say to yourself, 'Girl, you'd better make sure the rest of your life is darned interesting. Make it so yourself—don't depend on these relationships. Make sure work means a lot, and if you're not doing anything Saturday night, be prepared to go anywhere alone and do things on your own and be able to love it!'

"Yes, it's better to adapt to their style—it's the only way. I believe it goes back to the fact that women were in their little settled nests and men were out there hunting. I'm surprised couples ever really get it together. Because I know how often married men say to me, 'Gee, I'm tired of this'—their married life, their family life. The typical thing. And then they come running to us available women. I don't think the whole monogamous thing is that natural, so I'm going to back away from it in my own life.

"I do meet a lot of men here, but not many of them interest me. Their jobs are not that interesting, they don't read like I do, they don't go to plays like I do. I'm past the stage where I'll hang on men, their opinions or whatever, I'm more than willing to disagree or even decide he's not worth the effort.

"I think I've come into my own. It's taken me a long time, but it's true. I sense my life is at a crossroads in several ways; I'm looking over some of my various premises, looking at myself. I'm looking forward to the future, though maybe I'll make some changes. I've got some new beginnings started already."

As Diane Harrison hints, it seems that the period of the late thirties-early forties marks a transition period for many women. More subtle than the painful drama of the Age Thirty Crisis, and not as sharply defined as some women's crisis over childlessness, the midlife transition may be more selective in the way it manifests itself. It may first appear as a vague sense of unease. Or it may take the early form of a slight depression, for no known reason. There may be a sense of foreboding, shifting, change.

Gail Sheehy describes the midlife transition at length in *Passages*. Not surprisingly, she wrote mostly about the experiences of men, or married women. Among the women, the transition was often described in terms of its manifestations within a marriage or couple relationship, or how it affected a woman's role within her family. Sheehy described the struggles of such women to examine old values, move away from traditional patterns, and gain a stronger sense of self. Clearly, the struggles of never-married women will be played out in a different context and within different roles. Yet both groups will reexamine long-established values, reassess familiar roles, encounter a sense of self that is somehow changing. Both will be affected by a sense of disquiet, upheaval, and renewal.

A major hallmark of the transition is its marked interest in reassessment of everything accessible. Career, companions, life-style, life-strategy, life choices—all may be called into account. On a deeper level, one's life values and philosophic outlook may be trundled out of the recesses of consciousness and held up to a new light. Religious values may be reexamined; a number of women seemed to mark this period as a time when spiritual things took on a new or changed meaning.

Some parts of the midlife transition may manifest themselves as acute crises. One woman described her confrontation with the meaning of the passing of time in her life: "For the past fifteen years I hadn't had a birthday. We'd always opened a trade show the Thursday before my birthday and I'd immerse myself in that and I'd always been too busy to notice I'd become a year older. But we canceled the show this year, and summer was long and quiet and I had a birthday this year—my forty-first—and it nearly did me in!

"I was so depressed! I went into a depression thing I couldn't get out of. That probably was the end of the affair I'd been having right there! I didn't know exactly what it was all relating to except I suddenly woke up and realized My Lord! I'm forty-one!

"So many things went through my mind—is this what I want to do with my life—my God! It's half over! Am I headed in the direction I want because all these years have just vanished and I've never even noticed them! When you're young, you're sure you're going to do great and remarkable things and halfway through life I knew I hadn't done anything that great or remarkable, and I realized I probably never will.

"And I remembered when I thought anyone over forty must be *dead!* When I was in college all these men would break in on me at the country club dance, and they all thought they were so cute and I thought 'Look at that old guy—he think's he's so cute and he's so old!' And here it was, I was that old and it was a real shocker."

Another woman said, "My fortieth birthday set up questions like where am I going to go from here, in an undefined way. I couldn't really say I wanted to do anything different from what I was doing, but at the same time I started thinking what if. You don't want to let it all slide by, you know.

"I suspected maybe I was in a rut. My friends in New York and Houston kept telling me to get out of Knoxville because Knoxville was really a rut for them. It really played on me. I finally concluded it was all right for me to stay here because my family interests are here and my business can't be duplicated elsewhere. Besides, I like Knoxville, so I concluded my problem wasn't geographic.

"My friends and I had joked about a midlife crisis for years—we could put *anything* off on that. It became a catchword joke, a scapegoat for anything that went wrong. Well, this was a midlife crisis I was going through, all right, and I'm probably not through with it yet. And I don't know what the offshoot or upcome of it might be. I'm just sort of leaning into the wind, trying to do whatever is right."

Another woman looked at her late thirties from a longer perspective. "For many years my professional goals had taken precedence over my personal values—the professional ruled the personal—and actually I'd met and gone well beyond what I'd started out to do. I was a manager of a small social service agency, a decision-maker, well paid and moving toward a Ph.D. My parents hadn't expected this much from me and were pleased with my success. I confess I was quite ego-involved in how important I imagined myself to be on the job. I saw myself as a sort of majordomo in my agency.

"I became seriously ill in my mid-thirties—it was a severe muscular disorder something like multiple sclerosis. It threatened paralysis but I made it into a life-threatening disease and asked myself if I really wanted to live and, if so, what was really important to me. I decided my goals were about people and the arts. And I decided when the time was ripe and I had my degree, I'd quit my job. I began saving money. When my position was moved to Chicago I was pushed into action and quit, though actually I couldn't have gone because I couldn't move my degree program. It took me longer to do all this than I had planned. I was thirty-nine when I left.

"I took up a slightly nomadic existence and moved to a beach community near San Diego, got a roommate, rented a cottage near the ocean, and sort of kicked back, dropped out, and more or less relaxed for a year. I lived on my savings and a small inheritance I had. I cut back on my wardrobe, cut down on things for the house, and spent time doing more natural things, like sort of hanging out around the beach. I did a lot of furniture refinishing, reading, and listening to music. I bought a dog and trained it. I was a flop at the arts—you don't do everything you think about, and I never really got into it. Gradually I began to pick up part-time work as a consultant, and now I have enough offers to pick and choose between them. I'm quite happy with the way things are now. I needed a change, and I made it."

There are many responses to the midlife transition. Some women change or adjust their careers. A woman physician I met decided to move away from private practice and became more involved with preventive medicine. She began writing magazine articles, doing public speaking, and is considering designing video approaches for teaching about health needs to emotionally disturbed teenagers. Another woman tired of the competitive atmosphere of the district sales office and became an independent practitioner in a new holistic health field. Another moved from college teaching to a religious life at about this time. Recovering from a harrowing breakdown from wrongly prescribed drugs, she found a new life with the support of a strong religious faith and is now moving toward a vocation as an Episcopal priest.

Changes happen in many ways. A teacher in Indiana in her early forties discovered she felt reborn when she shed excessive weight she had carried all her life. Another found a new sense of self: "Only recently I see I'm much less inclined to take shit from people, not let myself get sucked into certain kinds of arguments, things like that. I think that putting limits on what I'll accept from other people is maybe the most pervasive note in this. I stopped talking to a couple of friends of mine who were getting on my nerves. When they're ready to behave I'll be delighted to be friendly with them. At first that scared me. But as I get older, I'm less willing to be hassled, less accepting of other people's nonsense."

Other changes are smaller and less dramatic, but satisfying because they meet newly realized needs. One woman moved from the city to the suburbs, another started an oft-delayed plan for financial security in retirement, a third adopted a Little Sister. Martha began to study voice seriously; Joleen bought a camera and began a diligent effort to record "my world as I know it."

Although it isn't clear that all single women go through a midlife transition, many do. The transition is like a shaking-out process, a seventh-inning stretch in the middle of life, a time to make some adjustments, take a longer view. It would be interesting if we could know the effects of biology and hormones on all this, because the midlife transition is sometimes caught up with a final concern about childlessness and may directly precede menopause for some women— or it at least foreshadows the beginning of the premenopausal period for most.

At any rate, in time the changing and shifting will subside. I believe a period of life begins then which for many women may be compared to a smooth crescendo. Building evenly and gradually, it will grow into the rich forte many women find in their older years alone. En route will be years of stable, calm growth.

Louise Ide

From the window of Louise Ide's apartment you can see the Capitol, the Mall, and the Lincoln Memorial. Jets roar out of National Airport, taking home people tired from a day's business in Washington. We sipped a Scotch, pondered the skyline, and Louise, a ranking administrator in a federal social service program in her late forties, ruminated over things as she saw them.

"I think one conflict of being a single woman is the feeling you have about yourself, compared to how others seem to see you. I mean, I see that most single women are relatively satisfied with their lives. Compared to other women, we have a good deal of freedom and opportunity to do what we want, and we usually can have material things we otherwise might not have, but at the same time the outside world has this peculiar, almost pitying attitude toward us.

"So there's conflict of having that certain satisfaction within, yet the outside world wonders how we live as we do. There's an ambivalence you don't know if you should explain, or even if it really matters.

"As far as men are concerned, I was thinking the other day about that tired cliché that as one grows older alone, one is less secure. That's just not based in reality. The notion of security tied up in marriage and a man isn't upheld by the example of many of my friends who have experienced great difficulties with their husbands. When those marriages start to go, their security in life is much less than mine. I know the myth of the ideal life maintains that a good woman marries and lives happily ever after. There are still a few women who have these good marriages and I wish them well, but they're getting harder and harder to find.

"My closest friends are all women: my sisters and my girl friends. They meet my need for personal intimacy. We go shopping together, have lunch out, or spend the holidays together. Men are important to me as sources of ideas, someone to talk out plans or strategies associated with work. I've nearly always had a man in my life and I feel women need men for intimate physical reasons.

"So many people assume single women are lonely. They confuse aloneness with loneliness. But I find being alone is restorative, it helps me get my insides together and synchronized, to be the way I want to be physically and mentally."

She paused, and we watched the lights come up on the Capitol dome. "In terms of work, it's interesting, the kind of quick movement that's taken place because of the women's movement. Women of my age are an anomaly. We understand the values and life-styles of the old-fashioned, pre-1960 male—those same ideas were a part of our lives for a long time. That makes us sometimes seem not as much a part of the current women's movement, which is more avant-garde and con-frontive in the way it approaches men. The younger women I work with are much better educated at an earlier age than my generation was, and older women wonder about the competition from these really bright women. I feel secure enough to welcome them, but I sometimes regret I didn't pursue my academic career further, and I realize my chances for growth are more limited than theirs.

"Still, I feel for them. They meet a lot of frustration in today's job market. The public service sector is shrinking; there aren't that many good jobs, which is different from my time, when the recruiters were out literally shaking the bushes to find young talent.

"And once they found us, our expectations were lower. Very few of us thought in terms of top jobs as women do now. They begin with the premise 'why not the top' which is good. I like to think in terms of the top too, but I don't have the same kind of drive they have. In fact, I'm less driven now than I was in my twenties or thirties, when I thought nothing of putting in a ten- to twelve-hour workday, or spent all weekend behind my desk. It was exciting to work for the government in the sixties during the time of the War on Poverty, when we were really out there promoting growth and change.

"Compared to those early days, I can see that my horizons have broadened. I'm more efficient now too. I used to think in terms of rendering specific programs or projects or such. Now I'm more interested in the broader issues, for example the value systems which affect how money gets divided up so that some poor people will never get their basic needs provided for. We used to grapple more with issues like that but the government doesn't even address philosophical issues any more.

"I think a great deal more these days about the social issues that have affected my own life. How could United States citizens be interned during the war years? I'm very interested in the strategy of the Japanese-American Citizens League in getting reparations for those of us put in concentration camps. I go around and talk to law school students about the constitutional issues, how it could be that the

Supreme Court declared the act constitutional when obviously it was not. These kinds of issues concern me more than they did when I was younger.

"I find I like to do things with my hands. I have an almost botanist's interest in plants, studying their growth and what you can do to encourage that. Maybe it has something to do with the fact that I was born on a farm. Touching the soil is therapeutic to me in some way—my potter friends say the same thing about working with clay. And I like to work with crafts, and I'm interested in various oriental arts. I work on my family history.

"We were farming people. I was the youngest of five girls and a boy. My mother died when I was two, and my father raised us alone. We lived in an all-Japanese community in rural California, quite self-contained and cut off from the rest of the world. We didn't interact with American families at all; I didn't learn to set a table American-style until I took home economics in the eighth grade.

"I was brought up to be a typically nice Japanese girl, who without the war would probably be the wife of a Japanese-American farmer today. My father lost everything in the war, including my dowry; he had no control over my life and couldn't really even support me. We stayed in Arizona after our internment ended and Dad tried to farm again. But the climate, the land, even the crops were different, and he couldn't make a go of it.

"I wanted to go to college, and fortunately my teachers encouraged me, steering me toward academic things and away from the pitfalls of secretarial work, which was virtually prescribed for most Japanese-American young women at that time. I was interested in political science and government from the start.

"My dad, thank God, encouraged me fully, though he put his foot down when I talked about joining the CIA. He was satisfied to see I had serious intentions towards my education and career, and never especially pushed me toward marriage. My sisters all got married and became topnotch secretaries.

"That's a funny thing: I visited home once again when I was in my late twenties and saw again my childhood companions, now grown. The men seemed quite desirable, quite comfortable to me, and I understood with a flash of regret how men and women could somehow 'fit.'"

I asked Louise to tell me about marriage and singleness in the Japanese-American community. "Well, in the very early days, immigration was restricted entirely to men, and women came over later as picture-book brides, so truthfully there weren't any never-married women, and I'm sure widows must have been snapped up pretty quickly. Divorce was undreamed of. Later, single women tended to be seen as a backup to marry an older sister's husband if the sister died. There was an attitude of great sadness on the part of her parents—who will look after my daughter when I die? That was tied into not being provided for—in those days a woman had no honest way of earning a living and simply couldn't take care of herself.

"At one time there was something of a colony of never-married Japanese-American women here in Washington. So many had been trained as clericals and it seemed attractive to them to come east and work for the government—it was part of our old proving-our-loyalty-to-the-United-States thing. There weren't as many jobs here for Japanese-American men because of prejudice, and at. that time intermarriage with Caucasians was virtually impossible.

"It's an interesting thing, this mixture of culture and marriage. An Italian girl friend of mine said that in her community, without a husband, you're regarded as nothing! I never understood that—being a Mrs. isn't acquiring an identity, it's absorbing someone else's. In Japanese, the word for wife is 'woman in the back,' which isn't the kind of role I'd want. There is no word for never-married women. She'd be viewed in relation to the next generation, not her marital status, and would probably be called auntie."

She mused over that a moment and went on to speak about the women's movement. "Something else it's done—it's added to my psychic security and freed me from the cautious fears I used to have in the fifties and sixties of being seen as a sex object. Now that thinking is passé—I don't concern myself much about it. Relationships between women and men are more comfortably and freely expressed, without all this nonsense imposed. There's more choice in the whole thing; I now feel you can refuse a man without having him fall apart and I can accept his acceptance or refusal. At least, that's my more recent experience. I used to so fear hurting a man I would put a lot of energy into assuaging the tender male ego at the cost of my own.

"And I don't think women have to be afraid that as they grow older they'll be seen as less attractive. I don't fear this myth, in fact, I'd like to be a model of a woman who refuses to accept a 'used-up over-forty' model. I don't hide myself or dress less attractively or become less visible in any way. But other things are less encouraging. Take work, as a primary example.

"One thing I've noted I think of as the evolution of the old boys' network into a form I call the Harvard Business School syndrome. Men are brought up to have a male-herd interest in making the real decisions—the hard stuff, decisions with real power or importance attached to them. Younger women claim younger men are better at overcoming this, but I doubt it. Men don't use the sexual clichés, they don't make the obvious mistakes of class and caste they once did, but when it comes to policy-level decision-making, it's the same old game. I find our younger male managers are just as bad as their fathers.

"It's related to the business school syndrome of what a good manager is all about, which is to talk a great line about running a good shop and being a good team player. But the old business of looking out for Mr. Number One by any means possible hasn't changed. And the number one spot is measured in terms of the bottom line—their grade or their salary or their position on the organization chart. You can see all this reflected in the management best sellers.

"Something women can learn: I think people don't 'float' to the top, but know far in advance where they're going. Young women must learn the discipline of goal setting, just as men do. That is just as clear to them as making money or becoming president of the company. Women are much more tentative and are content to be facilitators and supporters while they're deciding. They'll make general goals: getting some academic degree, some skill, or whatever. But if you plan to get what men get out of life, you have to have clear, specific goals.

"One of the most satisfying and positive things women can add to the work environment is that we often have the training and background which makes us good interactors with people, and supporters of people. That lowers the competitive atmosphere. I find the longer I work with a group the more trusted I become and the deeper the friendships go. I'm not perceived as cutthroat or expedient. And I last longer—the other types win a few battles, but I hang in for the long run. Women do this well. We can work trustfully and add gentleness to the environment, and that means we're valuable.

"And one more thing. We can know that things need to be changed without being so arrogant as to think we know all the answers of what should be done. And that's hard. We see things are not as they should be, yet the women's movement is not like the civil rights movement, it strikes into people's lives more intimately. We know the need for care for children while mothers work, but we don't know what working mothers and institutionalization do to kids. I feel strongly about freedom of choice, yet I'm alarmed when I hear of women having two and three abortions a year.

"Yes, I see myself now as a different woman, and as a matter of fact, I always have. I knew when I was young I wanted to be more. Perhaps this has something to do with my background, or how I related to my background. In the Japanese tradition, there is an old saying that the most valuable person may never be rich, but will be priceless to those around him or her. When I was growing up, we had an elderly minister's wife—she was a notoriously bad housekeeper—who had the ability to really do good for the community. Wherever she went, things happened. She had a way with words and could give much better sermons than her husband. Her kind meant more to me than the classic role of the minister's wife as a nice lady. She's one of my models.

"Well, I feel there's something noble about serving others, being more than just useful to your own family and taking care of just your own. Somehow you must do something for the community. Somehow I knew within my family that responsibility somehow fell to me, to be more than just a wife, just a sister."

Helen Nardozzi

"I've always felt that inside of me is a person who is far more interesting than the person other people saw and knew, and since I've really gone into painting, I feel this person emerging more and more. In fact, I call myself another name when I paint; I use my name as it is in Italian, which is Elena. And just the sound of the name itself conforms so much more to my image of this hidden person. So I see myself as a woman who is beginning, you know, to emerge. There's a lot of pain involved in it, though."

Helen Nardozzi paused and looked around her small studio apartment. A slender, graying woman of fifty-four, she lives in a neighborhood of artists and students in a large Ohio city. Her home was filled with what interior designers call visual interest; tapestries, prints, and large canvases she had painted covered the walls; a clutter of basketry, ceramic objects, art reproductions, photographs, books, shells, and miscellanea of all descriptions filled every available space. A fire smoldered in the round Hansel-and-Gretel fireplace. She arranged the folds of her long skirt and continued.

"I had an interesting experience last Saturday. An ecologist was giving a course for women artists: writers, dancers, potters, visual artists, anybody. It was sort of a multimedia type thing: to get these different women together and then do things in several forms. So as kind of a takeoff she had us list numbers one through nine on a paper, and then she said, 'Number one, write down "Who am I?"' And you were to answer just the very first thing that came into your head. And 'Number two, who am I?' and all the way down to nine. And every time she asked the question, you were just to give a very spontaneous answer. And in the answers it became clear to me that I was expressing two different people inside of me. One is a person who has, you know, a very good self-image, who is assertive and kind of looking ahead and feels positive about herself, and then there is the other person who is frustrated, fearful, holding back: two different people. What followed from that little exercise was that you were to take your answer and do anything with it you want; express whatever came out, however you wanted to. So I wrote something like a prose poem that really says where I am at the moment, that expresses all those things:

> I pain from the yearning to be free
> As alone in my search
> Unsure of my footing,
> I stumble on this unfamiliar terrain.
> Yet I begin to feel
> The sparks within me kindle
> And I must dare to
> Bring forth Life.

And I guess that's the place I'm really at.

"All of my life I've always felt that I was someone who was swimming counter-stream. All my life. As a young girl, I was shy. And as a teenager, I didn't know how to play all of the games that were necessary for dating and such. Either I didn't know how to do it or I didn't want to do it; I was uncomfortable with it, so I always felt different from other girls my age. You know, one thing the women's movement has done for me was to make me realize finally that my instincts were healthy and what I was doing all that time, unbeknownst to me, was preserving the real me.

"Another thing that made me feel differently from the other girls was that I was on the stout side, and I really didn't have a good body image of myself. I have been working on that lately, trying to rid myself of that old self-picture by working in dance movements. American men have such a fetish for slimness that if you're not in that range, you feel like a misfit. So I compensated for any differences I felt by developing my intellect. I always got good grades throughout high school and college, and I graduated *magna cum laude* from the small college I attended. I then went into teaching.

"I haven't been involved with a lot of men. My father died when I was twenty-four, and I became the sole support of my mother and younger sister. I didn't feel I could get involved because any man would have to take on responsibility for all three of us, so I never allowed anything to happen.

"My teaching job was in a suburb of New York City in a private high school; at that time the public schools wouldn't take you unless you had a master's degree. I couldn't support us on my salary, so I quit and went into the business world. Since then I've always kind of swung between the two, doing either teaching or various kinds of office work. I started out as a secretary to the treasurer of Columbia University, worked in a real estate office in Manhattan for a while, and then picked up a position in a research institute. I began to attend Hunter College at night and got my master's degree; that took three years. About then I began seeing Harold Barnes, a teacher I met when I was at the private high school. He was six years younger than I and rather well-to-do. I was quite taken with Harold, but at about that same time my mother was diagnosed as having cancer and slowly began to die of it. I was really spaced out. Harold came down and made many blood donations to help her. But I became aware he was being pursued by a twenty-three-year-old girl, and about the time Mother died, their engagement was announced. Harold came around and apologized for the timing of their announcement; he felt I also disapproved of the match, which I did. I was cut in half; everything ended at once. To lose them both at the same time was a blow and created a terrible void.

"I returned to teaching, but then got a sabbatical leave and came to Kent State to begin a doctoral program. I think at the beginning my intention was to have a Ph.D. instead of an M.R.S.; later it changed into wanting it for its own sake. Fifteen or sixteen years ago there was still a feeling that if you were not married there was still a stigma, or at least you tended to lay a stigma on yourself, although I think it's much easier now, because there are so many single people and it's more or less acceptable. But getting this Ph.D. was to me a kind of way of compensating.

"But I must say, I think from the time I started working on my Ph.D. I was fighting the program subconsciously, and that fight continued through the whole time I was at Kent State. There were several problems in the whole setup that made it difficult for me.

"First of all were the politics of the thing. I learned that in order to jump the many hurdles of the Ph.D. program, and there were plenty of hurdles, you had to project the image of being somebody's protégé, that some important faculty member was your mentor. I still remember asking the chairman of my orals exam how I could best prepare for that exam. And he said to me—I'll never forget this— 'Meditate on the architectronics of the department, and how you fit in!' And I thought, what the hell is he talking about? What are architectronics? Finally I figured he meant, you know, the setup, the politics of the department and how I fitted into that. And I knew I didn't have to meditate about that, I knew I didn't fit in! And that has been a real problem for me all my life. I talked about having difficulty playing games about getting dates and that kind of thing—well, I have a need to meet a person on a person-to-person level. I don't like to manipulate and play games, because it implies that I'm in a subordinate role trying to control someone more powerful. And then I see that I've become something less. I can't be one of those women all full of smiles, pretending to be happy in those kinds of situations—putting up a phony front diminishes me and I just revolt. I'm sure that's one reason I've never married. I want to meet and deal with any person on an equal footing. And those feelings got very stirred up by the academic setting I was trying to operate in.

"And another thing was the very fact that I've come to realize more recently, that buried within me has always been the artist. For a very long time I questioned it. I felt there was something stirring, but I tended to repress it, and told myself I was imagining things.

"In graduate school these feelings were just starting to emerge. There was rumbling deep inside, telling me that I was not a creative person in my own right; I was just using other people's creativity in this academic pursuit. It made me feel like I was exploiting someone else's talent for my own ends—like I was a parasite feeding off another person's creativity. That feeling bothered me very much.

"And in order to get through a Ph.D. program, you have to develop real tunnel vision, you have to focus all your energy on this goal exclusively. It's almost like agreeing to wear blinders for five or six years, and it worried me. I wondered what would happen to me as a person after all this time of restricting my relationships with other people, letting my own creative outlets go, and just living for term papers and exams and the dissertation.

"The time I felt the most disparity between what I was doing and the outer world was during the crisis we had at Kent State which finally culminated in the tragic shooting of our four students by the National Guard. The campus was so upset that spring, and it was such a grim time—I remember crossing the campus with a friend not long before the incident happened. I could imagine what it would be like to live in a totalitarian state. A National Guardsman with his bayonet fixed stopped us and told us to walk elsewhere, we were too close to their headquarters. I don't know what he possibly expected us to do just walking there, but I remember feeling tremendous anger and being terribly, terribly frightened. And all this time I was supposed to be immersed in seventeenth-century Spanish literature and English romantic poets and such. The whole thing seemed so unreal, and totally irrelevant to me. There was no way I could touch base.

"I finally ran out of money and left at the end of that semester. It's a shame I didn't try to get a teaching position six months before; just then the job market for English teachers became glutted and closed. And, from then till now, I've only been able to find work teaching for about a year and a half as a sabbatical leave replacement in a junior college.

"I've had a hard time getting satisfactory work. I had a one-year position at the world affairs council as a school services coordinator, trying to enrich the high school social studies program. I edited a newsletter to teachers and sent speakers to schools to talk about international affairs. I worked in the school district for a year with in-service education, and after that I just did a lot of secretarial work. When your whole orientation is in the humanities, it's very hard to find that bridge between teaching and the outside world. Everything is so very, very specialized.

"Actually, I began to feel changes just after I lost the junior college job. The future looked bleak; all I could imagine was standing in unemployment lines and the fact that I was also turning fifty about then didn't help any. I was puzzled why fifty seemed like a magical age; I never felt that way about any other birthday. But I got this strong sense of shifting—it was a little scary—and I knew life was going to change. I was facing a clear unknown. I did get in touch with the fact that I had used my head all my life, and I wanted to move away from that and use my body, and also do things that were tangible.

"I still can't get over how it happened that one weekend the museum had a symposium entitled 'The View From Within.' It was about the Japanese Americans who were interned during the war. I knew very little about their experience—maybe it was suppressed in the eastern papers—so I was interested in finding out what went on. The first day a seventy-two-year-old Japanese-American woman spoke of her experiences. She was an artist, and her words had great impact on me. 'Life and art are asymetrical,' she said. 'When we make a flower arrangement, we begin in an asymmetrical way to bring harmony out of the whole. Out of bitterness and discord we emerge whole.' I believed her. All I had to do was to look at her and know that she was a whole person. She mentioned that during the camp years her colors were all somber but now they were bright and clear. Afterwards, I visited her at her studio and got to know her on a more personal level. I told her I had just begun to dabble in watercolors, but I was frustrated and disappointed at my efforts. I still carry with me the image of those gentle hands pointing inwardly and then outwardly as she spoke these words of encouragement: 'You have it within you to bring forth. You are a beautiful person.' Then she traced her finger on a blank page of the guest register and said, 'We have this much space, and we must fill it as best we can.'

"Well, I heard what she was saying very allegorically: we have this much space in our lives and we must fill it in the best possible way. That resonated within me because I was thinking, 'I'm fifty, and whatever direction I'm going to go in, I must start soon.' I was very aware that time was running out, and whatever I was going to accomplish, I had better be about it soon. Really, when she spoke to me, it was like the voice of a prophet or guru or something.

"Later I attended another of her shows and she introduced me to another artist, Ann Hamlin, who is seventy-two years old and just a dynamo of energy. Again, I expressed my hesitancy. Ann is very positive, very much an individual, and she said, 'All you need is the proper environment.' She eventually became my teacher, and much of what she has done has been to help me create that environment and learn to see—I came to realize I didn't know how to see. I who had spent my life in letters suddenly found myself an illiterate in the language of vision. The skill with which I had so facilely analyzed a literary work no longer served me to penetrate the internal structure of a painting. It was a humbling experience.

"So I began a journey into artistic expression, a new terrain. The attitude of 'what would happen if?' seemed alien to me. Although I was happy to explore and experiment with any type medium, I wanted perfect results. I wanted to fly before I had even learned to crawl. I was familiar with the concept that literary figures have autonomy—what a surprise to discover that a painting has a life of its own. Learning to let go—to know that at a certain point one must allow the birthing to occur, learning to respect the work as an entity unto itself, learning how to part with a painting—these have all been difficult lessons. Even more baffling to me is the very nature of creativity itself. Sorting out those feelings which are part of the creative act—anxiety, depression, frustration, anger—from those things which make me feel like giving up sometimes is still a challenge.

"Well, art has been the major growth process in my life in the past few years, but there have been other changes as well. I'm aware that I've been in process for a very, very long time; there's been a kind of steady progression, a sort of development, through my adult life. Twenty years ago my mother died. I was extremely close to her, almost a kind of shadow of her. Our thoughts and feelings were so similar, we'd react almost the same way to the same situations—we had a kind of an ESP, you know.

"As she got older, our roles became switched and I became the parent, and she became more childlike and became very emotionally dependent on me. It was a heavy, heavy trip. I realize now the best years of my life—the years from twenty-four to thirty-four when most young women really blossom—were kind of erased for me because of my responsibility to her. Of course, I have enough insight to realize that was partly my fault; I took the responsibility too heavily and let it interfere too much with my own life. But when she died and my relationship with Harold ended there was a terrible void, and it forced me to realize that I really had to find out who on earth I was—I was no longer my mother's daughter. Nor would I find my identity through Harold. I was thirty-four already and it was late in a lot of ways, but I had to find out who I was and begin to build a life of my own. That was one reason I left New York and came to Ohio, to leave old memories and make a clean start, separated from the rest of the family. So that was my first break, you know, away from my family background.

"Then the second thing that happened was a problem with religion. I realized that little by little I really did not hold to the major tenets of the Catholic faith. It was a gradual erosion, but I became basically anticlerical. I viewed the priest as an intermediary between me and God, and again, I didn't want that intermediary. It was my old problem of relating to authority roles—a real turnoff.

"I wanted to be engaged in my own search for God, or the Spirit, or whatever you want to call it. I think Providence intervened in this search. During my graduate days I knew a woman from Kenya who was a Quaker. I remember asking her what it was like at a Quaker service. She described the unprogrammed meetings, which are meetings in silence. Well, I didn't think much more about it at the time and then about four years later I began having troubles with Catholicism. I was struggling with what I really wanted. I knew I didn't want a priest. My first impulse was to go to a Protestant church, but then I realized there would be a minister there, and he wouldn't be too different from a priest. I wanted to get away from all this ritual, and I knew there would be ritual in a Protestant church. I wanted to do my own searching in a kind of communal setting. And all of a sudden this woman's description came filtering back into my mind. I went to a Quaker meeting, and the seed she had planted in my head just blossomed forth. So that was another move forward, a positive development in my life.

"And the third step forward was this business that happened to me in graduate school. It has been a steady progression, you know, of moving away from authority and controls in the family, in my church, and in school. Over the years I have been working to free myself and find out who the hell I am, and to be responsible, you know, for my own self.

Now I find I don't need the meditation from the Quaker meetings as much because the painting gives me the same centering experience, in fact to a greater degree. Because when I'm painting, I get so absorbed in what I'm trying to do that I blot out any other pressure. It's terribly therapeutic, because those other pressures dissolve and my total being, my total concentration is on that canvas. There's a real stilling of being, a real centering that goes on.

"Another thing I experience is a very gratifying sense of power. In a very positive sense, not the kind of power people talk about like when you're trying to control someone. It's the power of creating something: I'm creating something that never was before! And I'm making it from within myself, from whatever there is in my being! I feel a marvelous high. When you have the strength within you to put something out there—it's a feeling of real power.

"So there's that gratification and sense of power, yet at the same time, it's a very humbling experience to feel you are simply the instrument and the canvas is an entity unto itself. I've become very respectful of that—of the canvas, actually. I often have such a funny feeling, I know that I've done it and feel a part of it, but yet, I'm a part *from* it too. I guess that's because I know it's become a thing in itself. That's a very nice, very good feeling.

"But I'm finding that through this art, I'm better off as a person. I'm beginning to find myself in a way I never did before in the academic world. Because I think you become so goal-oriented that you never really experience process; you never really have to undergo an experiential sense of what process truly is. I love that Paul Klee quotation 'Becoming is superior to Being.' It's that whole difference between a rational approach to living, starting from A and going to B and on to C, contrasted with a more intuitive approach to being alive. What's in between, in the act of being, is what's important. The becoming is crucial at any point.

"I'm very, very much into this art thing and I think it applies to all of my life, that sense of trying desperately to get beneath the surface of things. That's why I'm interested in abstract art, not in associative or representational art. To try and get at the essence and not be concerned about the appearance. In my own life, that's where I'm trying to get, trying not to be so concerned with the appearance of what I am, but more with the essence of who is this being.

"Oh, I'm under many pressures. I'm financially insecure; actually I'm financially bankrupt; I earned just over seven thousand dollars last year from temporary secretarial work. There's always pressure from the outside. It's like that whole question of why I'm not married; people wonder why; when you don't conform, it raises doubts: Why aren't you married, why don't you have a proper sort of job, why are you out there chasing this artistic thing anyway?

"So that's one part of me—the rational part—that sometimes says I'm on a collision course; I'm out of my head; at fifty-four, I should be scrambling around trying to have a certain kind of job that pays a certain amount of money no matter what. I should be saving for my old age. On the other hand, there's this part of me that's really on a discovery trip and says, 'Oh, what the hell! *Risk!* In order to be alive *you've got to risk!*'" She laughed heartily. "And then I break out in a really cold sweat when I realize what I've chosen to do!

"I tell you, if I were twenty years younger, I wouldn't have a moment's hesitation, because truly I feel so much more alive at fifty-four than I did when I was twenty, it's incredible. Many artists say it's the creative act that makes you really live spiritually. That's the way I feel. But there's also that side where you deal too with the fear, the hesitation. You have to have a lot of guts. I feel that either I've got the guts, or I'm crazy, I don't know which. But I tell you one thing—I'm alive, I really am alive and I mean *here* and *now*. Believe me, it feels good!"

Annette Falk

A full moon lights the road through the gentle hills and hollows of Appalachia. It is past midnight, and though the car can only creep along, its driver is eager to be home. Annette Falk, fifty, a community developer, is returning from a conference in Washington.

She has a special aura about her, and I struggle to define what I see. On one hand is the unlined face, the self-effacing manner of service I associate with a nun (and she was one, once); on the other, a contemporary activist, going places, making things happen. I asked her about her work.

"My approach is built on the belief that if anything could be done in Appalachia, it would be identified in the local communities, and any change would be built on the strengths of the people. When I came here, there was little beyond a road, a few strip mines, a general store, a church, and many poor and discouraged people. For about two years I tried to listen and see what people really wanted. And I felt the things they wanted would be the things they could do. So when I found five or six people with the same interests, I'd put them together. And when they wanted a clinic, we learned to form one type of corporation, and when we wanted to have some light industry, another kind. In time, I encouraged the man who runs the general store to open a laundromat; now people can easily wash their clothes. We have a crafts co-op which pays people for their handiwork. We're working on getting a garbage collection service going. Today I look more at things like land acquisition issues and the ramifications of the control of strip mining by these big international corporations. I work more widely around the region: I'm interested in networking. I get called to a number of conferences so I travel quite a bit."

I guessed from her speech she was from New York. "Brooklyn, though I spent my summers at my grandparents' home in rural Kentucky. My parents were musicians and ran a music studio. Mother had strong beliefs about what she thought was right, though she gave my sisters and me a lot of freedom to form opinions and make choices.

"I was brought up during the Depression, when things were tight, and they were just starting their music business. Mother made our clothes, and even to this day she never wastes anything, nor does she want anything just to have it. I'm amazed when I go home and see her cutting a loaf of Italian bread and picking up the crumbs and putting them in a jar so she can use them when she makes meatballs. Now I'm in a society where people don't have things to waste and must be careful, so it's not that much of a change.

"Music and my parents' appreciation for the arts and cultural things influenced me a lot. I remember how out of sync the geniuses who produced the arts were. It made me understand that when people become that unusual they don't relate to the world of people who do the everyday thing. And the pain that causes in their lives because people don't understand. That gave me a certain perspective.

"I joined the sisterhood when I was nineteen. It was a new group, all younger women, organized to work in the rural South. Having been exposed to rural Kentucky, I really liked country living and thought it would be fun to be a sister and help people. I was religious, of course, but I didn't join the convent just to be joining a convent. I was in it for the service and the action.

"When you grow up in the city and are taught by Catholic sisters, you develop a sort of awe for the religious life; Catholics tended to treat sisters as though they were a little better than most people. But in Appalachia most people had never seen a Catholic, much less a sister. There was a historical tradition of bad feelings between Catholics and Protestants, going way back from the old country. They had all sorts of stories about witches and webbed feet and carrying off babies and Lord! I don't know what all! And there we were in all our splendor, black habits, wrapped heads, and all. But we were filled with a frontier spirit, and we willingly plunged in.

"We started out with sort of the usual proselytizing things—summer Bible schools and all—probably because we didn't know how to make other kinds of approaches. We'd affiliate ourselves with the few Catholic congregations around the area and teach Sunday school and sing in choir. But in time we saw it just wasn't appropriate to be thinking about convert kinds of things. We saw how deeply spiritual and religious the people were without any institutional affiliations. When we saw their whole culture and some of the things they were struggling against, we realized it could cause a lot of discomfort to people if we tried to drag 'em into a Catholic church to give their souls some peace. Though I have never lessened my interest in the spiritual side of people, I saw myself more as part of the servant church, the part that identifies with the powerlessness of people.

"I stayed with that group eighteen years and enjoyed every minute of it. I regret nothing! When you joined, there was this sense of giving up your past life and melding into this whole new world. Anything we went into—finding new houses, expanding our work, getting training for our younger members—we did it as though this were our family, our whole world."

I asked her what change caused her to leave. "Well, it's oversimplifying it a bit, but in time the structure we were working with sort of overwhelmed our mission, which was to serve the real needs of Appalachia. Because we were really serious in figuring how to do that better, without realizing it we were breaking a lot of conventional laws about how sisters should behave.

"At that time we were working with Appalachians in Cincinnati, organizing community groups. Well, we had to work at night because that's when working people are available. Twenty years ago sisters weren't to leave the convent after dark. This running around scandalized a lot of Catholics in Cincinnati who complained to the bishop who complained to us.

"And we lived in a convent, and what the heck did Appalachians know about that? Certain areas were cloistered—how did mountain people know that your dining room in the back of the house was a place where other people weren't allowed? It created all sorts of suspicions. To impose those sorts of behaviorisms, mannerisms, and stuff among people to whom Catholic tradition was just so alien didn't make sense.

"The original idea of our founder was that we should not wear long habits, but just dress in a skirt and blouse. She had enough sense to know what the scene was. But we felt we couldn't be sisters unless we looked like sisters, so we put on this long habit. Later we realized it was really in the way and wanted to shed it.

"Well, about that time all these changes were happening in the church. Other groups also wanted to stop wearing habits and modernize their ways of doing things. Well, when we threw our habits off the bishop had a fit, because he thought we were trying to lead the revolution as it were. So we got into all sorts of trouble and in the end we spent more time coping with these sorts of issues than doing the work. After a while we decided it wasn't worth it. It was a question of whether we were committed to the traditional church and the bishop, or to our work with Appalachians.

"Different women made different choices. Eighty-four of us left and of that, forty-four reorganized into a new Appalachian federation, and seventeen remained in the order. I joined the new group. The bishops in the South had no problem accepting us as lay people; they would go along with the choice we made. But to the bishops in traditional Catholic areas like Chicago and Cincinnati we were just bad news.

"Yet there was a sense in which leaving the convent was like a divorce experience, because when I joined the convent I felt it would be a lifelong thing. Some of my friends made different choices than I did, and that was hard. They wondered why we should leave the order to form another organization to work in Appalachia and decided to go their separate ways, finding other work. Some of our personal relationships continued, though in a much different context. About half the women who left the order eventually married."

I asked Annette about her personal adjustment to leaving the sisterhood.

"I remember that sometimes men pursued us, and in the convent that never happened. We were sort of shook up by the fact that someone was trying to make eyes at you, trying to get a date, oh! wow! Some of our gals decided they wanted to get married so they had to relearn behavior they hadn't used for years. I wasn't interested in egging things on. I simply didn't care to establish dating-type relations with men, yet I didn't want to be rude. I remember it as a shock, not knowing how to react when it happened.

"And in the convent we never handled money, and I wasn't sure how I would manage it, pay household bills, but that came very gracefully.

"One thing I didn't do gracefully was getting my own wardrobe. I hadn't been that observant of styles for eighteen years, and I really didn't know how to tell if something looked good, or even if it fit.

"I remember when I first got out of the convent, Mother thought she'd buy me a suit, and I remember saying to her about three years later, 'You know, this thing must have stretched or something! It's so baggy!' She suggested maybe it looked like that when I first had it and didn't realize it. I said, 'Oh! Mother! it probably did!' She didn't have the heart to tell me at the time. And then, I would get a little confused by trying to decide the kind of clothes to wear here; what to wear in Knoxville, what to take to New York.

"Well, after we got down here, those of us who wanted to continue realized we needed some sort of a support system. So, we organized ourselves into CISTA—Communities in Service to Appalachia. We didn't want to be an organization in the usual sense, so to show our looseness we called ourselves a community, and emphasized the service part too.

"CISTA was at first a support group for us in our transition period. We had a little house in Knoxville and people from the counties around here would get together once a month. The transition didn't happen to all of us at the same pace, but as we got more involved with our local communities, there was less need for that. Now we're used to the fact that we can be in touch. We meet two or three times a year and we know if there's any trouble, sickness, or if someone lost a job, got divorced or whatever, the word would get around quickly and we'd know our CISTA friends would be there to help.

"I didn't know I would soon need that support. A few years ago there was talk of banning strip mining in the region and things were tense. Miners were told to lobby against the ban; their jobs might depend on it.

"One night during an organizational meeting, a woman who was living with me and I were accused of being a source of trouble in the area. 'We wouldn't have so much trouble if Annette Falk were run out of town!' someone remarked. After the meeting, we found our car windows smashed and a terrifying time began in which varying threats were made against us. We were shot at—the holes are still in the house. Our windows were broken. A car with a loudspeaker drove by one night with the speaker threatening to burn us out and rape us. The steering mechanism on our car suddenly failed, and the car ran off the mountain."

Annette left the area a few days to think things over. "I realized the groups I had worked with were becoming uncomfortable with me. Some of my friends were afraid to say hello for fear they'd be harassed.

"It was all so tense and awkward and terrifying. I had tried to work behind the scenes, but when the violence erupted, I saw I could no longer be inconspicuous. I seriously thought of leaving, not out of fear for my life as much as for the good of the people and their land."

I asked about her means of support, and her salary. "The local diocese supports my work as a layperson. I'm paid three thousand dollars per year, plus certain expenses."

I was stunned by this answer: Selfless dedication or no, I found it difficult to believe anyone could survive on so little income.

So I asked her about personal rewards. I was concerned about where Annette might find intimate sustenance, the meeting of needs beyond public recognition and the pleasure of seeing work well done.

"There have been years in my life when those needs have been very satisfactorily met. I've found some beautiful relations with people here.

"Like Henrietta Duncan, who works in some of these projects also. Now she is a person who is extremely creative. I get turned on by people who are not confined to certain ways of doing things, and she's so freewheeling that anything can happen and some great idea will bubble out of her. I get so turned on by her, it's like something somebody might get from a great composer.

"We can get together and go on forever. Part of the closeness is because there have been some family problems I've been able to share. When her mother died, for instance, we felt we had to be more supportive of each other; we saw ourselves as both continuing a legacy of service she'd left us.

"The mountain people are wonderful. At first they'll be suspicious of you, but when they accept you, it's total accepting. I was thrilled when a couple told me they wanted to take care of me in my old age. Another man offered me a spot in his cemetery plot.

"The times I have with the CISTA people—we're meeting for the weekend in North Carolina. We'll spend the night with Tom and Susan O'Mara, they're married, he's a doctor, they have two children. They just got a new house and we'll oooooo and ahhhhh over their kids and their house. They'll be delighted to see us, and we'll hear how he's doing with his doctor business and she with her pottery. There'll be two other couples with their kids from North Carolina, a gal from Knoxville, Carol from the Development Council, myself, and Marie, a film maker from Gatlinburg. We'll just be very busy sharing what we do and how we're feeling, how our families are. Most of the women are former sisters, so it's a coming together of CISTA interests and personal things.

"Besides the former sisters, we've picked up a few other members; women working in the mountains with a sort of religious orientation; some husbands have joined too. Over the years, some people have left us, so there's a coming in and going out. CISTA is like a family in some ways, people weave in and out, with different emphases at different times in their lives.

"When we get together one woman always wants to know about everyone's love life." I asked Annette what she replied. "She doesn't ask me. She figures that's not where I am and if I were, I wouldn't be one to talk about it. Everyone knows that for a few of us, that isn't the first thing on our priority list, although now and then, someone will hear that someone else went out with someone and they wonder what they might mean. Sometimes we ask, or tease about it. More often, we just watch.

"There have been a few men I've been very close to in terms of sharing ideas and goals, men I've felt very attracted to because of the wonderful things they were into. But for the most part those men were married, or priests, and there wouldn't be any thought of having a relationship which wouldn't be thought of as right, in the old-fashioned way. Strong feelings develop. But it never moved to the point where I've talked about love, or it's been any sort of a sexual relationship or anything like that.

"I've gone out with one man around here a few times, but I'm very inconvenient for anyone from Knoxville, or other places where I generally meet people. Every so often someone's attracted to me and they pursue it to a point where I don't particularly appreciate it.

"My real appreciation for men is very similar to what I feel toward certain women. My strongest relationships are not built on a sexual thing, but an appreciation for the person, a sharing in terms of achieving certain other goals in life. It's nice to be part of a movement. That sort of drive, that sort of passion is really quite fulfilling."

What about the future? "One thing I'm determined to try to control is not getting scared or insecure, thinking, 'I can't do this or that!' which would force me from the scene as an activist or even into thinking I couldn't stay in Appalachia. On the other hand, I want to be careful that I don't get so possessive of my position that I couldn't move on if something seemed to call me someplace else. At this point I don't know of any place or anything else to go to that would help me make a better contribution to Appalachia. I still believe whatever creative eruption will happen, will happen locally. So I see a value in staying here; it keeps me honest as I move in and out of the scene.

"I also see there's a certain period of life when you're more likely to do the activist thing. The life is physically hard; I wonder how many more years I can keep it up. As people get my age, you tend to think more about the future and want to move beyond the kind of money you can get for doing these things. You worry about the future and look for stability. I try not to think about that too much.

"Yet, almost every time I turn the corner and come up the country road, I feel good about it, and I'm conscious of feeling good. I sometimes wonder if a time will come when I'm not happy to come in. Because I've lived through a scene like that—when something that was beautiful all of a sudden was not, when suddenly people who could share so much found the home we came back to was not the same happy place. That could happen again someday, though I've no idea how.

"But I certainly don't feel trapped here, largely because I have a close network of friends, people who would help me in any way. I note a new kind of relationship with families. As they've gotten more established they've become more concerned about some of us. I'm not sure I'm entirely comfortable about that, though I appreciate where it's coming from.

"I think of our shared concern to look at some of the problems of Appalachia—we see it's been messed over to make the American system work. We're not only concerned that Appalachia gets its fair shake, but also that the country be awakened to the abuses it has laid on one part of our system, in a way very similar to the way America and its corporations have used and abused the Third World. We want to awaken our country and also help Appalachia speak for itself. So whether we're young or old, married or single, in a good position or otherwise, we're all willing to help, we're all working for that."

Judge Margaret Kennicott

She's the person they'd love to have as keynote speaker for the United Way kickoff dinner; everybody knows her name, she's a great draw. She's the person to present the Scout awards; her interest in young people is well known, she'd have something interesting to say. She's the judge young women attorneys call if they need a court internship; she always has twenty minutes to ponder out a placement. She's Judge Margaret Kennicott of Denver, a distinguished jurist, a widely respected figure in the community.

I talked with her late one afternoon, waiting in the back of the courtroom as she finished a jury selection process. She's a small woman, and both the bench and her robes seemed to emphasize an impression of frailty and vulnerability. The darkness of her robes underlined the fatigue in her face. She thanked the jurors sincerely as they filed out. The aura of the court wasn't one of fearsome power, but of human dimension.

We went into her chambers, which were littered with houseplants, small figures of animals, children's crafts projects, travel mementos. She removed her robes, spoke to the bailiff, and drew in her breath, as if going for a second wind.

I asked Judge Kennicott how she saw her life, as a single woman at the age of fifty-seven. She looked up, smiled, and said, "Basically, I see that I have secured what I wanted to have almost all my life. I wanted to be a lawyer from the time I was very young, and I marvel that I was able to identify whatever it was that attracted me to this way of life, because whatever it was, I was right on the beam. It was like I heard this drummer, this distant voice within me. I mean, I never knew a lawyer, so I couldn't be that sure of what they did, but there seemed to be a fascinating aura around the whole thing. I thought maybe I could learn a lot through the cases lawyers take on, and that's true, I wanted a job that would always be interesting and that excluded me from teaching— I guess I thought I'd get tired of teaching the same old thing all the time. And then, I wanted a job where I was in control, not a job I might have to leave, you know, where somebody could call you in and that's it! Don't ask me where I got those ideas, but to this very day those things are the most significant things I'm aware of, and they weigh very heavily with me.

"And oh yes—I thought that if you were a good lawyer you eventually became a judge. That's not necessarily true, but that's the way I planned it. And all these things came to be. I don't want to appear smug, but if I had it to do all over again, I would go through all the difficulties and all the struggles to do the same thing. I'm very satisfied, very happy with my life.

"I never believed I had the ability to combine marriage and my work—I felt I would jeopardize my career if I married. I think now that I have more fixed hours and this sort of thing, maybe I missed a little bit, some in-depth, long-term companionship. But when I look around among my friends who may have these wonderful marriages, I'm not at all sure they don't miss the same thing! But I have no regrets. I would do it this way again. I'm satisfied and happy—that doesn't mean there aren't good days and bad days, but I wanted what I wanted badly, and I'm not disappointed.

"My life is extremely full. I'm normally at the courthouse at least by a quarter to nine and I might never be alone again until I leave, which can be as late as eight or nine o'clock at night. You constantly have people waiting to see you, who need to get authority to do something or have to get some questions settled or whatever. My assignment changed recently to jury work and this is less hectic. I generally go out on the bench as close to nine as possible—we do routine court business and generally we get going at nine-thirty or ten. I usually have about an hour and a half for lunch. Many of my lunchtimes are taken up with various community meetings or meetings here. Running a municipal court is big business. Each judge is his or her own executive; we're all equals and this requires meetings and committee meetings to keep the court as a whole functioning. So I'm here now certainly until five, sometimes later, depending on what's on my desk. Then I go home and I may have as much as three more hours to spend because of extracurricular activities that have to do with law.

"I was an officer of the state group to provide for judicial education and research, and I just completed chairing a committee that puts on a workshop for judges in domestic relations. Sometimes I do lecturing, and every lecture requires hours of preparation. I occasionally do some writing. And it's not all work and no play—I sometimes see friends during the week, we may take in a theater performance or go to a concert. But still, I'm not home a good deal."

I knew she had much influence in the community and had many activities that were not involved with her work. "Let me tell you why that is—I wasn't the first woman judge in Denver, but I was an early one. And our first women judges were highly skilled, extremely able women. But they were of a generation when judges were far more reserved and did not involve themselves in community affairs. Almost all those women withdrew from women's groups and other forms of community involvement when they became judges. I know they had many problems and obstacles to overcome just by having succeeded that far. They blazed an early trail, and that was very helpful, but that wasn't enough anymore.

"The contribution I decided to make was to continue to work with women's groups to convey not only verbally but by working with them that there was nothing different about me at all; that I wasn't a judge in spite of being a woman, I was a judge, and as a woman I thought I brought new dimensions and perspectives to the job. But I also did all the things they did in running a home, or in worrying about problems, or whatever, and there was just nothing that different. And if that would help them aspire, or if they already aspired, perhaps it would encourage and help them get through those dark days when they are struggling so hard toward a goal. So I decided to remain very visible.

"I'm a strong feminist. I didn't start out that way. But I soon learned as a lawyer that I basically couldn't go much further than my team did. So I committed myself to helping my team and I think for some thirty-two years I've never turned down a speaking engagement or some form of participation if I could say yes.

"Originally I worked strictly with women's groups. I held club offices and district office in various business and professional women's clubs. I owe a lot of my development to groups like BPW and Zonta International. Then I branched into community activities that were more broadly based. One of my first was the Volunteer Bureau of Greater Denver. We developed a program that became very successful and was widely written up and copied across the country, and was even used in England. We worked out a system of allowing traffic offenders and other misdemeanants to work off what would otherwise be fines or jail through various services to the community—we put the need of the courts together with the need of community agencies for some help. We're real proud of that program.

"I do a lot of things that are sort of miscellaneous. For ten years I used to lecture at Girls' State, which is sponsored by the American Legion Auxiliary for junior high school girls. It's been a constant joy to me that some of the young woman lawyers I see now got started in things like that. They'll come up and tell me they remember seeing me long ago, and thank me. And that's what I wanted—for them to at least take a look and see a woman in public life, a woman no different than they are. If getting to see me and know me helped them get where they want to be, I want to do it.

"I'd like to overcome the idea that to be in public life you have to feel you're something different or special. It's not true. I don't think you have to be much above average to succeed. The biggest drawback for any man or woman is not to be in the game, not to try. More people fail because they feared to try, in my opinion, than failed because they tried and couldn't do it. It's real exciting if you think there's some possibility and you get out there—you win some, and lose some, but the important thing is to have the thrill of having some control over your own destiny. Because that's what living is all about.

"One of the things that struck me in handling volumes of people in the criminal court is that so many of them only vegetate and drift, it seems to me. For them, happiness is probably the absence of pain, never the positive, affirmative thing. They see themselves as leaves blowing about. I think reading probation report after probation report verifies that conclusion, and that's sad. I thoroughly agree with Mary Wollstonecraft's idea that the whole purpose of living is for the opportunity of fully developing our potential. Men or women. I subscribe to that!"

I asked her how she came to be a feminist. "Well, I came to fully realize what it meant to be a woman in law just in my first few months of law practice. When I got out of law school, I served as a law clerk in the Circuit Court of Appeals until I passed the bar. I finally decided to open my own office. I had looked for jobs in existing law firms. It may sound funny, but I didn't dislike the firms that put it on an impersonal level: 'Sorry, we don't hire women.' I didn't agree or didn't like it, but you know, I understood. What got me was those lawyers that would interview me and play with me by saying things like 'Do you think that you can carry a big briefcase?' or 'What would my wife say if we had to work late?' Their rejection hurt so badly. I had worked my way through both undergraduate school and law school. Law school was touch and go; in those days, you weren't allowed to attend and work and if they found out you had a job, they made you quit or go to another school. So I ran scared! I wasn't always sure I could last it out from week to week and yet I managed to come out with reasonably good grades. So not being able to be hired made me feel pretty bad.

"So I opened my own office. It took time to get business. Many of the people who supported me were little people, too. I appreciated their assistance, but in all honesty the work they had to give me sometimes amounted to cases it might have been cheaper for me not to take. So I appreciated their assistance, but it was slow going. And there were many other problems—judges were not always as unprejudiced toward women attorneys as they should have been, or agencies dealing with me might be slow. When someone called, they would always assume I was the secretary. I would be greeted by my first name while male attorneys were addressed as Mr.—things like that.

"Being single complicated the picture further. I think that single women in almost any occupation face more acute problems than married women have, though married women may well have additional ones that single women don't have. I'm not putting the married woman down by saying that her life is easy, it's not! I know the culture keeps telling her to go home and have children and if the kids get into trouble, it's all her fault! That's terrible! But I'm talking about business conduct. Single women are often perceived as being a threat to other women, and may be suspected as being after their husbands, or something like that. In the past, this put a great deal of pressure on the single woman to dress and conduct herself in the so-called old-maid style so she wouldn't be misunderstood. I think that's still a very real problem today, especially for very attractive women—just by being themselves, they run into problems and that takes away from their professionalism.

"But say a single woman is invited to a dinner party. She's a real problem for the hostess—how does she match her up? She's neither fish nor fowl at dinners and things. At those occasions, you may well get shunted over to the women's side of the room, while the talk I enjoy is with the men—if lawyers are there, it's lawyer-talk, obviously, and I want to be a part of that, not struggling to talk about formulas and dancing classes. I'm not disapproving of that, but it's not where my interests lie.

"As a lawyer, I used to go to the state bar association functions. I was interested in going out to dinner to talk with other lawyers—nothing immoral, just business talk with a few social pleasantries mixed in. How do you pay? No problem when I was a lawyer—everybody just put his money out on the table. Now in the judges' association, this has been made into a constant problem for me. I've been asked to join and I go and when it's time to pay, the men gather around the cash register and it gets terribly difficult. They insist on paying for me. Their wives look at me and think, 'Why does John pay for her, she makes the same money he does and we've got kids in college and she doesn't have any' or whatever. So what I do now is clue one of my very close friends to pick up my ticket in advance and pay it, and then I pay it back, or I may take a woman friend with me and we just go off to dinner by ourselves and we don't have a problem. Or if we stay with the men, it's understood that I would take care of my own guest. These are not critical problems, they're just awkward problems.

"Back in the days when I was practicing law, some of the cases were settled by the men in the steam room at this leading men's health club on the same floor as my law office, and many things would be taken care of on the golf course and in chance social meetings. Women generally were excluded from informal contacts on those levels, but especially single women were left out, because there was less opportunity to invite men for activities or join in things where a couple would be part of the crowd. If a woman were married, she could have dinner parties and such with her husband in attendance, but we single women didn't feel we had that option.

"I must have been in my thirties when I realized I probably wasn't going to choose marriage—my first choice was in favor of my career. Like everyone else, I was at first interested in marriage and planned on it. There was someone very nice—we're still friends. But I came to perceive rightly or wrongly (and probably very selfishly) that marriage was more than I could handle. We would go out on dates, and I would be so tired. Actually, I sometimes didn't even want to go out on that date, frankly, I just wanted to be left alone. Sometimes dates would have to be canceled or postponed because I'd get a call saying I had to go to trial tomorrow and I naturally would drop everything and get ready—like mad you get ready. And I thought, 'How would I handle this if I were married and planning a dinner party maybe for a husband's benefit and I'd get a call to go to trial tomorrow?' Would I call up and say, 'Honey, you're on your own—maybe Mrs. Jones can help you get dinner on the table'? And what if you had children? I had no doubts in my mind that if I had a sick child, I could not go to the office in the morning, yet clients require that. My ambitions and goals felt threatened. I know many, many women combine it and certainly in many ways they succeed. But I could not see my way through and decided I couldn't! I didn't need more problems—I needed rest."

I asked what the decision felt like when she made it. There was a very long pause, and I studied her face for a clue to feelings perhaps her words wouldn't reveal. At length she said, "Well, I don't know. I had wanted to be a lawyer all my life, when it was practically unknown for women. There had been so many problems, all the way from the school counselor who wanted me to become a legal secretary to all the other discouraging messages and barriers society had given me. To keep my sanity, I had developed the habit of analyzing painful or unfortunate situations, and of looking at myself objectively. I tried to be objective about my own decision-making. I think I retreated pretty much to that. I'd think, 'Who says you have to get married? What do you really want?' 'If I got married would I come to resent it, and have that festering underneath?' 'What do you really want out of life, Margaret, *what do you want?*' And I knew what I wanted! What I'm doing now! So I thought it was more honest and proper for me and the others concerned that I do it this way." Neither her face nor her voice gave me a further clue.

I asked what kind of an issue childlessness had been for her. "None! Absolutely none! Though I love kids—I love to play with them. I used to take my cousin's children camping, and my love for children accounts for my work with Girls' State and my Y work. I'm glad to make a contribution toward children's welfare. But I don't think that in this crowded world I have to produce a child to do that. It's a myth that all women have to have children or feel unfulfilled. I don't understand that emotionally."

So where does she draw emotional sustenance, where does the warmth in her life come from? "I don't know—I don't know. I try to expose myself to people and situations that I consider constructive and healthy. Because in criminal court you encounter so many destructive people, and I don't want to go sour. So I work with people, on projects, do my club work—common things everybody does. I enjoy gardening— just pushing the dirt around really, nothing fancy, and I have lots of animals.

"Men are very low on my priority list, except as close friends. I have a number of close men friends I like a lot. But not in a romantic way. I haven't been involved with a man in that sense for quite some time.

"I look to the future. It's obvious to me that I'm entering a new phase and it's kind of jolted me. In all my life thus far, everything was always ahead—sacrifice now for what it will bring you in the future. Now, the future is not as large as the past. And realistically, I doubt that I will progress much further in the judiciary than I am now, though I'd like to! But I don't think that will happen.

"What I'm conscious of doing now is planning a way of life that makes my future full and satisfying to me, for the very first time in my life I'm in a position where I can make decisions geared only to what I want and be totally selfish. Until recently, I had my mother, who was severely stricken with a stroke and paralyzed for over ten years. That was extremely limiting, because I had her at home until almost the very end. It was very hectic, I mean, I had to function around that. Now, I have pretty much the kind of life I want.

"Recently I've had a sense of wanting to learn more—there's so much information I feel I don't know—and once I thought I knew most of the answers! Either I'm regressing terribly or getting a better appreciation of the extent of knowledge, but—oh, I don't know, there are so many things. How do I enrich my life?"

I asked Judge Kennicott what had been the hardest thing for her as a single woman. "I don't know, I never thought about its limiting qualities. Last year, when I handled domestic relations all day long, I kept thinking, 'Oh, boy, such fictions and myths we indulge in about getting married and living happily ever after.' How poorly we prepare young people for marriage—marry the campus athlete or big wheel, marry for all the wrong reasons, and somehow everything will turn out beautifully. It's a terrible thing we do to young people. We never encourage people to decide what they want out of life, and to find a person who meets those requirements—to marry someone with similar desires and capabilities. I used to look down from the bench and see those people that were hurting so badly, and I thought, I never went through that. Yet I marvel how they spring back.

"The best thing about being single for me has been to do my own thing. If I want to work at night, or study, I can do it. And if I just want to stare into space, I can do that. And I've tilted at windmills—that was fun! It was exciting! That was my game, you know, it was I who won or lost or broke even. I wasn't only vicariously involved, with my husband tilting at the windmills—it was me! I've lived my life, and I don't mean it just in the past tense, I mean I've lived it all the way along! *I* have been the participant. And I think it's very important that I feel I have put myself in a position where I had that opportunity, at least, to develop my full potential. I was in the race. And I'm grateful for that."

* * *

Women in midlife; this period marks the beginning of many things; it also marks some closures.

For most never-married women, this is the time two issues we have followed through the tempestuous twenties and hectic thirties come to rest: the question of men in their lives as a heavy issue, and the possibility of marriage—both seem to lose their pulsating quality sometime in the late thirties to mid-forties.

This is not to say that women end all involvement with men; one woman I met, an attractive literary agent of fifty-five, shares an apartment with a man who lives in her building. Four days a week she lives with him; three days she prefers to live alone. He's careless about financial things and far from a neat housekeeper; she's fastidious about such matters. If they were married, those differences would, she feels, ruin all that is good in their relationship. This way she has the best of both worlds. And time alone is very important to her.

But men and marriage as a driving issue? Women do not often mention them as something that rankles. Well into midlife, women speak of these things as something they recall, not something that presses now. As the fifties progress, the sense of only past importance becomes greater; when questioned, women remember with vague difficulty when it was that they were last heavily involved with a man, or why it was they didn't marry; it is an issue which has been filed away in the personal archives of one's life and is spoken of in a distant and sometimes impersonal way. One finds exceptions, but not many; for women who still involve themselves with men beyond a friendship level, the sense of driving urgency isn't there; it's nice to be involved and the relationship is valued for its companionship or sexuality, but the sense of clamor is stilled.

Nature, of course, closes the biological possibility of childbearing in the forties and usually the issue passes to the background. Perhaps that's the key; no more raging of those hormones, the theory once so dear to those behaviorists who thus explained away any and all behavior of women in their forties. While these women sometimes mentioned menopausal effect and psychological and physiological changes, they seemed to take them in stride; the life-upsetting traumas attributed to menopause were few.

So for most never-married women I talked to, midlife is a good time. For many of them, as for men in their same age group, it is a time of high concentration on career and career advancement, a time when professional pinnacles are reached. The rewards for the struggle are good. And many, as we have seen, pour back gifts of service into the community. The altruistic purpose—the larger social good, the rectifying of adversity, cultural gain—sometimes becomes a *raison d'être* no less important than career goals. Midlife women are busy, busy, busy with myriad tasks. If I were an anthropologist and had to choose one artifact which best represents women in this age group, I'd choose the personal calendar most single midlife women carry in their purses, jammed with appointments to keep, things to do.

Since they lack a spouse and usually children as well, one asks where intimate support and emotional nourishment come from. Sometimes midlife women seem taken aback by the question and are not always sure of the answer. Most have extended family circles, close and long-standing friends, work companions whose association is valued beyond the workplace. They serve as leaders, mentors, models. Some claim to have little or tenuous close support. I think many of them meet their needs for emotional closeness eclectically; they pick and choose what they need from where it's available. They rarely volunteer this as a problem; they seem satisfied with this aspect of their lives and often claim a high degree of self-sufficiency: "Well, I really don't know where my support and closeness come from, though I have my family and several good friends who would be there if I needed them; but I get along all right, it's not something I think about much." Are their needs less? Are they not dealing with it but suppressing something very basic? It isn't clear.

They seem like happy women, sure and secure in who they are. They are in control and moving ahead. Compare them with the women described in Lillian Rubin's *Women of a Certain Age: The Midlife Search for Self,* an excellent book describing the coming of age and coming to terms of married women as their children leave home and they move to new identities not tied to traditional roles. These women seemed almost overwhelmed at the difficulties and risks that accompanied their attempts at even the simplest change; their sense of self seemed particularly rudimentary. I was talking to never-married women in midlife at the time I first read Dr. Rubin's book, and felt a wave of both sorrow and outrage as I compared the two groups. The married women seemed so pitifully hobbled so far into life; the never-married women were strong, vigorous, and healthy. The comparison of the two groups seemed to me a strong indictment of the deleterious effect marriage can have upon many women.

VII

I Reviewed My Life Alone
—and Found It Good

Belle Cunningham

Belle Cunningham was born the daughter of the president of a small women's college in the South. She describes her childhood as a happy and secure one, filled with good memories. Always fond of children, she "collected all the babies in the neighborhood" and played nursery school with them, and decided to grow up and become a teacher herself.

She received an excellent education; her father stressed she should be able to be self-supporting and be able to live on what she could earn. While she was in graduate school she became involved with a medical student, Ty Armstrong, who wanted to marry her. She wasn't ready; her father had just died and she couldn't yet meet his goal of self-sufficiency. Ty couldn't wait and married someone else.

It wasn't a crushing blow; Belle went on to have many men friends, but never seriously considered marriage again. Like several other women of her generation I met, Belle describes her singleness as a choice she made to accommodate her professional goals—an either/or decision that apparently was widespread fifty years ago.

Belle worked her way up in the Alabama public education system and was heavily involved in various federal childhood education projects of the thirties and forties. Determined to maintain a comfortable standard of living, she always resided in an apartment or house, "not in a back room on the west side of the house where the old maid schoolteachers traditionally roomed." She was determined never to fear the associations linked with spinsterhood or growing old.

She appears to have succeeded admirably. At seventy-eight, she has the appearance and energy of a woman twenty years younger. She talked with me one afternoon in the living room of her home.

"I retired in 1969 and took off for Africa—Ethiopia, to be exact, the Haile Selassie University in Addis Ababa. I went through the Teacher Corps; my field was in-service education. There had been some question about my selection because of my age, though the Ethiopians didn't mind that, and the fact that I was a Southerner going to Africa— they were afraid I wouldn't be able to get along. And the Ethiopians had doubts about Americans. My job was to teach elementary school principals how to train their teachers. Most of the teachers hadn't gone beyond the seventh or eighth grade, so the principals had to show 'em how to organize their classes and teach school. My, I can't tell you what an experience it was. I got to see Ethiopia inside and out. I got to know the people in a way a tourist never could, all the way from visiting my students at home in their little floorless thatched huts to attending state dinners with Haile Selassie's relatives. Well.

"I found the students were much the same as everywhere—they wanted to test me out and see if I knew what I was up against. They had had teachers from France and Germany and the Soviet Union and Japan, but they hesitated about Americans because they thought everything we had here depended on fancy advanced ways that wouldn't fit a poor country. And I said no! When I first began teaching in the rural South, I had to make my own fire in the burner every morning and I taught seven grades and we sure didn't have fancy things. I took them out in the schoolyard to a muddy spot and picked up a stick and I showed 'em you could write and communicate with almost nothing if you had to.

"And I showed 'em you could teach everything—even subjects like math—with an emphasis on democratic values in the classroom—that was real important to me. Not to just stand up and lecture your students, but to also show your respect for them by giving them a supportive hand in learning to work things out for themselves. I told the dean I wanted to divide my class into groups and have them use a discussion group approach in their own language. 'Oh, no,' he said, 'they would never do that, they'll just talk about whatever they want, and they won't learn anything.' So I invited him to send observers in and we'd try it—and we did, and it was real successful. Teaching those kinds of values was real important to me.

"I'd go out into the countryside taking every means of conveyance available—I wanted to see the missionary stations. And we'd be invited to neighboring countries by government officials. It was all so amazing for one born and brought up in the briar patch! I went to Nairobi and took some tourist trips to Tree Tops and the big safari parks. I met the most delightful Australian girl there who later paid me a visit in the United States and I returned the favor and visited her in Australia. I turned down the chance to go to South Africa out of sensitivity to Ethiopia's stance—they were not in agreement with South Africa's policies and I wasn't either. That whole African adventure—it was wonderful.

"I came home and right away I got involved in a project involving a proposal for a tristate project in early childhood education. I felt if we were ever really going to get anywhere and do something substantial about this on a graduate level, we should do it on a regional basis—Florida, Alabama, and Georgia together. So I was the person for Alabama, and I ran around the region for two years and saw Florida in the winter at the government's expense and had an office with wall-to-wall carpeting for the first time in my life and we worked with the state departments of education and tried to strengthen the program. One of the good things that came out of it was that we set up a state committee on early childhood education tying in the health department and the welfare people—I learned in Australia that sort of thing is conducted through the health department—to get better coordinated and avoid fightin' over funds. I always said we were too poor to fight over money—we've got to work together for children!

"So I still serve on that state committee and I work with the retired teachers and an advisory committee on children and youth. I served as a consultant to church groups with day-care centers, and I'm also a consultant for welfare. But the last thing I did for money was the tristate project. I have found that if you don't draw a salary, you don't have status. Nobody thinks you have a job unless you're makin' money from it. Some way or another, we've got to figure out a way to give status to things people do because they want to do them, because they need to be done.

"Now I'm getting ready to go to England. I'm going over to see the relatives of the girl I met in Africa whom I later visited in Australia. I want to do more than tour and see the churches and historic sights, I want to meet individual people, so I'm going to meet her kin. And when

I travel I see the early childhood education centers and meet all these guys you hear about in the field—oh, oh, one of them is comin' over here soon and I guess I've got to do somethin' about that.

"That's what I do in my old age. I guess I'm in my old age.

"Now that I'm home, one of the main things I do is visit nursing homes. You know, people don't like old people, they're scared of 'em! So I go in and talk to them and find out what they're thinkin' about. Really, it's mostly just being friendly with 'em. Sometimes they don't talk normally, but I'm not afraid of 'em. I'm old too.

"Right now I'm responsible for an old friend of mine in Selma who's going through the last stages of dying. I went down this Sunday and arranged for everything with the funeral home so if I had to hurry away, I'd have everything done. But she's takin' her time so it doesn't look like that's going to happen now, so we can relax.

"Well, the visiting thing and the travel are the main things I do. One person said I'm the guardian angel of the old folks, but that's not true. I visit the nursing home, and I visit those who are living in their own homes or with their families. Usually they are at least reasonably well cared for, though I find when they live with their relatives they still need to be able to talk with someone from outside the family. They may want to complain about their folks a little bit—we all do. Or they just like to visit.

"Now I went to a funeral last week. My ninety-year-olds are all dyin' off; I've got to work on my eighty-year-olds. I don't do much with my seventy-year-olds because my time is filled largely with ninety-year-olds and eighty-year-olds. Well, I went to this funeral last week, I had known this person on and off for seventy years or so. I used to visit her and we knew a lot of people in common. When I'd go over we'd take all these people out of their tombs and dust 'em off and talk good about 'em and talk bad about 'em and when we were through with them, we'd put 'em back in. And then we'd take another one out and do it again.

"Her mind was very, very clear. She said she always looked forward to my visits because we had so much fun. She was a very happy-natured person, she was never bitter about anything. She told me one day, 'You know, Belle, I've quit going to funerals. I decided to stop that when I was ninety. I got bored long before then, so I just stopped. I said to myself, "I believe I'm going to stop now, I'm at the age where I can stop goin'—and I'd encourage you to do it too. It's good for you to stop." But I'll make an exception and go to hers. Another funny thing she told me—when she was ninety-two she said, 'You know the thing that bothers me most is that I can't do anything near as much as I could when I was ninety!' And it was true, it was true!

"But if you're going to work in this, you've got to have some fun. This lady in Selma whose funeral I'm arrangin' is a Methodist and she really dislikes the Baptists. Recently she had a falling out with the Methodist preacher and said she wasn't going to let him conduct her service. Well, she got so upset about the entire matter that she took to calling me several times a day and even at eleven o'clock at night. I finally got impatient with her, so I told her, 'Martha, take a sleeping pill, but before you take it, I want you to know I'm going to get you buried even if I have to get a Baptist preacher to do it!' And she got all excited and she said, 'No! No! Belle! Don't do that! You mustn't do that! I'll take Mr. Kennedy, a Presbyterian!' I said, 'Okay, I'm going to put him down!'" She laughed heartily, and added, "Well, it's funny but it's sad. But I keep workin' on one of my friends about this: You can't let death get you down. If you're going to live and enjoy life, you've got to find the fun in things—if you're really going to live and enjoy things. So that's that."

I asked her how she found her clients. "I work regularly with one nursing home, and I ask around and try to keep tabs on people I know. When I say I take 'em on, it doesn't mean I have to do it, and it *certainly* doesn't mean they have to see me. It's not anything of that type. I find out if they'd *like* to have someone come calling on them, and if they would, I do. I enjoy going to both the nursing home and the regular homes. I'm just curious to see what the problems of old age are and I'm learning a lot. Don't know what I'll ever do with it, though—do you have to do something with everything you learn?

"The Gray Panthers talk about an alliance between youth and old age, and I believe it's true. I have a neighbor, Linda—I knew her when her daughter Beth was born—I saw her come home from the hospital with her husband. After about fifteen minutes he left and I went over. Linda was alone and cryin' and the baby was yellin' bloody murder. The nurse couldn't come for three days, and neither her mother or mother-in-law were there. The baby was just two days old. I said, 'Linda, can I pick up that baby and do something with it?' 'You can *have* that baby—you can just take it home with you. I'm just about to scream!'

"Well, I got both of them quieted down. I'd worked with newborns as part of my training and I wasn't afraid of 'em. Lots of adults are. And as Beth came along, I decided I'd work with her in the matter of vocabulary. I'd always wanted to work with a youngster from birth on language development. So I started doin' a lot of babysitting with her. I'd go over with Beth two or three times a week or if I didn't sit with her, I'd run over before she went to bed, since I could just run across the street. And when Beth got bigger, she could just come over here.

Not too long ago Beth told me, 'Cunningham, you're my next-to-best friend.' And I said, 'That's nice, you're my best young friend—my youngest best friend.' And she said, 'Aren't you going to ask me who my best friend is?' And I said, 'Would you like me to?' because I know when they ask you a question, they want you to ask them a question. And I said, 'Yes, who is your best friend?' 'God is my best friend, but you're my next-to-best friend.' And I thought to myself, 'I rate. Not many people can say that.'"

I asked if childlessness was difficult for her. "I would have loved to have children. I remember when I was very young I wished I could have children and not have a husband. When I was at the stage where I could have adopted a child, the right age and with the financial wherewithal, there were legal restrictions—single people couldn't adopt. That law has since been changed, and if I were thirty-five years old, you bet I would adopt. I'd do it.

"I nearly came home with a baby once. I was in my thirties and was working with the WPA nurse and I heard that one of the teachers in the nursery school was pregnant. I knew there were going to be some problems there if everybody else found out, so I took her aside and talked to her. She was an awfully nice girl; she'd gotten involved with a college professor. I could have killed him; it was his fault, he should have known better than to do a thing like that. She was hiding from her parents. I was about the only person who could help her, to plan with her and help her recognize that the child would have possibilities like any other little person. I tried to work out some way she could keep the baby, but she was dead set on getting rid of it. I worked with welfare and got her into this home. On the day it was born I went up there and that was the sweetest, most adorable baby. I've thought about that baby so many times. I could have taken that baby and that baby could have been mine, as far as love and affection and everything else goes—the only thing I didn't do was born it. But I've seen babies born and I realized that wasn't any big deal. I wanted that baby so bad. I offered to keep it for a while, as a foster home situation.

"I couldn't legally adopt it, so I tried to get my married sister to take it legally and I would actually raise and support it. She didn't cotton to that idea and felt we were evading the law. She didn't want any responsibility for a newborn baby. I was concerned about the lack of a father in the child's life, but I have a number of male relatives I thought could fill that role. I saw all the people who adopt children and I thought, 'My Lord, I'm as good as any of them with this one exception.' But I would have given anything to have that child. Still, I've had my satisfactions otherwise.

"But anyway. You know, we were talking about the problems you have because the society is built up on the basis of the assumption that everybody's supposed to get married. One of the things you have to learn to get through is the stage in which your own nieces and nephews—they're not exactly ashamed of you, but they don't know what to do with you. You're not married, you don't have a husband. Consequently, when they're about fifteen or sixteen, they've been brainwashed that you must conform. Teenagers are very conforming-minded, and they need to learn a little something about everybody not conforming. When they've got a person they've got a little regard for, who up to this time they've adored—then they've got an example. It took my nieces and nephews about five years to get through that. And now they are simply marvelous to me—I couldn't ask for anything nicer than my relationship with my nieces and nephews, and grandnieces and grandnephews!"

I asked Belle what her perspective of single life was, how she felt about having spent her life without being married. "Well, I can conceive of a happily married proposition as being very fine, but *personally* I have *everything* that any married couple I've ever seen has. Like friends—I have more social life than I can handle. Now I know I'm invited lots of times as a second choice and lots of times as a substitute but I knew this was going to happen when I decided I wanted to be single, and wanted to be a professional. I wanted to do what I wanted to do, and I was willing to take the consequences. 'Course, that sort of thing doesn't happen much anymore—things have smoothed out and people are more used to seein' a woman making her own way and they accept it. And of course, now I'm in the company of plenty of widows and divorced women.

"I've had three boyfriends that I kept up with on and off over these fifty years. They were all married, but their wives had either died or they got divorced so they came back into circulation. Some years ago Ty Armstrong wrote me and said he was coming to see me. I figured he was coming to size me up and see if I was happy, if I was content or if I was starving or living in the west room of the back side or something.

"Well, he found out I was living about as well as most people live, about as well as I want to live. He told me, 'I came back to marry you but I don't think we should.' 'Well,' I said, 'you didn't ask me about it and I have no intention of marryin' here at sixty years of age. My Lord, I've had my freedom too long and now you have your freedom.' About a year later he told me he was ill and he died two years after that. But my Lord, wouldn't that have been a mess if I'd have married him only to immediately turn into his widow?

"And there was another old boy up in Tennessee—Howard used to remember me and send me candy and flowers and stuff like that—for instance, Valentine's flowers—he's gone now and I miss those! I'd still like to get 'em! Last Christmas was the first time I didn't get my candy. They don't know it, but my nieces and nephews are makin' up for those kinds of things now.

"But frankly I enjoy men's company, by and large, more than I do women's. One way or the other, I've worked with men most of my life. I was about the only woman in our division of the state department of education, and I used to travel with them. But I kept it absolutely clear that the relationship was strictly a business one, and I've always been accepted by their families. I remember the first time I went to one of the superintendent's parties, they put me in a room with all the women and all the men in another room and I was just like a fish out of water! I know all about diapers but I wasn't interested in diapers. And I've never been interested in cooking. I have no interest whatsoever in the latest casserole—if that's what you call it. Stuff like that bores me to death! I don't see why men and women don't have just good human friendships. Maybe I'm naive, I guess I am."

We got to talking about widows and widowhood. "Of course that's one of the phenomena of my age group—all these women becoming widows. They become single all right, and they're more single than we are because they're not nearly so independent. But one of the things single women can do and sometimes I do it—help those women bridge on over into independence.

"Originally this house was a duplex, and on the other side I used to have a very lovely couple by the name of Johnson, who had no children. They lived here eight or nine years. She was younger than he, very pretty, and very dependent on him and quite possessive of him too. He worked for a local insurance agency. Well, one day he dropped over dead—right there in the house, no warning or anything. She called me over and sure enough, he was gone, and we called the doctor and we got him buried all right. I had a woman friend living with me at the time and we were a little worried about Mrs. Johnson. We knew how quiet and shy she was and we could see she was not going out much. So we went over not long after he died and invited her out to dinner. 'Oh, no, I couldn't do that,' she said. And it was always that way; I could see she was becoming a recluse.

"So more time passed and I said to my friend, 'I'm worried about Mrs. Johnson. I'm going over there and *tell* her she's going out to dinner with us. I don't believe she knows how to make up her mind.'

"So I marched over there and told her to come with us and by

George, when the time came she was dressed up and sittin' on the front porch. Well, I found out that woman was immobilized—she hadn't paid her water bill, she hadn't paid her electric bills, she was just sittin' there waitin' for the world to fall in on her. So step by step I told her what to do.

"I asked her if she found the will and if she knew a lawyer, and this and that. I asked her if she knew any of the men her husband had worked with. 'Why I'd never turn to them—I couldn't do that,' she said. Well, I knew some of 'em and I said, 'They're some of the nicest men in town—look at the drove of 'em that came to your husband's funeral. They want to help him by helping you out. That would make them feel real good, they would be honoring his memory in a way they'd know best. Now get over there right now, because they're one of your best sources of help.' Well, to make a long story short, after three or four months she asked the insurance men to help her in various ways, and they helped her all right; they were just as sweet as they could be.

"Then she had to decide where she should live. All her sisters were up in Birmingham and they wanted her to come up there too. But she decided not to do that, she wanted to stay right here. 'I need to become independent, and how will I do that if I move in with them? I guess I'll stay around someone who's independent too.' I told her she was more than welcome to stay, and I helped get her a job as a receptionist in a dentist's office and that was the turning-around point. She did pretty well, though she said she would have never in all her life tried it if she were still married. At first the work exhausted her, but because she was so tired she got some rest, and that helped her get past the stage where she'd lie awake and think about her husband all night.

"And I taught her how to take the buses—she didn't know the routes. She had never learned to drive, so we sold the car. I'd never done that, so we both learned something. She said the reason she stayed was because she needed to learn and she did. It was a real gratifying experience.

"There were others, too. A friend of mine was abandoned by her husband and spent twenty-five years lookin' for him—found him too, and they remarried. But she spent part of her transition time here with me. Transition is something single women can help married women with, if they want to.

"Well, the one thing I want to say about retirement is that it's a job and you have to work at it like any other! I can't understand people who don't enjoy bein' retired. As you get older, you cut back, of course. I still cut my own grass though I know eventually I'm going to have to give that up. I've already given up one thing: I don't go up on ladders unless there's somebody in the house. It's not that I'm afraid or that I can't; I just think it's the wise thing. I still drive, and I want to keep on driving. I took a defensive driving course twice because I want to feel safe behind the wheel. I want to stay mobile, and you have to be able to drive in order to do that. One habit I've never been able to break. I still do my laundry and grocery shoppin' on Saturdays, even though I know I could do 'em on Tuesday or Thursday just as well." She laughed and continued, listing her upcoming activities.

"Well, there's this funeral in Selma I'll get called to any day, and I have to get my income tax figured out. I'm involved in two concerts, and I have to get ready for those. I go with some older women. I do the drivin', since a lot of them don't want to drive at night. They have these big cars and I have this little imported one, so I go over and switch cars and pick up the women. That's what I do for the concerts.

"I have my organizations. I'm vice-president of my educational fraternity, which means I'm program chairman. I keep thinkin' the retired people should get out and let the younger ones take over, but they're so nice and keep insistin' we stay. I try to do the leg-work for them. I sure remember I used to wish I had somebody to do the runnin' around, pick up the projector or get the refreshments together or whatever, so now that I have my days free, I try to take care of that. And I go to various parties and cocktail parties here in the neighborhood and elsewhere. I'm busy a lot, my time is always full.

"But I tell you," she said, dropping her voice, "I've been so happy. I've had a lot of fun in life. I was happy in my work. Oh, I'm sure I wasn't happy all the time, there were bad times, but I can't give you any examples, not because I didn't have any, but because I can't remember 'em. Regrets?" She looked around the room. "I can't think of any—no, not a single one."

Betty Coburn

Like several other women in this chapter, Betty Coburn, seventy-four, would seem to have the world by the tail. She is a large woman, well dressed, and exudes an air of confidence, happiness—and power. We sat together in her attractive Omaha apartment one Saturday.

"The Coburns are one of the pioneering families of eastern South Dakota. Dad was a master farmer and owned a six hundred-acre farm. He was extremely civic minded and was a powerhouse in the community. All the time we seven children were in school—I was the youngest—he was president of the school board. We had a strong family feeling—achievement was always stressed. Dad said his motto was Industry! He said it was an honor to work, in fact, I think it was almost a religion with him. We were supposed to go to school and work hard and earn good grades.

"Mother was a dutiful wife and tried in every respect to please her husband and make a good home. Her hospitality was known far and wide; everybody called her Aunt Sally. Our family were members of the Church of the Brethren, a Quaker-like group, and at Christmas time, I'm sure we'd entertain at least seventy-five people at various gatherings in our fifteen-room home.

"Dad was something of a benevolent dictator, though he liked to consider himself progressive and open-minded. He held the reins; Mother didn't have any real power even within the house and literally didn't know how to write a check. She had to go to Dad for everything she wanted. The prohibition humiliated her and she wished she could be allowed to handle money. Father said that was his business, and I guess it was from that early conflict that I first questioned the role of women and money.

"I began to take an interest in Dad's business affairs. Because he prided himself on his progressive attitudes and his interest in young people, he let me sit in on bank board meetings held at the house, or go around the state to meetings he chaired of the Rural Electrification Association. I opened the door to his thinking in that respect, and he'd vigorously defend my interest in being there to his colleagues. As we'd bump over the rough South Dakota roads, he'd talk about his views of life. He taught me about livestock and emphasized the role of agriculture in preserving the good earth. I was the closest of the children in our family to Dad. 'You're everything I ever wanted in a daughter,' he'd say. And he was the important one to me, he was my man.

"I graduated from high school with good grades, traveled around the United States some before I went east to a private girl's college. Dad always emphasized he wanted the girls off the farm. I was interested in child development and studied several educational theories which were considered quite progressive at the time. The one that struck me most emphasized that children were to be respected as people, not as receptacles for their parents' ideas or just little listeners, views that were common at that time. Because my father had been so stifling when I was younger, I wanted children to be listened to. I began to think how I could combine my interest in progressive child development with my strong business instincts.

"I returned home one summer and quietly became involved with a fellow I knew locally. The second summer he proposed, and I seriously thought of accepting. True, his family had little status in the community but he had good qualities and I thought he'd go far. Dad caught wind of what was going on and curtly told me to end the relationship—he wasn't our kind. So I did." She looked away. I asked what happened. "Well, I think I was right. He's done very well, and the two of us could have really gone to town. I would have promoted his interests and I think he would have supported mine too, to a lesser degree." He was the only man whose proposal ever meant anything significant to her, the only man she could say she wished she had married.

"I stayed in the Midwest and got my master's degree in child development at the state university. I had decided I wanted to open a progressive nursery school for young children. It was no easy decision. It was the bottom of the depression, and it was not certain how much demand there would be for this kind of service. I acquired a partner in the enterprise who stayed with me only three years. She gave it up saying there was no future in it. I wondered if I should proceed and considered marrying a man I was seeing at that point, but I decided to redouble my efforts and go ahead. I had to know if I could really hack it.

"I always felt that I wanted a good program for the children and if I had that, the money would follow. I emphasized that everything should be top quality, and I always identified with topflight people and institutions in the field. I rented a thirteen-room house in the best neighborhood in Omaha for seventy-five dollars per month. The neighbors tried to run us out but we stayed. On the advice of the president of the university I attended, I set up a board of directors consisting of a banker, a businessman, a pediatrician, a psychologist, and the head of the child development program at the local college. Three other men offered to underwrite me, but I knew if I allowed them to do that, they could also control me, so I refused and built the business side up on my own resources.

"We soon had twenty children. The men were my boosters. I had to know if I could hack it, could really manage a business. I was never afraid. If you want to do things, you have to plunge right in. Doing that made me develop confidence. And I learned to find ways to promote the school. Sometimes I would be a guest on radio shows and I'd talk about new child development methods and relate that to things we did at school.

"I lived at the school, and it always came first. I had to make it go. I had to work around a few fathers who tried to move in on me in a too personal—sexual—way. I was tempted once but kept firm control of myself. It was a loving situation; the man was very attractive, and good to his child, though it was clear he had a roving eye—but it was no undying love and was never totally sexual. In those days, no margin of any kind was given for behavior that wasn't strictly acceptable. I felt any breath of scandal would surely jeopardize—would ruin—the reputation of the school. I just couldn't risk it.

"Perhaps it was rather predictable that I wouldn't marry, my business was so important to me. I didn't think I could handle a marriage and a profession so new to the world and still do a good job of it. My friends would sometimes urge me to get involved with interested men and I feel I would have had an easier time of it financially if I had a husband. I thought couples had more fun. Sometimes I felt I wanted to have a genuine shared joy with someone but I wasn't sure I could achieve that. I thought women in business had a disrupted home life, though maybe that's less true now. I'm not sure women have quite found their right place in life even now.

"As far as being stigmatized at work for having never been married, it didn't happen because my educational background overrode negative implications. I did feel a little discriminated against when I first came to Omaha, I guess because I had the ability to set up the school. But I chalked the people who criticized me off my list. I knew how to make choices!"

The years of building her school were satisfying ones for Betty. The school soon had a full enrollment and a waiting list. "The best part of my life was when I saw the school was succeeding. I had a part in a child's upbringing, and felt I was sharing in the lives of many families. Parents would come back years later to thank me for the fine start our school had given their boy or girl. It was so rewarding. I sometimes got Christmas letters from grandparents praising the school. Once we spotted a health problem in a child. The grandparents put in an air conditioner at the school in gratitude."

The school developed a region-wide reputation for excellence, and scholars and international visitors came to see it and study the methods used there. At the advice of the pediatrician on her board, Betty expanded it to include a small boarding school. She also opened a children's bookstore stressing quality literature for youngsters, and information about progressive child raising and educational methods for parents.

Along with her professional interests, Betty maintained a serious interest in business. She studied ways of making her school more efficient and profitable, and learned to make sound investments in stocks and bonds. She acquired a part interest in a milling business and owns a quarter section of land in Kansas, as well as real estate and business contracts. Today she is widely respected as a successful businesswoman. She conservatively estimates her net worth at slightly under half a million dollars.

Betty retired from the school eight years ago, and faced an inevitable transition period. Relatives had invited her to come live with them in Kansas, "but I faced the choice of being the odd person out, or staying in Omaha where I'm known for my worth." She chose Omaha.

She found her role had evolved from that of an active leader with a substantial reputation in her field who served on state boards and chaired active groups to that of a consultant, advisor, and honored speaker—"with lots of nice little things thrown in." Betty is called both to present honors and to receive them for her long work in her field, and in behalf of community causes in general.

I asked her how she now spent her time. Her list of interests was long; it was difficult to imagine she could be any less busy than when she was working. "Well, I got active with the Nebraska Republican Women and right now we're caught up in a project with other Midwest women's Republican groups on a library project honoring Mrs. Mamie Eisenhower. Mrs. Eisenhower was born in Boone, Iowa, you know. We're collecting books about White House families with a special emphasis on books about the Eisenhowers to be placed in public libraries. We're setting up a small library right in Mamie's home in Boone. Several years ago we invited Mrs. Eisenhower to meet with us and to tell her about our project. I think it's important to show that women appreciate each other. We wanted to help her see herself for her worth.

"Speaking of First Ladies, many years ago I had the opportunity to share a table and speak with Mrs. Eleanor Roosevelt at a Zonta meeting here. She urged me to go into politics, which is perhaps the basis of my present interest in political work.

"Well, anyway, I serve on the membership and scholarship committee of Zonta International, and I'm active in Delta Kappa Gamma, a fraternity for women in education. I have many retired women teacher friends, as well as being one myself, and we work on raising scholarship money and support some state fellowships for women.

"I'm a member of the board of the Omaha YWCA and I act as a consultant for the Y day-care center. I've got a cake in the oven for them right now, and I have to go down there tomorrow afternoon to hear a speaker we've scheduled. Afterward a group of us will get together and talk about the summer preschool and camp program.

"There's AAUW—The Association of American University

Women—I work on the membership and scholarship committees there. I used to do that sort of thing for the League of Women Voters, though I've dropped that. Someone called me about a group trying to promote the use of solar energy; I think that's important so maybe I'll give that a try.

"I have a pretty fair amount of business-related things to keep up with. I must keep books; I try to keep my finger on various trends which may affect my investments, and that involves reading and calling. I talk with my broker and accountant several times a week, and I consider my lawyer a personal friend.

"My family is very important to me. I wrote to my sister yesterday and tried to call my brother Jack—we're very close, we see eye to eye about many things, neither of us has children though Jack is married. We're working on a family reunion. I have several nieces and nephews and I love 'em all. For years I had hoped to have a niece to carry on with the school, but it wasn't to be. I did finance one of my nephews, Don, all the way through college to a Ph.D., and got him established. He's done so well; he's the vice-president of a college now, such a gentleman, so fair and decent. There are no strings attached to my helping him, but he understands I want him to return the hand of friendship to someone someday.

"I don't go to church; I haven't found I have a strong interest in it. Besides, there's no place for an unmarried businesswoman in most congregations, and in addition, I find religion too pessimistic for me! I may rethink that, though. Religion meant so much to our family when I was growing up.

"I enjoy traveling some, and I've made a few trips abroad, to Central America and Alaska, and down to Australia, New Zealand, and Fiji. I hope to go to the Holy Land some day.

"I'm thankful I've got my health and can move around freely; I'm at an age where I see many of my friends declining and facing various handicaps; I want to keep active while I can. My friends always assume I'm busy, they know I'm very involved. 'When are you going to stop running?' they ask. 'When I have to,' I tell them.

"As far as my personal friends go, I have many women friends, though in all honesty I wouldn't call any of them intimate friends. I find it hard to confide in others—I'm very self-reliant, perhaps too much so. I tend to be comfortable around women who are business-oriented also and who have done well at it. I see myself as an achiever and I thrive in that atmosphere. I know there are women in Washington or New York who have done better, but by the standards of a city the size of Omaha, I've done well."

I asked her about her relationships with men. "I like to deal with men on a business basis, but I'm not as comfortable with businessmen once we're on a strictly social footing. I find they tend to ask me for advice about business and that turns me away. And I remember all those years when it was very awkward to be in social couple settings with them. Sometimes their wives would assume their interest in me was something it really wasn't; I used to get tired of them leaning on the glories of their husbands' positions.

"But I'd like to expand my social relations with men—develop intimate relations I can feel comfortable about. I'm not sure I've ever really done that. There are men I still know from school and we've lived through the same era and I'm sure we've experienced some of the same things together.

"I was seeing a man socially a few months ago, a retired realtor. We'd go to a dinner and a show. There was no great emotional or physical involvement. He wanted to be closer but I didn't want that. He'd say 'Is there anything you want in life you don't have?' and 'Where can I help you?' He knew I'd done a lot and I guess he admired my accomplishments. But I wasn't quite sure what all this meant, where it was leading. It made me uneasy.

"I wouldn't entirely rule out a companion-type marriage—it might be something I still should experience. Men still attract me, and vice versa. But the relationship would have to be long term and very comfortable. I have a fear of being used otherwise." As if sharing a secret, she lowered her voice and confided, "There is a husband of a friend of mine—he has many quite desirable qualities and I'd hope to see him if something ever happened to her. *He* is *it!*" She laughed rather mischievously, yet she seemed to feel strongly about this man.

"My concerns for the future are few. I'm secure, and I don't have to worry either about money or my health. Old age will be all right—I think I can hack it like my parents did! My father lived to be ninety-eight. I'm a little concerned about nursing home care and I realize I'm basically isolated here in the apartment, but there's a phone by my bed, and so those concerns don't amount to much.

"I'm happy, and I feel good about my life. I have no real regrets. I have a deep concern about the well-being of others—I want people to realize that. I'm glad to give what I have, and help others. And I'm happy to be a woman today. I've seen women go from apologizing for leaving home and taking a job to wanting to have more information about how I made a successful go of it, and let's face it! I love to brag! I tell them the sky is the limit—in fact, there are no limits if you have intelligence, perseverance, and goals. We women of my generation have set the groundwork for you younger women. Now go to it!"

Hypatia Bennett

Two women from a small Massachusetts women's college told me I should talk to their classics professor, Hypatia Bennett. "She has her views on this subject," one said, bit into an apple and winked. "Maybe not everybody's views, but *views,*" said the other, and they both grinned knowingly.

Hypatia Bennett lives in a section of a Victorian mansion that was once part of a grand estate on the east side of town. She has lived there forty of her sixty-seven years. Her apartment is tastefully furnished in an eclectic mixture of antiques and immediately put me in mind of medieval Spain. A handsome woman—one might even call her patrician—she looked me over appraisingly and questioned me sharply about my work. She said she would tell me not about her life, but about the historical and cultural forces affecting marriage and women.

"In searching my memory it's perfectly obvious I got my role model for my attitude on marriage at the age of nine. It was then my grandfather told me the meaning of my first name. He was a professor of Greek and as a special favor my parents had allowed him to name me; he chose the name Hypatia; she was a very famous person of the Hellenistic age. It seems Hypatia's attitude became my own. She was a famous mathematician, a professor at the University of Alexandria, and she was also known—which I'm not—for her charm and beauty. She had a great many very flattering offers of marriage, all of which she refused on the ground that she couldn't marry because she was already wedded to the truth! That illustrates, of course, the problem of the intellectual woman in all times. So from the first my attitude on marriage was probably taken from the role model of Hypatia; I had no need for it.

"I think the next great influence on my thinking must have been when I was around twenty-two. I was in a seminar with a very great social psychologist. The subject of feminine psychology came up in class, and he said very flatly there was no such thing! I questioned him about it; I didn't completely accept it. He said, 'There is nothing.' There is no psychological difference between men and women; it's all conditioning.' I said, 'What about athletic competition?' 'Given equal training there is no difference.'

"I'm still not so sure: Male hormones, androgens, give men more muscle power than most women can aspire to unless they have a hefty supply of androgens in their system, and some women do. There *is* a difference in the matter of tennis, for example; women's tennis is much more interesting to watch than men's because in men's tennis the serve is so strong. In other words the game is played more by force than by skill. But men don't play that way because they are men; mostly it's because they have been taught to play that way. So what passes for psychology is largely conditioning. People are socially conditioned to feel that if you're a woman, you're supposed to react one way—be intuitive, for example, while men are supposed to be another—be rational, in this case. But it's mostly a matter of conditioning.

"The other great influence or key idea came when I was around forty. I heard a lecture by the great anthropologist Ashley Montagu. He gave a definition of love which is one of the most challenging I've ever come across. According to him, our first ancestors, whoever they were, shed their instincts when they made the transition from humanoid to human—all except one! Survival isn't an instinct, he said, not sex, not anything—except this: 'Come close to a small baby and don't reach out at all; that small infant will reach out and pat you.' Most people don't realize this, because they are busy reaching out and patting the infant. *But we need to give love to other human beings.* To be human, every one of us has to take care of each other. This is the best definition of love I have ever heard.

"This abstract but all-embracing love is perfectly possible for some people. I'm not saying it's advisable for all people. It may be. Perhaps the people who have been able to do this have had special circumstances which have led them to it, special training, special God knows what. But those of us who choose not to marry and are able to give this love need not feel it's in any sense a choice of frustration or inhibition; the word is not even sublimation. Our private lives may be perfectly chaste by choice, we may have love affairs by choice, but that doesn't alter the fact that we may be able to give enormously widened love. It's perfectly possible! Think of Mother Teresa, the humanitarian who works with the abandoned dying and unwanted in Calcutta, or Mufi Murasati, the Turkish woman who achieved fame working for the relief of the devastated children of World War II, or Gabriela Mistral, the Chilean poet who spent her lifetime teaching native children in the rural schools *after* she won the Nobel prize. Some men are able to do it—fewer, perhaps, but Pope John is a perfect example. These people have a great affectionate concern for humanity. It's not affectionate in the normal limited sense of the word. The idea that marriage is necessary for someone's fulfillment is conditioned; pure social conditioning.

"You see, I question our Western idea that you can be an individual separate from the rest of humankind. I don't see any individual existence apart from the rest of the entire human race. I think of feral children who grew up in the wild—they're not human! Even though they are born from human parents, they have no language, they don't eat food as humans do, there's nothing human about them. Therefore you can't be circumscribed—closed in—as an individual. Everything we have is a part of the entire fabric of human culture.

"I never had much notion of myself as belonging to this or that sex— I never had a very developed sense of sexual identity. I once heard Dr. Mary Calderone, the sex educator, speak on this subject: She said sexual identity is taught! Sexual behavior is taught! All of it! Like walking and feeding—now we're coming back to Ashley Montagu—all such beahvior is taught. Obviously there is a necessity in the human race for sexual behavior, simply for the perpetuation of the species. But sex in the human species is extraordinarily wasteful; it's biologically wasteful and has received a really exaggerated attention in our culture.

"Our sex customs are comparable to the ancient Romans' attitude on food. They subscribed to the notion that you eat food for pleasure—a corrupt and ignorant idea. They ate a meal and then took an emetic, vomited and ate again. Can't you just imagine a social survey in ancient Rome: 'And how many times did you disgorge this week?' and 'How much pleasure did you have from your food?' You'd think we'd know better now, but we handle sex in much the same way. Sex is totally exaggerated in our society. It has a role, not nearly as important as many think; eating is more important, sleeping is important, playing is important, work is important. But sex is exaggerated out of all proportion.

"In Crete, before the rise of Greece, marriage was not a permanent condition. It was a brief connection for the sake of having children; women had equally high social status, held all sorts of positions as we see them in the bold frescoes—there are both women and men in athletics, in anything. Some have speculated that the origin of marriage as chattel slavery comes from the invention of iron. Before that, you had bronze which limited fighting to an elite. However, when iron was invented a large warrior class sprang up who brought home booty from wars. The idea was to lock up the treasure and from that people learned to lock up what they had, including their wives and children, because you've got to keep what you've got! This is believed to be the origin of the cloistered notion of marriage.

"I once heard a woman lecturer say she thought the golden age of Greece was the noblest time in human history. I mentally spat at the thought! Because to be in a position like hers, an intellectual woman in the Golden Age of Greece, you would have to be a hetaera, a high-grade prostitute. The hetaerae were the emancipated women. You had a limited choice; you could be a chattel slave wife, all locked up—you didn't go out, you didn't even go to the marketplace, you know, you were just nothing. You were property yourself and were there to guard whatever else had been acquired.

"But if you had some education, if you wanted to be somebody, you had to be a high-grade prostitute. So I wondered if the lecturer would have really enjoyed life there. After all, the Golden Age of Greece rested on the labor of slaves at the silver mines at Laurium. Greek society was really plenty revolting.

"The enforced enclosure of women caused women to develop and master nurturing functions. Not because they are less selfish than men, but because it was forced on them, and they learned it. They were deprived of other things. And enclosure has to do with the fact that men, not having been enclosed or required from childhood to learn nurturing skills, had to learn to do things by their wits, and they still tend to do things with their fists. The enclosure of women was more or less also to protect them from marauding bands of men, who were less evolved. You see, it's the old story of conditioning once again.

"There was a whole period in the Middle Ages where the women ruled abbeys and used to ordain priests, so women had the function of bishops. The Council of Trent changed all that and the position of women altered very greatly. There have been repeated periods in Spain where there were intellectual women and women rulers. My most amusing illustration of how unnatural the condition of women has been in many ages of our Western culture—Eastern is bad too—are the women in Shakespeare's plays. Of course, they were not played by women but by male transvestites. The sopranos in opera, right up to the time of Rossini, were castrated males. Women were not considered fit to sing soprano or play women's parts. There was nothing wrong with castrated males singing soprano parts, but you certainly couldn't have women singing them, women weren't fit for anything! You can see that is exceedingly unnatural and artificial; I find every taboo against women in various occupations laughable and exceedingly cruel and also unnatural and unreasonable.

"A friend of mind who had researched the subject once told me 'There is no trait which is considered feminine in one culture that isn't considered masculine in another.' Weeping is feminine in our culture, but in other cultures only men will do it. We have wrongly conditioned men to be brutal and women to be subservient; and in their conditioned traits, women show a certain superior ability to show emotion, to feel compassion—the worthwhile things—but they have lost aggressiveness, the urge to develop themselves and be themselves. Men have been made overly aggressive and have lost other skills. Basically, there should be no segregation of traits; the traits of self-assertion and consideration for others must be developed equally. I look forward to the day when men can learn the so-called feminine virtues and women can learn the so-called masculine virtues, and we can stop being half-people.

"As it stands today, marriage is a very confused institution. Our society no longer gives opportunities for teamwork marriage. The good marriage today is a toughy! Some particular cases I would call *mariage d'art*—they put the teamwork idea into effect.

"Joan Sutherland, the great Australian diva, is married to Richard Bonynge, a conductor and musicologist. He always conducts when she sings; her career rests on his skill as a conductor and his knowledge of the flower *bel canto*. The tragedy of Maria Callas was that her husband was a businessman. If she had married a conductor, they could have built their lives together.

"Katherine Cornell was another perfect example, married to the playwright Guthrie McClintic. There again you have the complementary profession, in other words, the mutual helpmate. Not just the wife helping the husband. The wife helps the husband, the husband helps the wife. Cornell and McClintic had a very happy marriage. They had a brownstone house with three stories. She had her own floor, and he had his, and they had a mutual floor. They maintained their integrity, their privacy and their personalities, and their shared life.

"But I wouldn't wipe out marriage as an institution; not at all! There has to be some order, some continuity, some emotional security in human relations. I think marriage has some real and perhaps marvelous possibilities. But it's in a very bad state right now, very bad. Because of all these hangovers.

"Probably the best kind of human relationship is the small group of people in a rather close-knit but not totally intimate relationship who share large parts of their lives. Our notion of the nuclear family is very limited and very limiting. And too, there is something in the illusion of separateness that is very wrong: the notion of 'I'm an individual, complete unto myself.' But the idea of just a couple and their children being an all-inclusive supportive group is too limited, and marriage suffers very badly. In an extended family there's not that emphasis.

"And there's always the question of child-rearing—we have to have better methods than we have now. Children need the love of both parents, and men need the value of the experience of being with children, but I think in the future a family will be seen as a group of people loosely connected to each other who can be called upon to support each other. The main problem is to find a system for nurturing the children which does not fall so exclusively on one woman and one marriage; aunts, uncles, grandparents, friends, neighbors, other couples could put several groups of children together and look after the whole group. With the family as it is now, it's still cloistered, still closed in. Everything is 'mine,' 'ours,' closed in.

"So I hope with the proper attitudes of women, and the proper development of men—and a changing of the traits that are wrongly attributed to each sex—I think marriage could have a very good future, once it comes through this bad period.

"But I do think people should be able to say no to marriage!"

Marian McClelland

High above San Francisco Bay on the downslope of the Hayward Hills is the neat pine-paneled-cum-maple bungalow of Marian McClelland. I knew before I met her that she was an activist for senior citizens and women, and that her life work had been affected by her singleness. As I drove to her home, I couldn't help wondering how. She greeted me at the curb; a smoky-haired woman in her early sixties, she was dressed in a trim seersucker suit. She led me into the house, and we settled ourselves among the welter of correspondence, bulletins, newspapers, and the paraphernalia of a busy woman. Her cat, Jerry, luxuriated on Marian's lap, exuding the comfortable assurance that comes from being The Cat of the household.

"Retired? You might rightfully say I'm *double* retired! The day I walked off my job, I not only left my position, I left my security clearance far, far behind. I had been a cryptographer decoding secret documents in a national security agency for twenty-six years. Even today, the work is considered so specialized and secret that I can't say any more about it than that. So when I retired, I was released for what has turned out to be a very expansive and fulfilling time in my life.

"I was the second of five children born and raised in a company lumber mill town in Idaho. It wasn't an atmosphere of what you'd call grinding poverty, but a sort of poorness, a pervasive poorness, blighting everything. The Company held everything and everyone in its grip. The roof over your head was Company, the debt outstanding at the grocery store was owed to the Company, your job and your whole way of life could be terminated in a minute if the Company said so. There wasn't any union or any kind of protection against the power of the mill owners.

"It was an austere existence, strongly flavored with the stringent messages of fundamentalist Protestantism: Believe in God and work hard, live in humility and piety. They told us to expect suffering in this world and bear it silently. Children were told not to talk about unpleasant things, and quarrels and arguments were never allowed. The need for self-control was constantly emphasized.

"When I was about ten, our family suffered financial reverses and Mother went back to work in the office of the Company. She typed and filed all day, and came home to face a demanding household and a husband who never helped. In time, she developed an attitude of defeat and martyrdom."

But sometimes the tedium of small-town living was broken by the appearance of a lively guest. "Mother's sister, Elena, would arrive. She was single and seemed like a woman from another world to me. She had an interesting job, traveled, and always wore bright-colored clothes. She and Mother would sit up half the night, Mother drinking in Elena's tales. Mother's own life must have seemed bitter by comparison. She would repeat Elena's doings to her friends for months afterward. I know both Mother and Aunt Elena influenced me to remain single.

"You know, this story of my aunt as a role model came to an interesting ending. Mother died some years after I left home, and Dad married Elena. The marriage lasted about ten years, and then Dad died. I went home to help settle the estate, and I was shocked to discover how much Elena had regressed. She simply couldn't cope. She had let her driver's license expire and forgot how to drive. She didn't know where to pay the utility bills, or how to balance her checkbook. I remembered her as a capable, clever businesswoman and I really thought her regression was because she had married and let herself become dependent on my domineering father. I swore I would never let myself get into such a state.

"The Depression struck when I was in my early twenties; it hit our family and the region hard. Life was grim and we thought constantly about financial security—better use your wits and look out for yourself, hang on to whatever little security could be had. I got a job as a life insurance accounting clerk for ten dollars per week and eventually became supervisor of the department. When the war broke out, I left Idaho to join the Women's Army Corps.

"I joined the WACs for some of the usual reasons—war fever, the possibility of travel, job training—but I was also motivated by my health. For some time I had had the general sense of not feeling well. I had trouble sleeping, and a poor appetite. I felt very anxious at times, in sort of a vague, free-floating way, but I couldn't put my finger on it The doctor at home had checked me out but couldn't find anything wrong. These spells would come and go, and they worried me. With more than half the doctors in the country in the military, I figured somebody there could get to the bottom of it.

"I liked basic training, being outdoors and moving around, and I felt better than I had for a long time. Then I got an office job at a large base. I suddenly began to develop terrific headaches and felt awfully jumpy. I woke up paralyzed one morning—I couldn't get out of bed. Finally, the problem was diagnosed as being emotional in nature, and I was sent off for a long rest in a hospital ward. I stole a look at my chart one day, and it said I was psychoneurotic.

"I was given a medical discharge and reported to the Veteran's Administration Hospital as an outpatient, where I talked with a psychotherapist. He encouraged me to talk about my childhood. That was hard work, because I had blocked out much of my early past. But little by little I dredged up my childhood events, especially fights with my brother, who now appeared before me in dreams of death.

"We talked about growing up poor and my belief in the need for endless self-control. We talked about the denials and repressions that were part of everything. And the Depression. And the constant struggle. Learning to express my feelings was one of the best things that ever happened to me and my life smoothed out some. That experience taught me the value of psychiatry."

In 1948 Marian was looking for a new career direction and applied for training as a cryptographer at a national security agency. She was surprised by her acceptance for training, because she thought her history of psychological treatment might interfere with her receiving the extremely high security rating the job required. Apparently, it didn't matter. The rating meant leading a highly restricted and circumspect life: no unorthodox opinions or beliefs; no unusual friends; no behavior that could cause concern in the security-conscious era of the Cold War.

"You might say I had succeeded in putting myself in a nice bind. After I passed my original clearance, I had to be reviewed regularly. If I didn't pass, I could be fired with no recourse. They simply called you to the front office, told you you were dismissed, and you weren't even allowed to return to your desk to pick up your personal things. My skills were such that the United States government was my only potential employer, so you can see the position I was in; I had to keep my rating."

The 1950s are remembered as a time of fear, repression, and conformity. Of war, hot and cold. And a senator from Wisconsin was watching security agencies for any signs of deviance which might suggest "Un-American" sympathies.

"The security agencies responded by tightening the screws on their staff. My phone was tapped. My car was sometimes followed at night. Agents would enter my home during work hours, slightly moving and rearranging things so I'd know they'd been there.

"Being single played into all of this, you know. If you weren't married, you were thought to pose a security question from at least two angles: On the one hand, you might become involved in liaisons with men who might have a subversive influence. On the other hand, if you weren't at least known to be dating men, you might be suspected of being homosexual. Homosexuality equaled subversion; the FBI had *that* down pat. Homosexuals were thought to be subject to blackmail, even if they acknowledged their preferences. It was a damned-if-you-do, damned-if-you don't position.

"If I found a man I cared for, the agents would soon call him, asking pointed questions about what we had talked about, the degree of intimacy we shared. How many men could cope with that? Many couldn't; they didn't know why they were being questioned and it made them suspicious of just who I might be, anyway. And most often your relationship would abruptly end, with blurted comments about what business was it of anyone's anyway? There was one special man I really cared for and had a wonderful physical relationship with who got scared off by these calls. I was heartsick when it happened, but could say nothing in the way of an explanation to him."

Women friends, too, became enmeshed in the surveillance. "I once had a friend living with me, who, after an interview with an agent, suddenly took to wearing decidedly frilly blouses and fancy hairstyles. I couldn't imagine what had suddenly gotten into her. Finally it dawned on me that the agent had probably made some suggestive comments.

"Because of restrictions on our social lives, people in the agency relied on each other for social contact. Single people and families shared trips to the zoo, sometimes had picnics in the park, and went sailing on Chesapeake Bay.

"The group I always felt had the best status were the single mothers with a child or two. Somewhere back in their private histories, they had had a husband, but they didn't have to bother with the demands of one anymore. So they lavished a lot of care on their children. Involvement with their kids gave them a little more base in the community. They fit into more things, school, church, all that. I think they were regarded as a little more normal or acceptable than the never-married women, because they had Mrs. in front of their names. I also think the security agents paid less attention to them. They must have believed their kids would keep them out of trouble!"

In the 1960s things eased up for Marian to a degree. Supportive of the civil rights movement and activities centered around the emerging human potential field, she nonetheless had to remain a bystander. But some of her stress problems were manifesting themselves again, and she decided to reenter therapy. "The security agencies are like that. They breed a lot of psychological problems for the people who work in them. The agency imposes a need for constant control, and many people will consciously or unconsciously extend that self-control to injurious lengths—lay an even worse trip on themselves, tie themselves in knots. People have to learn to deal with the stress, the tendency to paranoia.

"But this time there was a new wrinkle. The security agents contacted my therapist, wanting to know what I was talking about. I was infuriated. I hit the ceiling. I put an ad in the *Washington Post* Personal section: 'Government employee who is being harassed by security agents for undergoing psychological therapy is considering a new job.' They never missed a thing; soon they were at my desk asking me what *that* was about.

"I decided to retire on rather short notice. I had lunch with a friend who was a former coworker at the agency, and she described her freedom in almost delirious terms and pointed out that my pension would be more than reasonable.

"Retirement brings upheaval to most people, but to me, it also released me to face a challenge about something I had placed on myself concerning my credibility with all these movements and actions I had admired and supported from the sidelines. I nurtured a picture of myself as this useful activist all those long years I had to be so carefully noninvolved; now that I was free, would I live up to this glorious image of myself?

"I decided to work at things close to my own interests. The women's movement was gaining momentum about then, and people were organizing around the needs of the elderly. Feeling deliciously wicked and free, I joined the National Organization for Women (NOW), and Maryland Chapter of the National Women's Political Caucus, and the Gray Panthers. I couldn't tell myself to restrain my actions to protect my security rating: My treasured self-image was on the line. During the first weeks of my retirement, I made a special point of going to demonstrations and displaying my placard or whatever in front of the television cameras. I could imagine the agents out there watching me, but I was out of their reach—and censure. It was a wonderfully fulfilling time."

Seeking a more benign climate and a more activist social atmosphere, Marian moved to California. She sought out projects affecting older women and volunteered on a full-time basis to work for a project creating a shelter for battered women. She managed the office, coordinating volunteers, and joined efforts aimed at creating a national coalition to support legislation for centers for these women.

"I thought my single days might be ending when I was in my mid-fifties, during the last years I was working. I had bought a house, and wanted some companionship—a man to live with, and to make the place more secure. I joined an introduction club for singles and spent an hour talking with the counselor, a guy by the name of Jack Watson. He was friendly and nice to talk to, and I described the kind of man I'd like to meet, thinking that he himself would do nicely. But I assumed he was married and unavailable. The agency didn't produce any contacts, and I called to complain and request a refund. Jack suggested himself as a Sunday date, and told me he was divorced. He came over and spent the day, and we hit it off immediately.

"We felt completely comfortable together. He was a happy-type person, full of warmth, full of stories. He made his living as a self-employed salesman, buying wholesale lots of slightly damaged clothes and reselling them as seconds to stores and individuals. He dealt in jewelry, too, and gave me this emerald ring. In time I came to realize that some of his activities were of sort of border-line legality and that some of his sources shouldn't be looked at too closely, but the first part of our relationship was a very happy time.

"Jack moved in with me, and we went out with other couples and traveled around the country. I bought him a car, loaned him some money and took care of him, keeping house, cooking, looking after his personal needs. When I bought him pants, they were always much too long—he was actually a rather average-sized man, but in my mind he was ten feet tall. For a while I hoped we might marry.

"But I discovered he wasn't as dependable as I thought, and his business deals, which he often was evasive about, worried me. Loans weren't repaid and he quit his job and leaned on me for financial support. I didn't like that and asked my sister for advice. She said I should be glad to support him for the company, but I didn't feel that way about it.

"More importantly, I guess, Jack turned out not to be very responsive to my feelings. We would get into quarrels. He wouldn't listen to me or go along with my requests. Then when he saw I was really upset, he would attempt to win me back by turning on his charm, being Mr. Personality with me again. I was feeling pretty used and exploited by then, but I found it difficult to turn him out. He had no place to go and was becoming increasingly sickly. Finally, he saw a doctor and a diagnosis was made; Jack had bone cancer, a terminal case.

"So, of course, that changed everything. We put all our differences aside. I resolved to do everything I could to help him, and Jack met the challenge of his illness and death with great courage. He had to travel hundreds of miles to take painful experimental chemotherapy which involved inserting thick needles into his flesh. Jack would sit with the other patients waiting for treatment, joking with them to keep their courage up, bringing them food. He never allowed himself a moment of self-pity. It was as though he realized that if he leaned heavily enough into his extroverted self, he would not have to deal with his own misery. Between stays at the hospital I nursed him at home, irrigating and dressing his sores until he was hospitalized for the final time.

"There had been other men in my life, but none who meant as much to me as Jack did. When things were good between us, Jack was so warm and such a good companion; I was always happy just to be with him. So sometimes he really lighted up my life. I had had teenaged crushes and hometown sweethearts and GIs and sailors during the war: I was involved with an amateur artist during the war too. There was a married man who used to squire me around during his wife's illness, a sort of Casanova the security agents scared away. But I think of Jack as best."

I asked her where the turning point in a relationship lay: When is it, in a caring relationship, that one decides or feels not to go on with it, not to pursue it to the point of marriage? She responded immediately: "I've always needed strict control of my own life—and I can't give that over. I have the confidence born of seeing myself come up the hard way. I'm rooted in a poor family who had little to offer, and I've developed my own life through the Depression and all. I've had my bad times psychologically and emotionally. I've gotten through it all by exercising strict self-control—not too strict, of course, because that's bad too, but I feel I want to continue to do that by remaining single, which translates to me as being in control.

"You know," she continued, "the bonus I could never have figured on in staying single is old age. I mean, you wouldn't expect it, I guess, but a real good time in life to be a never-married woman is when you're getting up there in years. You've had to work so you probably have your retirement pension and Social Security, with probably something put back in investments or property; I could pay off this house if I had to. I'm not used to thinking of being dependent on anyone else. At the stage of life I'm in now, I see a lot of women becoming widows, or losing their husbands through divorce. It's heartbreaking to see their loss when their husbands die or walk out on them. Often they've been counting on their children to help them out; sometimes the children are a major disappointment.

"It's not only the loss of these relationships they face but the demand to face life on an independent basis. That's not to say that having a husband or children isn't a good thing, it's just that it's real tough to gear over into independence when you are sixty-five or seventy or seventy-five or whatever and you aren't prepared for it. I'd rather have to do my coping when I'm younger and have it all down pat by the time I'm facing old age.

"I saw something in one of our retired people's magazines that pretty well proves my point. A sociology professor did a study of older men and women who have never been married. In general, they were doing very well: They were rarely lonely and were relatively unafraid of death. They were reported to be especially active and didn't see themselves in some sort of a decline because they were growing older. The study concluded that the loneliness associated with old age is related more to the desolation of losing a spouse than just from being alone.

"I plan to stay in my little house as long as I can. I want to remain active. I have lots of plans with the Center and my other projects; I hope I can take a few trips. I have only one real fear: getting sick or hurt in the house, and being unable to get to the phone. I can't imagine anything worse than being seriously ill and feeling trapped or isolated; it happened to me once, about a year ago. I got a virus or something and passed out in the hallway. I also have some fear of someone breaking into the house, but who doesn't nowadays? Eventually, I imagine I'll move to a retirement home and get a room with a little kitchen. I expect to live a long time because everyone in my family is very long-lived.

"I've discovered as I grow older I fear death less; partly that's a lesson I learned from Jack. I used to skirt the subject, but no more. I've learned to take things as they come, and death is just another step, although a final one. I worry more about incapacitation, or living in pain, or being unable to care for myself or becoming dependent on my family. My sister says she'd rather pay someone to hook her bra or give her lunch than ever have to accept help from the family or an agency. I feel that way too. Still, with a government pension and my health insurance, I'll make out okay.

"I've made out my will and joined a burial society. My family knows I don't want any unusual measures taken to prolong my life. I just want to live out my days in a natural way, taking things as they come—and taking my end as it comes too.

"A philosopher once said that we come into the world alone, and we go out of it alone. In some ways, we are always by ourselves, whether we are married or single, or have a family or don't. One way or another, we can all share our lives. I accept that, and I live by it."

I commented in Chapter One that I found the never-married woman in their twenties more different and more interesting than I'd imagined they would be. But no less different and no less interesting were the women on the opposite end of the scale—the senior women. I hadn't figured on them at all and they astonished me! What dynamos some of them are—how courageous and strong!

How improbable the stereotype of the elderly spinster now seems— the notion of the sad and forlorn figure spending out her years bitter and alone. As a group, the older never-married women seem quite the opposite—vigorous, in control, happy and satisfied with their lives. I wonder what the image of the aged spinster is based on. Some, of course, are quieter and more reserved than the women portrayed here, but I never met one who fit the stereotype; indeed, they are models of what older womanhood can be.

Friends who work in geriatrics tell me the strength of older single women is predictable, for as Marian McClelland and several others pointed out, older never-married women are master copers. They've spent a lifetime dealing independently with life's contingencies, plotting out their futures, making plans for themselves, finding their own way, coping, coping, coping. That process makes them resourceful and strong, ideal attributes for old age.

They are spared the transition to independence that strikes women unexpectedly when they are widowed or possibly deserted or divorced late in life when transitions are most difficult. Single women have almost always worked all or nearly all their adult lives, a factor which teaches a great deal about surviving in this world and provides pension, Social Security, and other financial benefits for retirement. And most single women have been able to accumulate other kinds of security for later years. At least they know the need for preparing for it well in advance—not for her the startling discovery of having to provide for the future when a husband dies and leaves few or reduced benefits for his widow, or when a husband announces a divorce and suddenly an older woman must find her own way.

I think finding out about the relatively good space and good times of older women is one of the most important contributions this book can make to our knowledge of never-married women. I say this because the negative stereotype of the forlorn elderly spinster is so pervasive—and so wrong—and because anxiety about the future is one of the most prevalent worries of younger single women. This fear is often mentioned in sort of a generalized, nonspecific way. Twenty-year-olds worry about being thirty and never-married as sort of a status question, but after that, women ruminate and fret about growing old alone, and see increasing years as a menace.

I used to worry about old age. I wondered especially how the older women assessed their lives alone, if they were sorry they had not married. In the darkest hours of my own Age Thirty Crisis and in the turmoil and disappointment of failing relationships with men, I have feared that perhaps my life would be seriously blighted, even ruined, if I spent it alone and never married. So the feelings of older women about the importance of not having married were of special interest to me.

Virtually none of the older women I met seriously regretted not marrying. When I asked them if they had major regrets about their lives in general they had some. A number wished they had children, a few wished they had had a better education or had prepared themselves more thoroughly for work. A few had wishes that were personal in nature—for better health, to have been spared certain traumas or tragedies. But they were not a self-pitying or regretful lot.

So, I asked them specifically if they regretted not marrying. I would get answers such as "Well, I can imagine if I'd have run into the right person, it might have been nice" or "My sister is very happily married; I can see how a setup like hers could be real pleasant" or "Well, maybe—under the right circumstances, with the right man—but it didn't happen."

But burning regrets, a heartrending sense of loss or deprivation? I didn't think so. I sensed some of these comments were made out of a sense of tipping one's hat to social convention—a sort of acknowledgment that "marriage is a desirable institution so I'll pay homage to it." Certainly few never-married women are hostile to marriage and are often willing to pay a certain lip service to it, to hymn its general attributes.

But I never had the faintest inkling that any woman I met felt her life was ruined because she hadn't married.

It's possible some of these remarks may have had an element of self-justification in them; certainly some of the same women had spoken of suitors lost, love affairs they hoped might have terminated in marriage but were gone forever. Maybe they were keeping a stiff upper lip, shrugging away a failure. But it didn't have that feeling; it seemed instead the pain of these earlier hoped-for relationships had faded or been forgotten, swept along and washed clean of hurtful regrets in the current of time.

More often the older women were quick to affirm the values they found in remaining single throughout their long lives. They pointed to their accomplishments with a deep sense of satisfaction and pride. They were proud they'd done it alone, on their own terms. Some of the preceding interviews carry this almost triumphal note. I think of Belle Cunningham and Betty Coburn who, when I interviewed them, displayed an almost tangible sense of joy about their lives.

The one thread of regret that runs with some regularity through the lives of some elderly single women is the loss of children. It seems clear that many who were strongly motivated in their childbearing years to become mothers and who did not do so carried that regret with them through the remainder of their lives. I would hear comments like "If I could have had just one thing different, I wish I could have had a son or daughter—it's something I never got completely over." "I so envy my friends when their children come to call or when their grandchildren are around—I would love to have grandchildren now." "I know children are no guarantee of company in your old age, but I wish I had a family—my nieces and nephews are wonderful, but it's not the same." "Of course it would have been difficult at the time, but if I had it to do again—" Certainly not all older women feel this way, but for those who wanted children, the persistence of this desire deep into old age seems both striking and touching.

I want to comment on the sexuality of many of the women in this group. A fair number of them were quite without sexual experience— by that I mean they were technically virgins, had not experienced sexual intercourse. Their relationships with men were quite limited and even stunted; a few professed to never have had the slightest interest in them, had never dated or even had what could be called purely social relationships with a man. Nor had they had homosexual experience, or any interest in homosexuality.

At first, I was quite surprised by this finding. A product of a sex-saturated culture which urges, urges, urges women and men on to ever more and fuller sexual expression, I found it unusual—even abnormal—to discover women who had never once been in bed with a man. I wondered if it was an error or quirk in my sampling, if for some unknown reason I had come across a group of women who were atypical in this respect. The question bothered me enough that I talked to sociologist Jessie Bernard about it, describing the age and background of the women and the information I was finding.

Dr. Bernard commented that my findings didn't appear off to her. She thought the experiences of my group were probably representative of women of this age and background. After all, these women were born in the Victorian and post-Victorian age and were influenced as well by a society with a strongly puritanical base, and the sexual taboos of their formative years and young adult life were many and strong.

Reassured by these comments, I pressed on. I got bolder, and the next time I came across this situation, I challenged the woman about her lack of sexual experience. "How can that be?" I asked. "I should think in the case of an intelligent woman like you, you would at least be curious enough about sex to want to try it." She laughed at me, a little patronizingly, I thought. "You have to remember that in my young days the whole attitude toward sexual things was about opposite of what it is now. Sex was associated with base appetites and lust and was something to be ashamed of and repressed at all costs. When I started menstruating, I was terrified and thought I was dying, and Mother was so embarrassed she could barely tell me that it was something normal women did. Sex outside of marriage equaled sin, period. The taboos against it were very widespread and very deep and if it were known or even suspected that a single woman was involved with a man, your reputation could be ruined. That affected your whole standing in the community, and could affect your job and your whole future. Such things went on, of course, but were kept deeply hidden and became a source of scandal and shame if they came to light. Sure I was curious about sex, but the price was too high to risk finding out much about it.

"And there were practical problems. Knowledge of contraception wasn't widespread, and women were known to commit suicide if they got pregnant and weren't married. I personally remember a case of that in the late 1940s. You didn't just go to the doctor and ask for birth control. Doctors were as moralistic as the rest of society and often denied protection to women who weren't married on the grounds that they didn't want to encourage immorality. You had to know the doctor's reputation about this before you asked. Often women went to a strange doctor and pretended to be married. It's difficult for you young women today to realize how strong those taboos were and how slowly they changed."

Another woman remembered, "I had men who were attracted to me but I pushed them off a good deal. I enjoyed men as friends, but I had a horror of a man thinking I was running after him, so I was a little standoffish. Oh, I went with some, and I called 'em love affairs, but I never slept with one! I never have had sex, really I haven't.

"People were appalled with women who got involved with men sexually. Absolutely horrified. I can remember—I won't say her name—I had a friend who was ten years younger than I. She was the sweetest person. Once she said, 'I just hate him'—the man she was going out with—'he'd never want to go out on a date if it didn't have some sexual thing in it.' And I just looked at her—I was the most naive thing. My mother would tell us all about where babies came from but the things beyond that just weren't discussed.

"Now my sister who was ten years younger than I knew a lot more about life and all than I did. I could see a big difference in women that way about every ten years, it seems to me.

"There were various stories I can remember going around. My aunt was a social worker and sometimes she would tell us, 'If I could tell you girls some of the things I see and hear from my work, if I could tell you what has happened to some of these poor girls at men's hands—.' And there was some boy who was talking like having intercourse was so cruel. And I thought, My Lord! So maybe I heard things like that that scared me, I don't know.

"Oh, I sometimes wonder what would have happened if I had married one of these boys I went with. I often have wondered about that. Now if I had married, I think the sex would have been all right, but as long as I didn't, to me it's just taboo. But I don't have any regrets, I can tell you that in all truth. I think I read enough to know about it."

Not all elderly never-married women are sexually inexperienced, of course. Some were probably less affected by the taboos of their youth, some were able to free themselves from their influence as ideas changed. Some few seem to have developed sexually expressive lives— one woman, well past her seventieth birthday, spoke with evident pleasure of a liaison with a professional colleague who lived in another city which had continued for over thirty years; another in her late sixties indicated in an indirect way that a male music student clearly some twenty years her junior was also her lover. But as I interviewed women of different age groups it was striking to see how deeply the mores, taboos, and ideas of their formative years had affected them, and how long and pervasively that influence lasted. The range of behavior from the younger women with their open, experimental, and almost insistent sexuality to the repressed and even nonexistent sexual experience of the older women is remarkable indeed.

Yet I'm not certain I see it all as a trend to liberality and freedom and the finding and possession of our sexual selves that women speak of. Sometimes the frenetic quality, the almost forced range of experience younger women report seems to have some of the same imposed quality that the older women speak of—only the older women's impositions went the other way, into repression, restriction, and shame.

Where lies the sexual balance and fulfillment women look for? Some find it, some don't. Perhaps as the pendulum of social influence that affects the sexuality of single women swings into a less defined position, perhaps as the sexual behavior of women is less prescribed, a chance for growth and expression that is truly individual and unique will emerge.

VIII

THE NEW WOMAN

People sometimes ask me, What things were most interesting about the women you met? What things surprised you, what things stand out?

Some things I knew about, or could predict. I could see them in my own life and in the lives of women around me, I could find them in the media and in the small amount of research that has been done about never-married women. The Age Thirty Crisis. The heavy involvement of single women in work and careers. The variety of our lives—the great range of life choices singleness makes possible. The differing kinds of relationships women have with men. and our close involvement with other women. The generativity and gregariousness of single women—our interest and participation in the world around us.

Some things were new: the fact that most women have a permission-giver, usually their mother, in their background who says, "It's okay to be single." I think it would be interesting for all women, married or single, to examine the messages we received about marital status from our mothers especially and from other women or men close to us. Once we recall what these messages were, we usually see how strongly we have been influenced by them.

When I began this book, I wondered about backgrounds—if the quality of our parents' marriage or if something about our home life influenced our marital status. I wondered if singleness ran in families, or if the kind of family we came from (whether a tight-knit nuclear family or a large extended one) affected our thinking about marriage.

Perhaps birth rank—first, middle, or last born—might influence single-ness. I don't believe any of these factors has much to do with it, though other researchers may wish to probe these questions further.

The intensity of one issue surprised me. I could guess some women were deeply interested in motherhood—it is an issue I feel strongly about myself. But the insistent quality, the heat of the issue startled me. For women still in their childbearing years, and especially those nearing the end of their reproductive period, the subject was often introduced into the interview with no prompting from me and discussed with great feeling. I conclude that motherhood is a major issue with many never-married women, much more than has been recognized in the past.

I was pleasantly surprised by the good space and the good times of the senior never-married women, and I was very interested in their assessment of their lives alone. How heartening their stories are, how inspiring their example of lives lived creatively and well! Younger single women often told me they dread growing old alone; I see now there is little to fear.

I was delighted to know the younger women better. Not all of them will remain single, of course; many hope to marry and some will. But those who remain single will be supported by the perspective they already have about the value of autonomy and self-determination in their lives. The most direct beneficiaries of the women's movement, they will blaze ahead less deterred about expectations for marriage, less affected by pressures to uphold social norms.

As if to refute an old cliché, never-married women themselves sometimes asked me to include a discussion of sexuality in this book. It has been woven into the text, appearing as it should in the context of the stories of women's experiences. I hope readers have seen the vast range and diversity it covers, all the way from the asexual and repressed behavior of some women to the fully expressive and exploratory activity of others.

People sometimes wonder, What is the incidence of bisexual and crossing-over behavior among never-marrieds who are basically hetero-sexual? It is hard to know. It is not, of course, a subject easily discussed, or something a writer always feels entirely comfortable in probing, especially among reticent or older women. But younger women will sometimes discuss it, and occasionally, after the tape recorder is turned off and the notepad put away, things are said, directly or between the lines.

One woman saw her physical relationship with a woman friend as a way of having a more committed sexual relationship in her life; she felt her relationships with men had lacked this quality. Another woman had lived with a gay man and understood something of his sexuality. She felt she wanted more physical closeness with women, but at first didn't know if her feelings were sexual. She sought out a woman she knew to be gay and they became roommates; she remained involved with men as well. She found she could be self-revealing to her woman lover in a more basic way, letting down barriers, walking new ground. "I don't have answers for what's ahead, but my relationship with Jill has spark and excitement and intimacy that's different from just sharing words, as I do with my other women friends. I like to let her know she's a very important person in my life; we have a sense of being closer in ways I haven't been before." Yet she feels the relationship is "new and scary" and wonders how open she can be about it in the small Indiana community where she lives. Expressing herself physically with Jill at a New Year's Eve party was uncomfortable; lesbianism isn't part of her self-image.

Any researcher in human sexuality would confirm there is a good deal more such activity than is commonly acknowledged. A rating scale appearing in *Sexual Behavior in the Human Male* by Kinsey, Pomeroy and Martin showed that of 100 women, 72 would be exclusively heterosexual, 22 would at times be involved in varying degrees of bisexual behavior, 2 would be exclusively homosexual (figures rounded off). The same figures for men are 63 exclusively heterosexual, 33 bisexual, 4 exclusively homosexual.

Such figures include all women and do not take marital status into account. But it would be risky to make assumptions based on marital status; it is certain bisexual and homosexual behavior occur in married, widowed, and other single women, just as it does among never-married women.

One of the questions that interested me most when I began this book was the question of the self-esteem and self-perception of never-married women. How do we picture ourselves; what might our self-image be? The signs were ominous. Clearly our position was stigmatized, and a stigmatized social status should logically affect self-concept. The names used about us are largely pejorative; as a group, we're often overlooked and discounted. We barely acknowledge the special circumstances of our lives to each other. Before I began this book, I rarely if ever had heard a woman speak openly and proudly about being never-married. So I braced myself for the worst.

I questioned about half the women I interviewed (cross-cutting all ages) about this issue. First, I asked what association they had with the words spinster and old maid. Not surprisingly, the associations were all negative, usually very much so. "Awful," "distasteful," "sounds like a shriveled-up old witch," "very bad," "something you would never want to hear." On the other hand, the term never-married was seen as being more neutral and less value-laden, describing a situation or choice. Some women objected to its negative connotation in implying a standard or norm, a criticism I agree with entirely. They pointed out an old problem: We don't have a good name for ourselves and we need one. But no one had suggestions beyond "always-single" or "on-her-own" or variations on that theme. Like other groups who in recent years have assumed proud new names to signal a proud new identity—blacks, Chicanos, gays, Asians—never-married women too need a new name. Yet we lack a word that sparks.

I asked the women to rank four categories of women: Who did they think had the highest status in the eyes of most people: married, divorced, widowed, or never-married women? Not surprisingly, never-married women believed married women had the highest status, followed by widows. They thought so because married women were seen as meeting society's expectations, were essential to family life, and were "chosen." "Women are supposed to get married and they get rewarded for doing it." "That's the standard, that's the norm." "Human society is pretty much based on the family and that seems to require that a woman get married and have a spouse to support her and the children." "Marriage is the keystone of family life." Others said, "A married woman has more status because it means somebody wanted her, somebody chose her." "It means she was picked." Old ideas die hard. Did they feel they haven't been chosen and thus are outcasts? They didn't seem to imply that.

Widows were felt to have nearly the same status as wives because their singleness was involuntary. "A widow has done the expected thing and the fact that she is single is not of her own choosing." "It's interesting to note that widows tend to go on carrying their married status long after their husbands are gone."

Never-married women were not sure who ranked next; either themselves, or divorced women. It depended on which they felt was more negatively valued: failure at marriage, or failure to marry at all. There may be a slight tendency to imagine that divorced women outrank never-married women, because divorced women once had married, done the right thing. In these cases, of course, they saw their own status as being lowest of all.

I asked the women to rate the quality of life of most never-married women they knew. "Most of them lead good lives. They have their freedom and can do as they wish. They can make whatever they want out of their life situation and they pretty much do so." "As a group, my never-married friends are well off. We have our problems, or no better or worse than the general run." "I think most get along well—they seem stronger than many women." One college professor in a small town was less sanguine about her colleagues. "I wouldn't be happy leading their lives, which I see as constrained. They have only school and social activities with each other. Their relationships and involvements are limited." An older woman said single women in her age group could be divided into two groups—those who had their health and were financially secure were well off, those who didn't could be facing real problems. But generally, never-married women saw the quality of the lives of most of their peers as being quite good.

Then I asked them to compare the quality of their own lives with that of other never-married women they knew. Their answers fairly sang out: Almost always, they saw their lives as being as good or better than that of their peers, and they generally regarded their peers as being well off. They'd tick off their strengths: "I have my freedom, and can do as I please. I'm lucky to have had the kind of parents I have—they always back me up—and I got a good education, and my career has worked out well. That means a lot. I don't see many women doing better." "I'm not dissatisfied, I'm doing okay. I feel good about myself in relationship to just about anybody. Oh, I think married women or women who have been married may have done better financially, but that's not so important to me; I've had my successes and little triumphs in life. I'm satisfied." "I don't really lack for anything. I've had love in my life, and joy; being single has its rough spots, but you could say that about marriage too. I've been happy and I make a practice of counting my many blessings." One woman laughed and threw up her hands. "Count me happy," she simply said.

I wish now I had asked them to compare their lives directly with those of married women. I think their answers would have continued to show satisfaction with their own situation. I did ask them to estimate the proportion of truly happy married couples they knew, and despite the strong tendency of never-married women to speak benignly of marriage, I received a pessimistic answer: No one believed over fifty percent of marriages to be truly happy; one woman guessed as low as ten percent. Whether this is a sour-grapes, self-justifying view— dumping on a social status she couldn't attain herself—or is simply a fairly realistic assessment of the state of marriage today seen by women who have observed many marriages and considered the institution from a certain distance, remains to be seen.

I do want to emphasize that the self-esteem of never-married women appears to be quite high. Even without these questions, I would judge it to be high from the process of having met, interviewed, and talked with over eighty never-married women. Their pride, their sense of self-respect and well-being came through. They felt good about themselves;

they were happy with their lives. True, they sometimes talked of problems, heartaches, disappointments, and hurdles they had not been able to overcome. But defeat, "downness," and depression were rarely the tone of our encounters. Most often I heard about assessing, coping, drawing on internal strengths and external resources, setting goals and attaining them. They were proud to relate the story of their lives, pleased that a stranger was interested enough to ask. Many told me they enjoyed being interviewed; it was good to air a subject so little discussed, to look at one's life and tell how it all came to be.

And the interviewing process was an enriching, enjoyable experience for me, too. It was wonderful to have talked intimately with so many women; I know I sometimes heard things that had never been shared before. Sometimes the things we talked about touched on matters that reach into my own life and struck deeply responsive chords: my feelings about childlessness, my struggle to balance work and achievement with more personal, intimate needs; the question of how much marital status really matters, over the long term, in one's satisfaction in life. We tend to imagine we live in a world of unique problems, unique situations; I was reassured that we share a lot in common. The older women, especially, gave me confidence to go ahead on my own, unafraid.

When I was finished, I knew I had listened to a group of healthy, whole women, and I remembered Bruno Bettelheim's model of mental health: self-mastery and wholeness, or autonomy. These women had those qualities in abundance.

I want to add that despite the women's feeling that never-married-ness carries a low status, most of them believe this is changing, and changing fast. Indeed, a recent study published by the University of Michigan Institute for Social Research shows that while in 1975 eighty percent of people had negative attitudes about people who did not marry, by 1979 less than twenty-five percent felt that way. Older women especially volunteered how much things had changed, particularly in the last fifteen years. The awkwardness they remembered in some social situations—being partnerless at a formal dinner, being systematically excluded from the world of couples and shunted to the sidelines—is fading in today's more informal social atmosphere, although some women in the South and in small towns and rural areas still report this as a problem. Many pointed out that varying life choices and life-styles are more widely accepted now. The large presence of divorced, separated, and other single people rendered being solo more accept-able everywhere. Few women reported overtly discriminatory behavior or could recall comments that made them uncomfortable about their marital status in recent years.

* * *

Let's pause and consider once more the question which this book is largely about: Why don't some women marry? The first answers women give are as varied and individualistic as the women themselves.

There are a multitude of reasons: relationships that never worked out—"I loved him but he didn't love me" and "He loved me but I didn't love him"—the matching that never quite occurred. One woman described what she called "the windshield-wiper theory": "First he chases you and then you chase him and then he chases you and you chase him"—the actual catching never quite happens. There are women who don't marry because they feel they've never met someone they wanted to marry. Some remain single because of the death of a suitor, or because of parental disapproval or interference. Sometimes, mostly among older women, women remained single to assume family responsibilities caused by the death of a parent, or because they were needed to provide economic support to other family members. Sometimes role models had an influence: unhappy parental marriages or persons who set a particularly strong example of what marriage or singleness could mean, good or bad. A few women felt they were physically unattractive to men; often they cited weight problems. A few women claimed no interest in men; others, especially those of small and distinct ethnic groups, lacked a suitable selection of partners. Some struggled with the nature of marriage itself or the kind of marriage being proposed. Others had strong career aspirations which they felt precluded marriage. And a few were simply puzzled: "I can't tell you why I never married; I wish I knew myself. I'd like to be married and don't know the reason I was never able to bring it off."

Most of these women have received marriage proposals. We can conclude that most women have thus had an opportunity to marry if they wanted to badly enough. There *is* an element of choice in almost all women's singleness.

But let's look for deeper reasons, attempt to identify motivations perhaps not so immediately explained. When we move onto this level, we begin to hear something else time and time again—a struggle, often a deep and difficult one, with the need, indeed the demand, for autonomy, independence, and freedom versus the restrictions conventional marriage implies. "I need space," they say, and they mean it both figuratively and literally. They talk about their need for time alone, and for privacy, the need to be able to close doors. One woman said she had to live in a house with big rooms—an interesting comparison, I thought, with the expansiveness of her own life and aspirations.

And they need time alone, and elbow space to do what they feel they must do. "Don't crowd me; don't fence me" say even the most social and gregarious among us. Many women mentioned the need for self-direction and self-control—the ability to set one's own life agenda, to follow a different drummer, or even to be able to follow the muse.

The struggle towards autonomy and independence rarely appears to be a simple one, however. Younger women especially develop a self-conscious style of threading their way, and often experience a very considerable amount of ambiguity and conflict about whether to marry or remain single. The painful clashing may go on for many years. I have heard women of forty-five describe this conflict with all the pain of a twenty-year-old whose boyfriend is placing demands upon her freedom she can't accept. One woman joked about the seesaw nature of her conflict between marriage and singleness: "I'm the forty-nine-fifty-one-percent woman; on some days forty-nine percent of me wants to be married, and fifty-one percent of me wants to stay single; on other days it flip-flops. And I'm never quite sure which day is which." It is a question which usually requires much working through, and will only gradually take its place in the scheme of one's life.

Few women reported loneliness as a problem. They differentiated between aloneness and loneliness, pointing out that aloneness had restorative and curative value; loneliness was something negative and damaging that one could learn to overcome. As if to refute an old cliché about never-married women, they said that whatever loneliness they did experience was the "loneliness of people in general" or the "loneliness of the human condition"; most did not feel it was a problem with special meaning for them.

I think given the proclivity of most of these women to autonomy and self-reliance, loneliness is a problem they have the resources to perhaps more easily solve; their coping mechanisms may be stronger. Being alone all one's life forces one to face and deal with loneliness as an issue sooner in life, at an earlier age, when we are more flexible and adept at meeting personal challenges. I personally cannot remember loneliness as being a problem since I was in my mid-twenties, when living alone in Los Angeles forced me to learn to reach out, establish friendships, plan my time, and face down this issue in my life. I learned to cope.

Above all, never-married women emphasize that they treasure their freedom. Freedom was cited as the most valued attribute of being single, by a wide margin. "I lead my own life, I'm responsible for my gains and failures. I can go where I want when I want, and do what I feel I should do." "Nobody is in control here except me, and it's sweet, I tell you. I couldn't live any other way." "I spend my money as I see fit—I'm spared all those fights my parents had over finances." "I don't have to jump around to suit someone else's fancy"—and on and on. The question about the worst thing about singleness did not yield a similarly clear answer. Responses tended to turn to personal problems and individual life situations. Loneliness was rarely cited.

But let's press one level deeper. People ask, and women ask themselves, for more final answers—why, *really why* doesn't any one woman marry. What's going on deep within her, anyway? I think the answer lies deep within the psychodynamics of one's own being, perhaps in the deep, hidden recesses of our psyche where our most basic life drives begin. It may be a product of complex early life experiences, emotions, perceptions. A final answer may be difficult to reach and interpret.

I say this based on my own experience. I spent a long time in psychotherapy looking for the answer to that question, among others. The psychiatrist probed and probed and tried to fit together the pieces of the puzzle, but I felt we never found a satisfactory explanation. "It must lie somewhere in the dynamics of your relationship with your father," he finally ventured. But in all that time, we hadn't focused much on my relationship with my father, which seems to be quite normal, except that my father spent much of my childhood either sleeping on the davenport or playing poker and was somewhat emotionally reserved and distant. But many women, single and married, have reserved, detached fathers—that was almost the standard of fatherhood for women of my generation.

I must confess that after having interviewed many women on this very subject I don't have a better feel, an intuitive hunch about why they *really* remain single—I have no better sense of an ultimate answer for any one woman or for women in general than I had when I began this work. I have come instead to question the question, more than the answer. When people ask, "I wonder why Jane never married—she seems like such a nice person," I think about the problem of the question itself, and all it implies about the Marital Imperative in our society. For few dictums are more deeply imbedded than the one that prescribes that people must marry, and especially, that *women* must marry. Not to do so, and especially not for women to do so, is to fly in the face not only of convention, but of the whole hierarchically arranged social order where women are invariably assigned to a position subordinate to men. There is no social institution where this is not so.

It is tempting to quote feminist ideology about the meaning of marriage for women; whole books have been written defining the position of women within the institution of marriage. We would be telling the tale of women's suppression. We could cite the Hebrew concept of wife and child as the property of the husband; or the Greek origin of the word family—slaves belonging to one man. We could cite the story of the struggle to overcome its most oppressive features—the notion of wives as chattel; and from that the inability of women to control their own bodies and physical existence once married (not to mention their property—still another extension of the idea of *themselves* as property); the notion of the indissolvability of the marital union, regardless of any consequences. Nor would we be cheered to examine it in most nonwestern cultures.

Or we could turn away from history and look at more recent sources and note the outcome of this suppression: studies showing the poorer mental and physical health of married women, poorer than their spouses, and poorer than their never-married sisters. We could read psychologically and sociologically oriented books describing the effect of traditional marriage upon women. Jessie Bernard's *The Future of Marriage* or Lillian Rubin's *Women of a Certain Age—The Midlife Search for Self* describe in different ways what happens to women in marriage.

I think that, without having to cite lists of evidence, most women realize that their role in marriage is a subordinate one. While some expect and have even been conditioned to welcome that position, not all women can or will accept it. True, we look with encouragement at modern marriage and at all trends which stress the equal partnership of two people within marriage. But we also know such marriages are hard to come by and their actual number is not high; they seem as fragile and subject to dissolution as more traditional marriages are. Women have learned that not many men are inclined to change a relationship bestowing advantages and privileges in the name of freedom and fairness, anymore than most whites are willing to surrender the privileges of racial status until they must. Not to marry is a form of withdrawal and boycott, and if the punishment is to be labeled an outsider, to be given a stigmatized name, to be marked as odd and apart, it has not been too great a price for some women to pay. We know how many women have been propelled toward the altar in fear of that very thing.

The Future

So what might be the future of never-marriedness among women? I think there are some very hopeful signs; to discern what they might be, we can look to two sources: trends developing among never-married and other women today, and developments in societies which tend to be more advanced around women's issues and thus have a predictive value for us.

I particularly refer to Sweden, which is generally regarded as leading the way in promoting equality between women and men and advancing the status of women. Admittedly, we want to use caution in comparing societies where social structures and the ideas they are based upon are different. We also don't want to paint a picture of Sweden as some kind of feminist utopia, an attitude which must surely become tiresome to the Stockholm housewife, lugging home groceries and fixing dinner after a hard day at the office, while her spouse remains prone before the TV set. For it is in the private sphere where Sweden seems most traditional. But thanks to progressive Scandinavian custom and body of laws affecting women and men in the workplace, in employment and leave benefits, in health care and maternity programs, in housing and day-care services, the faith placed in the system pulls the private sector ahead, and Sweden usually leads the way.

My predictions   *The numbers of never-married women will rise.* I would not predict the death of marriage; no reputable observer would, though there is much call for change in the nature of traditional marriage. But I think the number of women who remain single will become greater.

Indeed, the numbers have almost doubled in recent years, though the overall percentage remains modest. In the 1950s, in the era of great emphasis on togetherness in the bosom of the conventionally defined family, never-married women made up only 4.1 percent of the adult female population in the United States. By the late seventies the figure had risen to 7 percent. (In Sweden, 28.4 percent of women are never-married at age thirty, the traditional cutoff age for such statistics. It should be noted, however, that cohabitation of women and men—living together in a de facto marital arrangement—is widespread in Sweden and is rising here as well. And many Swedish women marry for the first time when they are between thirty and thirty-five.)

A number of factors will cause this trend in the United States to continue. Women tend to remain single as their dependency decreases. As educational levels rise and economic status improves, women are less inclined to marry. We know women are becoming more highly educated; now slightly more than half of all persons enrolled in institutions of higher learning in the United States are female. The percentage of women enrolled in graduate and professional schools is rising dramatically; some medical schools report 40 percent and more female enrollments; a number of law schools are half female. Under the aegis of affirmative action and their own abilities and ambitions and skills, women are forging ahead into higher-paid work, often in nontraditional areas. The very qualities which lead to their success—assertiveness, the drive to self-actualization, a healthy self-image, strongly goal-oriented behavior, the willingness to defer short-term gratification for long-term goals—are the same attributes I noted in many never-married women which appear in this book.

Social conditions and social changes will be more supportive of remaining single. No doubt the most important social change has already occurred: the women's movement with its affirmation of autonomy and self-determination, its constant emphasis on equality and freedom, its questioning of traditions which have subordinated half the human race. As we have seen, the women's movement has already played a major role in the thinking of women about marriage and singleness; there is every reason to believe it will continue to do so. It will buttress the gains we have made and encourage further development of the concepts which support autonomy.

Women feel the social attitudes stigmatizing singleness are fading. It is not unreasonable to hope they may disappear altogether in the future, as people learn to value individual life choices even more. And I think while the status of singleness rises, the status and value of marriage is more and more called into question. No need to recite the difficulties of traditional marriage today here, or review statistics which show that nearly half the marriages occurring today will end in divorce; that litany is well known. Young single women today are increasingly aware that living happily ever after is not guaranteed by a wedding ring, even though the rate of marriage remains high; fear of divorce is often cited as a reason women hesitate to marry. Young women today are more conscious of making choices about their lives and weigh out the pros and cons in a more pragmatic way. Perhaps since marriage seems to be so temporary these days, they begin to attach more importance to their own autonomy. Even if they marry now, they know they may very well be single later.

And what a flowering of choices they have! No longer are their options restricted to a dreary existence alone, or a conventional coupling arrangement. Extended families, cohabiting couples, single parenthood, homosexual partnering, sweet solitude, and shared living arrangements of every description offer almost endless choices. All these situations lend support to being single.

Single parenthood will increase. I think more never-married women will choose to become mothers, joining the more than seven million divorced, widowed and other never-married women who are already single parents. I sense choosing to bear one's own child openly as an unmarried woman is an issue which now lies only slightly beneath the surface of social acceptance. The almost total lack of adoptable children available to single women together with the fading of mores which label such decisions as shameful or sinful will accelerate this trend. From a feminist point of view, it is impossible to tell a woman she does not have access to her own reproductive system because she is not "owned" by a man.

I think of the old saying "First comes love, and then comes marriage, and then comes Mary with a baby carriage" and see that the inevitability of marriage irrevocably linked to children, and in that order, is entirely a matter of social convention. Neither the desire nor the ability to produce and adequately care for children is tied to marriage; it has no place in the natural order of things; it is no irrefutable law. We have increasingly recognized that women may marry and not desire children, and therefore do not have them; the converse is true also. Women may not marry and ardently desire children and may have them. I think it is time we moved to recognize and validate this need, so strongly felt in a good portion of never-married women whose adequacy for parenthood is unquestionable. In Sweden, unmarried motherhood, including child-bearing, is not frowned upon on moralistic grounds but is addressed in terms of the best interests of mother and child. All parents—married, divorced, widowed, never-married—have access to assistance in housing, child care, medical benefits, leave, welfare, whatever, regardless of the circumstances of their parenthood, based on their individual needs and the availability of services.

Laws and regulations may change. In Sweden, the drive toward nondiscrimination in the public sector tries to make the law neutral not only in terms of gender, but in terms of marital status as well. Laws and regulations are coming to consider dependency—how many people you are supporting or if you are dependent yourself—as basic criteria for social benefits.

A recent change of laws emphasized this trend toward neutrality in marital matters. The law is about name changes at the time of marriage. It stipulated that the name of either spouse, male or female, does not change automatically, but if there is to be a change in any direction—hers to his, his to hers, a combination, whatever—the court must be petitioned separately. The marriage does not bestow a name change in itself. Children bear whichever names the parents agree upon, and if a child's surname isn't registered six months after birth, it receives the *mother's* name automatically.

In our society, the concept of neutrality in marital status and the greater emphasis on dependency status is less well understood. Oddly enough, at the present time, tax laws, Social Security regulations, credit regulations, retirement and pension plans often make certain assumptions about need because of marital status which ends up shortchanging married women, widows, and sometimes divorced women. Never-married women fare better.

But there are some situations where the burden of inequality falls on the other side. I think especially of the need of single mothers for adequately funded day care, a need created by dependency. Lack of adequate day care for single mothers isn't brought about by consideration of marital status per se, but it falls especially heavily on them because other resources (a second income, assistance with the child and in the home) may be lacking. Greater recognition of needs in terms of dependency could not only help single mothers who are especially burdened, but would benefit other mothers and children as well. As social planning increasingly considers the individual situation of those affected—be they married or single, adults or children, dependent or independent—our laws and regulations will become more just.

Single people have organized themselves in Sweden and several neighboring countries to protect and advance their interests in social, tax, and other legislative matters. What new meaning this gives to the concept of a singles organization! Instead of tiresome social events organized to "meet someone," the agenda concerns lobbying, letter writing, and planning for social action. In any society where daily life is intimately affected by social legislation, organizing to protect and advance one's rights and interests is bound to be important. Perhaps we should consider something similar here.

Single people have taken an interest in the Marvin vs. Marvin decision which protects the property expectations of women and men who enter into a marital-type arrangement sans a legal marriage. The case protects the right of the couple to contract to live together without having society's statutory or customary terms implied for their relationship. Couples may make their own contract orally, in writing, or even by implication and have their property expectations protected. Society no longer thumbs its nose at those who were once said to be living in sin. It brings cohabitation under the protection of law. The implications of this California ruling are being widely felt.

However, in California and several other states unmarried mothers have seen a loosening of some rights they once had. They have less absolute authority over their offspring, for unmarried fathers now have all the custody, visitation, and other rights and responsibilities of married fathers, with few exceptions. To California's and some other states' credit, the old notion of illegitimacy has been completely wiped from the books—a legal concept, it no longer has real meaning.

In closing, I hope other never-married women who have read this book will feel I've represented us fairly and well—that in some way you've seen facets of your own experiences mirrored here, that your feelings and understandings have somehow been reflected on these pages. I hope younger women still considering life choices will have found something of value, and your deliberations will take into account the options you truly have, and your choices will be made in freedom based on knowledge.

I hope other single people—those who have been married but are now alone—will see our present experiences are in many ways alike, though our backgrounds are different. Perhaps there are people reading this book who are now married, but contemplate that one day they will be alone. I hope you can see the strength that comes from a life that is your own, and the fulfillment that is truly possible when one seeks the self-realization that autonomy promises.

Never-married women are not a group without problems and shortcomings; we have dreams which remain unanswered, problems we cannot solve. But we know much about fulfillment, accomplishment, and the realization of hopes that seemed beyond attaining. We have stood alone or apart at times; but we have also taken our place in the great social forces which move humankind forward. Above all, we have our sense of self, and a realization of our own self-worth. We look in the mirror and feel good about ourselves, and as years pass, our sense of well-being grows.

We know who we are; we have led our own lives.

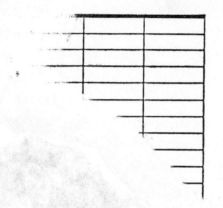